D1058972

Digger Phelps's
Tales from the
NOTRE DAME
HARDWOOD

Digger Phelps
with Tim Bourret

www.SportsPublishingLLC.com

ISBN: 1-58261-827-5

Publisher: Peter L. Bannon
Senior managing editor: Susan M. Moyer
Acquisitions editor: Dean Reinke
Developmental editor: Noah Amstadter
Dust jacket design: Christine Mohrbacher
Project manager: Kathryn R. Holleman
Imaging: Kerri Baker, Christine Mohrbacher, Heidi Norsen
Photo editor: Erin Linden-Levy
Vice president of sales and marketing: Kevin King
Media and promotions managers: Cory Whitt (regional),
        Randy Fouts (national), Maurey Williamson (print)

Printed in the United States of America

Sports Publishing L.L.C.
804 North Neil Street
Champaign, IL 61820

Phone: 1-877-424-2665
Fax: 217-363-2073
Web site: www.SportsPublishingLLC.com

To my family: wife Terry and children Karen, Rick and Jennifer. They stood by me and provided a great support system every moment of my 20 years as head coach at The University Notre Dame.

Also, to all the student-athletes, assistant coaches and administrators during the 1971-91 era who helped make the Notre Dame program among the best in the nation. Finally, to my coaches, mentors and my parents, who provided me with a guiding light through my youth, into college and beyond. They all helped me realize the dream of becoming the head coach at Notre Dame.

—DP

To the Notre Dame class of 1977. From our freshman year when Notre Dame ended UCLA's 88-game winning streak, to our final game at the Joyce Center when No. 1-ranked San Francisco and its 29-game winning streak fell, we knew what the spirit of Notre Dame was all about.

—TB

CONTENTS

ACKNOWLEDGMENTS

A lot of work went into the production of this book and I have to begin my acknowledgments with the sports information department at the University of Notre Dame. If I didn't, my co-author, Tim Bourret, a product of Roger Valdiserri's army of student assistants over the years, wouldn't speak to me. Of course, Roger, my confidant for all 20 years as head coach, is the first person who comes to mind.

John Heisler is now the director and was in the office as an assistant, associate or director for 13 of those seasons. He continues to follow Roger's great example and was inducted into the CoSIDA Hall of Fame in 2003. His current assistant for basketball, Bernie Cafarelli, secretary Susan Reed and student assistant Gary Paczesny were very important in this process, and their hours of work are much appreciated. I also want to thank former SID office basketball assistants Jim Daves, Eddie White, Bob Best and Karen Heisler for their help over the years and in their contribution of background for some of our tales. Tim Bourret, now the sports information director at Clemson, had a staff of workers in South Carolina who helped in the proofing process as well, including associate SID Anne Miller. Former Clemson SID office personnel Emily Rabon, Sanford Rogers and Samantha Carruth transcribed about 30 hours of tape and know more about Notre Dame basketball history than anyone who lives in the state of South Carolina. Tim's Dad, Chuck Bourret, a 1948 Notre Dame grad, also put in many proofreading hours. Noah Amstadter, our editor at Sports Publishing and a Notre Dame 2002 graduate, was also very helpful.

Finally, I'd like to acknowledge my student managers who made the daily administration of our program a much easier process:

"For Digger, who did for Notre Dame basketball what Rockne did for football!"

—Legendary *Los Angeles Times* columnist Jim Murray, signing a copy of his autobiography for me in 1996

Chapter One

COMING TO
NOTRE DAME

THEY CALL ME DIGGER

I was born Richard Frederick Phelps in Beacon, NY on July 4, 1941. I was named after my father, but he was known around town as Dick Phelps, the local undertaker. People called me Richie until the eighth grade, when I started getting interested in sports.

At Beacon High, the junior high and high school were combined. As a junior high kid, if you loved sports like I did, you wanted to be the water boy for the football team or the batboy for the baseball team. In the eighth grade I became the batboy and loved every minute of it.

One day I got bored...and a little hungry. We were on a bus trip, and while the guys were taking batting practice, I went back to the bus and started going through their lunch bags in search of cupcakes and cookies. I ate to my heart's content, but when I came back to the field, I was dumb enough to leave the chocolate evidence on my face.

When the team returned to the bus, they went straight for their lunch bags, only to find them devoid of dessert. I was dragged to the back of the bus, where some of the players started beating me up. When it appeared I was never going to get out of this predicament, I yelled for the coach, Jim Guariloff, hoping he would save me.

In the 1950s there were popular radio shows like *Amos and Andy*, *The Lone Ranger* and *Abbott and Costello*. *Digger O'Dell, the Friendly Undertaker*, was one of those shows. When Coach Guariloff asked what was going on, the team told him I had eaten half of the cupcakes and cookies. Guariloff said, "If you don't stop eating the team's cupcakes I am going to put you in one of your old man's boxes. Do you understand, Digger O'Dell?" The entire team laughed. The next day in practice it was, "Digger O'Dell, get the bats. Digger O'Dell get the balls." Soon everyone shortened it to just Digger, and that is what I have been called since that bus trip with the Beacon High baseball team in the 1950s.

GUESTS RESTING IN THE LIVING ROOM

I went to Rider College in Trenton, NJ and studied business administration. When I graduated from Rider in 1963, my dad wanted me to go to the Simmons Embalming School at Syracuse. You could get to my father's funeral home by walking through our back yard, so I had been around that atmosphere all my life.

I learned to cope with corpses around the house at a young age. When I was five I came downstairs and found a man in a casket in our living room. When we had a doubleheader (two funerals at the same time), the second one would be in our living room. I didn't mind the undertaking business, and I had a lot of respect for my dad and what he did. But I just never took to the embalming aspect of the job.

"I CAN DO THIS"

I spent four years at Rider and lettered in basketball as a junior and senior. I also lettered in golf my senior year. I was not much of a scorer, but, as it says in the 1971-72 Notre Dame basketball guide, "[I] gained a reputation as a fine defensive specialist."

The summer before I was supposed to go to Syracuse I met Tom Winterbottom, the new coach at my old high school. He was starting a local summer league, but state rules prohibited him from coaching in the summer. So he asked me to coach a team in the league.

I told him I had never coached before. So he gave me a book called *Swing and Go*, which was written by Ed Jucker, the coach at Cincinnati at the time. It featured the double-stack offense that Ron

Bonham had used to lead Cincy to the National Championship. Ironically, that was virtually the same offense Notre Dame used with Austin Carr the year before I got to South Bend.

I tried to get a high school job at the end of the summer, but struck out. I told my dad I wanted to put embalming school on hold and go back to Rider to get a master's degree and be a volunteer coach under my college coach, Bob Greenwood.

One of my assignments that year (1963-64) was to scout NYU. In that era, NYU was still a power in college basketball. NYU entered the game with a home-court winning streak that dated to 1941. They had lost in Madison Square Garden, but not at University Heights.

I scouted them twice, against Iona and Hofstra. At the time, I lived with Nick Valvano, Jim's brother. His dad, Rocky, was a coach, but he was also an ECAC referee. He refereed one of those Iona-NYU games and I remember picking his brain after the game.

I came back to Rider with a game plan, and Coach Greenwood let me put it in over the two days of practice prior to the game. We won to end the streak. That night when I came home, I sat in the apartment and said to myself, "I can do this."

AN EARLY HINT OF THE IRISH

After I earned my master's degree, I wanted to get a full-time coaching job at the college level so I started sending out resumes, but I didn't have much luck.

With the rejection letters piling up, I ran into Jack Gallagher, who was coaching at Scranton Prep in Pennsylvania. He told me about a high school job that was open at St. Gabriel's High School in Hazelton, Pennsylvania. He told me to call Father Ray Deviney. I figured I wasn't going to get a college job, so why not get some head coaching experience? He offered me the job and I accepted. At age 24 I was a head coach.

Like all high school coaches, one of my first projects was to design the uniforms. When I was growing up in New York, the biggest game of the year was Notre Dame vs. Army. When we played in the yard as kids, you were either Doc Blanchard, Glenn Davis or Johnny Lujack. I was always Lujack, who won the 1946 Heisman as Notre Dame's quarterback.

Notre Dame was in my blood at an early age, so I wanted to incorporate something about Notre Dame into our uniforms. Even though our primary color was purple, I put a shamrock on our game pants.

Writing Ara Parseghian

That part of Pennsylvania was a strong Notre Dame area. At St. Gabe's, the nuns were saying the rosary and lighting candles on Saturdays for the Notre Dame football team. In those days Notre Dame would play Pittsburgh every other year in Pittsburgh. Many of the coal minors in that area were in tough shape economically, but they would save all their money over a two-year period so they could make the trip to Pittsburgh and root for Notre Dame. That was their vacation.

About six weeks prior to the season, in a letter postmarked October 30, 1965, I wrote Notre Dame football coach Ara Parseghian a letter. In it I told him that my goal in life was to be the head basketball coach at the University of Notre Dame. I loved the essence of Notre Dame and what the university stood for.

I wrote a letter to Ara Parseghian in 1965 telling him it was my dream to be the head basketball coach at Notre Dame. Six years later, at age 29, my dream came true.

I am sure today it seems odd to write a letter to the football coach about a job as head basketball coach, but Ara had such charisma. He was the most visible symbol of the school and I identified with that. When I thought about Notre Dame, I thought of Ara. To some extent, I still do that today.

JOHNNY DRUZE

Other than me, Johnny Druze is one of the few people who is a common denominator in the athletic histories of Notre Dame and Fordham. As a student in the 1930s, he was one of Fordham's "Seven Blocks of Granite." He joined forces with Vince Lombardi and five others to form one of the most famous offensive lines in college football history. After he got out of school, he became an assistant coach at Notre Dame, working under Frank Leahy and Terry Brennan from 1941-55.

I got to know Johnny Druze through one of my best friends, Johnny Campbell. Johnny's father, Hugh, ran a brickyard in Hazelton, Pennsylvania, and I worked for him when I coached at St. Gabriel's. Mr. Campbell went to Notre Dame and we used to talk about his experiences there all the time.

One day, while I was at Penn—where I spent four years helping Dick Harter build some of the best teams in Ivy League history—I called Hugh Campbell and told him I always wanted to be the head coach at Notre Dame. I asked him how I could get involved in that job when Johnny Dee retired. This was a brash move, because I was only 27 at the time. I told Harter about it and he was upset with me, not to mention that he thought I was crazy. "Like you have a chance to be the next head coach at Notre Dame."

Hugh Campbell told me a good contact would be Johnny Druze, who was by now living in Asbury Park, New Jersey. He added, "His daughter is married to John (Hugh's son)."

So, I called John and we went to see Johnny Druze. I told him I just loved Notre Dame and that it was where I wanted to coach some day. We kept in touch over the next couple of years.

While I went to see Johnny Druze so he could some day help me with the Notre Dame job, I never dreamed I was also creating an in at Fordham. In March of 1970, Ed Conlin left Fordham after the season.

In those days the Final Four was on a Thursday-Saturday. When I got back home to New Jersey on Good Friday, my wife, Terry, said Johnny Druze had called. He had been at a dinner with Pete Carlisimo, who was the athletic director at Fordham. Johnny had spent the banquet selling me to Carlisimo. To make a long story short, I interviewed with Carlisimo over the Tuesday after Easter and he offered me the job the next week.

Last fall I was at Martin's Supermarket in South Bend and I ran into John Campbell and his wife. I asked them how her how her mom and dad were doing. She said that they were outside in the car. Johnny is 90 years old now. I went out to the car and told him, "Without you, I'm nothing. I wouldn't have gotten the job at Fordham and I wouldn't have gotten the job at Notre Dame. I am what I am because of you, Johnny."

EARLY SUCCESS

I inherited a Fordham team that had been 10-15 in 1969-70. We had a pep rally before the first game in one of the dorms. P.J. Carlisimo, who went on to coach Seton Hall to the National Championship game in 1989, was a senior on that team and the athletic director's son. He could get things done on campus and organized this rally. Jack Burik, our point guard, was one of the speakers as a tri-captain, and told the students about our 40-minute full-court press. When he said that to the students I told Frank McLaughlin, my assistant coach, that our players had bought into our system.

We got off to a great start and just kept on winning. Among the first six games of the season we beat Pittsburgh, Seton Hall and Syracuse. Bill Raftery, my collegue at *ESPN today*, was the coach at Seton Hall and we won 97-80. Dick Harter told someone in the media if Seton Hall had hired Digger they would be undefeated. I am sure Raf loved that.

A WORTHWHILE SCOUTING TRIP

Before videotape became a way of life, coaches would send assistants to scout future opponents. We didn't trade game film like some football coaches did then and still do today. We were going to play Notre Dame and Marquette on consecutive Thursday nights in February in Madison Square Garden, so it was a perfect scouting opportunity for me to personally scout Notre Dame at the Marquette game in Milwaukee on January 12, 1971.

Word was out that Johnny Dee was going to retire as Notre Dame coach at the end of the year and return to Denver to join a law practice. So it was a good opportunity to meet some Notre Dame people at that game.

I had been to Notre Dame in the fall of 1968 when I was on a recruiting trip for Penn to see Corky Calhoun, of Waukegan, Illinois. Johnny Druze had arranged a meeting with Moose Krause, so I made a side trip from Chicago to South Bend. Before I met with Moose, I went over to the stadium and walked in the tunnel onto the field. I walked to the middle of the field and mentally flashed back to my youth. I could hear Bill Stern calling games on WOR radio. I got goose bumps as I stood in the middle of Notre Dame Stadium.

When I met Moose I also made a point of getting to know his secretary, Elenor Van Der Hagen. What a wonderful person. If there were two people who helped me get the job at Notre Dame, it was Elenor working from the inside and Johhny Druze from the outside.

When it came time to scout the Notre Dame-Marquette game, I called Elenor to tell her I was going. She knew I wanted to come to Notre Dame some day, so she called the sports information director at Marquette and arranged for me to sit next to Roger Valdiserri, Notre Dame's sports information director, at press row. That Marquette game was the first time I spent any time with Roger.

I went to that game with Frank Mulzoff, the head coach at St. John's at the time, who was also going to be playing Notre Dame in New York just nine days after us. We called Al McGuire ahead of time to let him know we were coming and he invited us to meet him at a bar called Timeout prior to the game. It was right across the street from The Milwaukee Arena, which was later known as The Mecca.

Frank and I were having Cokes, but Al was having a beer. He had one beer, two beers, three beers. I said, "Hey, don't you have a game tonight?" Nothing phased Al.

He said, "Let's go, I want you to meet the guys." So he took us right into the Marquette locker room during pregame to meet his players. We were going to play them in a month. Those were different times.

So, I scouted that game and obviously followed Notre Dame's progress throughout the season. They (it seems strange to use they when referring to Notre Dame) had Austin Carr, the best player in the nation, and to this day the best player Notre Dame has ever had. He came to New York averaging over 37 points per game. The Irish had beaten UCLA on January 23 and Carr had scored 46 points in an 89-82 win to give UCLA what would be its only loss of the season.

BEATING NOTRE DAME

Ranked in the top 20 with an 18-1 record, we had captivated New York by now. Howard Cosell was the sports anchor at WABC in New York at that time and he adopted me. He had me in studio for an interview during his sports segment and compared me to Melio Betina, who was a light heavyweight champion from Beacon.

I remember him saying, "Digger Phelps, an undertaker's son, is bringing the bacon back to Beacon like Melio Bettina had many years ago." I looked at him and said, "Howard, I'm going to put you in one of my old man's boxes." Everyone on the set broke up. If Howard loved you in New York, you were in. In 1970-71 we owned New York, and Howard had a lot to do with that.

The game was a complete sellout, 19,500 people, toughest college basketball ticket in the Garden in years. While the first game of the doubleheader was going on, I was standing behind the scorer's table with Roger and Johnny Druze.

In front of Roger, Johnny asked, "So how are you going to beat Notre Dame tonight?" I said, "I can't tell you that, then Roger is going to go in the locker room and tell Johnny Dee." But Roger said he wouldn't—it was too close to game time and Notre Dame wasn't going to change its plan just before the game.

So, I told them that Notre Dame had lost six games all year and five of the teams that had beaten them had played a zone defense. You couldn't guard Carr man to man, so I was going to play zone for 30 minutes, then go after it with the press for the last 10 minutes. We hadn't played a zone defense all year, so I knew Notre Dame would not be expecting it. I also told them we were going to let Sid Catlett shoot from the outside and when Carr got the ball we were going to double team and make him give it up. We wanted to make someone else beat us.

That little interaction before the game might have helped me get the Notre Dame job, because the game played out just that way. Carr still scored 29 to lead all scorers, but we didn't let him penetrate and he got just six free throw attempts. We had a five- to 10-point lead most of the game, but Charlie Yelverton, our top scorer, fouled out with seven minutes left. He left to a standing ovation.

During the momentary timeout I got everyone together and told them I wasn't thinking about losing. Someone else was going to step up and I looked right at Billy Mainor. Down the stretch he scored 13 of our last 19 points and did not allow Carr to score a single point. We won 94-88 and it was party time in New York City.

We went to parties around town, cabbies were blowing their horns. At one point we went to the Webster Bar on Webster Avenue, which was just up from the Fordham campus. It was 2 a.m. and the students were still going crazy. My wife, Terry, and my high school coach, Mike Scoba, and his wife, Barbara, got home about 4 a.m.

That night I had sold New York City on Fordham's basketball program. I had also sold Roger Valdiserri that I could be the next coach at Notre Dame.

REALIZING A DREAM AT AGE 29

We finished the 1970-71 season with a 26-3 record and a No. 9 final national ranking according to AP, still the only season Fordham has had a final top-10 ranking.

We went to the NCAA Tournament and beat Furman in the first round, but Villanova's size was too much for us in the round of 16. They went to the finals that year behind Howard Porter before losing by just eight points to UCLA.

I was one of the hottest coaches in the country. My phone was ringing and the media was following my every move. First, Virginia Tech called and they brought me to campus. They had a $35,000 a year offer for five years. Then Rutgers opened because Bill Foster went to Utah. Then Dick Harter and Athletic Director Fred Shabel started to have problems to the point where Dick took the Oregon job.

I was the perfect replacement for Harter at Penn because I had been there and recruited those players who were leading the current team. I went over there for an interview and Fred had arranged to have the entire team meet me when I arrived. I told them with a smile, "Get out of here and get to class."

I met with Shabel and he offered me $35,000 a year for four years, a car and a preferential parking space at Weightman Hall. That parking space was big, it was a status symbol at Penn in those days. I was making $14,000 at Fordham, but they were going to offer me $18,000.

I met with Frank Dolson of the *Philalphia Inquirer* after I interviewed with Shabel. I told him all the particulars about the Penn job, but he just smiled. He knew I wasn't going to do anything until I heard from Notre Dame.

On Friday after the NCAA Tournament, Roger Valdiserri called and said they would formally announce Johnny Dee's retirement on Saturday, April 30. Father Edmund Joyce, the vice president of the school who was in control of the Athletic Board, wanted to meet with me on Saturday in Detroit. Notre Dame always worked quickly when it came to a major coaching change. The priests always had their short lists, and at Notre Dame you usually don't have to go very far down the list.

As Valdiserri was putting out a release that Johnny Dee was retiring, I was meeting with Father Joyce at a room at the Detroit airport. It was just like 1941 when Father Frank Cavanaugh, brother of Notre Dame president Father John Cavanaugh, met with Boston College coach Frank Leahy in Albany, NY to interview him for the football job.

The interview took place on the Saturday of the Blue-Gold Football game at Notre Dame. Fr. Joyce flew back in time for the postgame banquet. No one ever knew he wasn't at the game. We talked for two hours. I told him how I believed in what Notre Dame stood for. "If we can be great in football, why not basketball?" I was already saying we. He was very impressive. With his tall stature and Roman Collar, he had a presence about him. Even though I had never met Father Joyce, I knew of him because I had followed Notre Dame sports so closely. This was someone I trusted from our first meeting, and he trusted me.

I asked him what he expected. Father Joyce said, "We expect you to graduate your players, never get in trouble with the NCAA and be competitive." I asked what he meant by competitive and he said, "About 18 wins a year." I had just won 26 at Fordham, surely I could win 18 a year at Notre Dame.

At the end of the interview, not that it mattered, we discussed the salary. He said $18,000 a year for four years, plus an additional $3,000 for radio and TV. This was far below the offers from Virginia Tech and Penn, but I didn't care. I would have taken the job for food coupons for my wife and kids at the North Dining Hall. In fact, that four-year contract at the beginning was the only time I had a multi-year contract at Notre Dame. I just worked from year to year after 1974-75.

When I left that interview, I felt 95 percent sure Father Joyce was going to offer me this job, my dream job. He had to talk to the Athletic Board. Roger called me on Sunday and asked me about the interview.

On Monday, I called Fred Shabel at Penn and told him I was going to wait on Notre Dame. That afternoon he announced Chuck Daly as his new coach. Bill Conlin, who is a frequent guest on ESPN's *Sunday Sports Reports* program, asked Daly at the press conference how it felt to be second to Digger Phelps. Shabel jumped in and said he never offered me the job. The room broke up.

Monday night Roger called me to say it was going to happen. Father Joyce was going to meet with the Board on Tuesday and that I should expect a call that afternoon. It was a lock.

I set up a team meeting at Fordham's campus. At 6:32 p.m. eastern time, I got the call from Moose Krause, offering me the head coaching position at Notre Dame. I immediately went into the team meeting to tell them I was leaving.

I went straight to the airport with my wife, Terry. As we were going over the Triborough Bridge, a sports bulletin came over the radio. "Digger Phelps has just accepted the head coaching position at

Notre Dame." It hadn't been 15 minutes since the team meeting. At that point I realized how big it was to be the head coach at Notre Dame.

That June, I went to my first Notre Dame Monogram club golf outing. At the dinner I told Roger about the letter I had written to Ara Parseghian. Ara was also at the function and said he had a "crazy letter file" in his office and it might still be there. He gave Roger the keys and we went over to his office. Sure enough, the letter was still there. Roger made a copy of the envelope and put it in the press guide that fall.

At age 29, just six years after I had mailed Ara that letter, I was going to realize my dream.

FIRESIDE CHATS

Dormitory life at Notre Dame is a tradition. There are no fraternities nor sororities at Notre Dame. Heck, when I started there weren't any women at all. Coeducation didn't start until the 1972-73 academic year.

I wanted to take advantage of the spirit of the Notre Dame student body, and turn them on to basketball. The support of the student body was legendary at football games. Why not basketball?

So, I contacted the presidents of all the dorms, and my secretary, Dottie Van Paris, set up a speaking schedule. We started around October 1, taking one dorm per night. The dorms would publicize it with simple signs on the doors. I would go over to the lobby of the dorm, walk in and sit down and just start shooting the breeze with the students. Sometimes there was an introduction and sometimes I just started talking. Anyone who wanted to come in was free to do so.

The first of these "Fireside Chats" had small numbers, but soon the students would talk about it and the numbers grew and grew. We talked about the team, the prospects for the season, other teams around the country, but we talked about social issues also. I was always interested in politics, world hunger, the Vietnam War...you name it and we talked about it.

Turning Notre Dame students on to basketball was one of my first priorities, whether it was through informal talks in the dorms or pep rallies.

I genuinely enjoyed doing this. I think it got the students interested in our program. One of the reasons for Notre Dame's success has been the support of the student body, and the dorm system has everything to do with it.

I am glad to see that Mike Brey has continued to have his players live in dorms. In fact, when his team is introduced at home games, he has the PA announcer say what dorm they live in. It tells the other students that these guys are part of us, they aren't segregated in some glass house somewhere off campus.

In April of 2004, I was invited to speak on campus at Fisher Hall. I still do a good bit of speaking at Notre Dame when my ESPN schedule allows. A lot of my greatest players (Adrian Dantley, Gary Brokaw, John Shumate) lived in that dorm. I talked for two hours about my career at Notre Dame, today's Notre Dame team, the traditions of Notre Dame, and many other subjects.

Just after I had started, a 5-7 student who was not the most athletic-looking person in the world came into the room wearing a Chris Thomas jersey. Thomas and Torin Francis, stars of Notre Dame's current team, had just had surgery. I said to the kid wearing the Thomas jersey, "How'd the surgery go, Chris? Not too well I guess." The other students laughed. Then I said, "I can't wait to see Torin Francis."

"DIGGER, THE WIRE REVERSED YOUR SCORE"

When I took the Notre Dame job, I knew we would struggle the first couple of years. Notre Dame's 1970-71 team graduated six seniors who represented 93 percent of the scoring. Among the graduates was Austin Carr, who was second in the nation in scoring with a 37.9 average. He was a first-team All-American and the National Player of the Year. Collis Jones was a 6-7 forward who had averaged 24 points and 12 rebounds a game.

In the summer, my team captain and the only returning player with significant varsity experience, Doug Gemmell, was injured so severely in a motorcycle accident that he had to have his left leg amputated. We had three other scholarship players in Jim Regelean, Bill Hinga and Don Silinski who had a little varsity experience, or had played on the freshman team. John Shumate had averaged 22 points a game on the freshman team the year I was at Fordham, but in November of 1971 he was diagnosed with a blood disorder that was causing him problems with blood clots. Here was my star player in the hospital fighting for his life just after we had started practice.

That left me with an all sophomore starting lineup. My lineup for the opening game against Michigan consisted of Goose Novak, a 6-7 small forward who had to play center; Hawk Stevens, a 6-6 forward who was the most popular DJ at the student radio station; 6-7 Tom O'Mara; 5-11 John Egart and 6-2 Bob Valibus. Some of my top reserves were two guys from the baseball team, Tom Hansen and Bill Lucas, and later, three football players, Willie Townsend, Mike Townsend and Rich Allocco. We tried to run with Michigan and play the same pressing style we had played at Fordham, but it didn't work. The Wolverines beat us 101-83 at home.

The schedule didn't get any easier that first year. We lost at Kansas, at Indiana, at UCLA and at Kentucky all in December. Indiana, UCLA and Kentucky were all ranked in the top 15 in the country at the time we played them.

I never will forget the Indiana game of December 18, 1971. It was in Bloomington and they were dedicating Assembly Hall. I had beaten Bob Knight the year before when I was at Fordham and he was at Army.

We were awful...beyond awful. Let me give you a few stats to back that up. Indiana forward John Ritter outscored our entire team (31-29). We shot 13 percent from the field (8-61) and 48 percent (13-27) from the line. No Notre Dame player scored in double figures. Our starting backcourt that night was 0-16 from the field. We had the same amount of turnovers as points (29). We scored 13 points in the first half and just two in the last 6:23.

Indiana was not trying to run up the score, even though they beat us 94-29. It is still the largest margin of defeat in Notre Dame history. After the game I got a call from one of my buddies in New York. "Digger, the wire transposed the digits on your score last night." He thought the score was 94-92. I told him we had lost on a buzzer shot.

There weren't many highlights that first year. We played eight games against top 20-teams and lost them all, finishing 6-20. At one point in the season I told a writer at the *Chicago Tribune*, "We've got to scrimmage every day so I know what it feels like to win."

A LANDMARK VICTORY OVER KANSAS

Even with the return of Shumate and the addition of Gary Brokaw, Dwight Clay and Peter Crotty, we started out 1-6 in my second year with the only win at home by 10 points over Valparaiso. But at least we were competitive. We lost in overtime to Ohio State, by two to St. Louis, by two at home to an Indiana team that would go to the Final Four, and by two to Kentucky in Louisville.

When you are early in the development of a program you look for one win to turn your program around. That victory came for us against a Kansas team coached by Ted Owens on January 7, 1973. It was a nationally televised Sunday afternoon game in South Bend.

This was the first time that Shumate, Brokaw and Clay all clicked in the same game, as they would combine for 53 points in this game. We were down two, 61-59 in the final seconds. Brokaw missed a jumper, but Shumate tipped it in at the buzzer, sending the game into overtime. We took a four-point lead in the overtime, then tried to give it away when Brokaw had the ball tied up at mid-court with 19 seconds left. We lost the jump ball, but Kansas turned it over in the final seconds and we had finally won a close game.

There was a carry-over effect from that game. The following Saturday we beat Marquette to end their 81-game home winning streak on a jumper by Clay. We won eight of our last 10 regular-season games to finish 15-11. The NIT called and we enthusiastically accepted.

In those days the NIT took 16 teams and all the games were played in New York at Madison Square Garden. Only 32 teams went to the NCAA Tournament in those days, so the NIT first-round games were like NCAA Tournament games today. There were only 48 teams in the entire nation going to postseason play.

We opened against a Southern Cal team that had finished second in the Pac-10 to UCLA and featured All-America guard Gus Williams. The game was played on St. Patrick's Day in New York, how could we lose? And we didn't, winning 69-65. The game was televised nationally, and I remember being interviewed after the game by a young CBS announcer named Don Criqui, who was a Notre Dame graduate.

The next Tuesday night we played Louisville, coached by Denny Crum, and we won another close game, 79-71, as Shumate made nine of nine from the field. The following Saturday we played North Carolina and Dean Smith. Shumate continued his incredible play, as he made his first 11 field goals of the game in our 78-71 victory. North Carolina was ranked 11th in the nation entering the NIT, a team that would have been a No. 3 seed in the NCAA Tournament

The Final Four of the 1973 NIT included (from left) future Hall of Fame coach Dean Smith, me, future Hall of Famer C.M. Newton, and Virginia Tech coach Don Devoe. Both Hall of Fame coaches were eliminated in the semifinals.

by today's standards. But in those days, a conference could only send one team to the NCAA Tournament.

That sent us to the final against Virginia Tech, ironically the school I had turned down just two years earlier. They had hired Don Devoe and we were both Cinderella teams. The Final Four teams at the NIT that year were Notre Dame, Virginia Tech, North Carolina and Alabama. Alabama was coached by C.M. Newton. Out of the four teams in the Final Four of the NIT that year, two were coached by men in the Hall of Fame and two weren't. The two future Hall of Famers watched Devoe and I battle it out.

The championship game on Sunday turned out to be an incredible game. It was an overtime game and our lack of depth caught up to us. I played just six guys and four of them went the entire 45 minutes. Virginia Tech beat us in overtime by a point, 92-91. On the last possession Bobby Stevens missed a jumper, but the ball rebounded back to him and he nailed the second shot from the left wing as the distinctive Madison Square Garden horn sounded.

WELCOME HOME

We knew we had accomplished something, but we were still disappointed as we flew back to South Bend on Monday morning. It had been a great run to close the season, winning 17 of our last 23, including wins over Kansas, Marquette, Michigan State, St. John's, South Carolina, and the wins in the NIT. But that last play was just a bitter ending to the season. We were so close to a national championship, and for a program that had started out 7-26, that was an accomplishment.

Our spirits were lifted, however, as the bus turned up Notre Dame Avenue and moved slowly towards the Golden Dome. Over 3,000 students, including the entire Notre Dame Band was at The Circle (the main entrance to the school) to greet us. That was the beginning of a tradition. There would be many more occasions when the student body met our team at that same spot whether it be 3 p.m. or 3 a.m.

Those evenings in the dorms were paying off. The campus was not quite there yet, but the students were getting almost as excited about the basketball team as they were about the football team.

Even though we had lost, Shumate was named the MVP of the NIT. He never smiled when he accepted the trophy. He wanted the team championship trophy. That was the reaction I was hoping to see because I knew he would be our leader the next season.

With all five starters back, plus the addition of a recruiting class that included Adrian Dantley and some other top-100 players who would fit into our system, I couldn't wait for the next season to start.

Despite the loss to Virginia Tech, the student body met us at the circle at noon on a Monday. I couldn't wait for the 1973-74 season.

Chapter Two

71-70

THE MAKING OF A RIVALRY

When I came to Notre Dame in May of 1971, I was determined to make Notre Dame basketball the best program in the country. It had the best football program under Ara Parseghian, why not in basketball? The first thing I did was look to UCLA. They were the Yankees of college basketball, a true dynasty.

When I came to Notre Dame we were already scheduled to play UCLA home and home. I wanted to continue that series and we did, playing the Bruins twice a year until the 1982-83 season. John Wooden's first job in coaching was at South Bend Central High School in the 1940s. That school does not exist today, but in the 1970s he still had a lot of friends in the area. It gave him an opportunity to see them every year.

At the time we scheduled those games, he figured we weren't going to be very good. They never lost to anyone, and I am sure he wasn't afraid of a program that had just been wiped out by graduation and was now coached by a 29-year-old who had just one year of head coaching experience.

ROUGH START

As I said in chapter one, we were horrible my first year. Goose Novak was our center at 6-7. To see him go against Bill Walton...it was ugly.

The first time we went to UCLA, in December of 1971, we were coming off the 65-point loss to Indiana. Two days later we were flying to Los Angeles to play UCLA and of course they were No. 1. When we landed I bought a *Los Angeles Times* and the pregame story included a cartoon that had a Notre Dame player about to face a guillotine. "Watch a live execution in person" was the headline.

This was Walton and Keith Wilkes's sophomore years, their first year of eligibility. We were starting five sophomores and had walkons playing 20 percent of the minutes. We were supposed to have Shumate, but he missed the year with a heart ailment.

With eight minutes left and ahead by 41, Wooden was still pressing and had his starters in the game. We couldn't get the ball into the frontcourt, never mind score. I still remember poor John Egart trying to break their press. They beat us 114-58, the second largest margin of defeat in Notre Dame history. Nice start for me, the two worst defeats in Notre Dame history back to back within the first seven games of my career.

Late in the game, I was in a crouch in front of our bench and looked down at UCLA's bench. I caught Gary Cunningham's eye (assistant coach at the time) and I mouthed two words to him. It wasn't thank you...but the second word was you. He did a double take, then I said, "and the guy next to you, too!"

After the game, Wooden sought me out after the media interviews were finished. Obviously Gary had told him I was upset. Wooden started in by saying, "Now Digger, this past week we were in our final exams and we didn't get to practice that much. We have our conference season starting next week, so I needed to work on my press."

I knew that was bull, they were getting revenge for last year when Notre Dame beat them in South Bend, their only loss during a National Championship season. So, I just looked at him and said, "John, you do anything you have to do to beat me, because someday I am going to kick your ass." Then I just turned and walked away.

For the second meeting in South Bend that year I was bound and determined that we weren't going to lose by 58 points. In those days there was no shot clock. I knew Wooden would play man for man but wouldn't chase Walton away from the basket. So, I just held the ball for long periods of time with Gary Novak dribbling the ball by the 28-foot mark on the court. I know we missed two TV timeouts because of it. A couple of times Novak caught Walton napping and just drove by him for a basket. Of course all that did was make him mad. The final score was 57-32. It was boring, but we didn't lose by 50.

YEAR 2: BRUINS SET A RECORD

The next year they beat us by 26 in Los Angeles two days before Christmas, then they came to South Bend in late January. There are many ironies in this series, and one was this game in January 1973. They had won 60 in a row and were tied with San Francisco's Bill Russell teams of the mid-fifties for the longest winning streak in college basketball history. A win over us in South Bend would break the streak.

We stayed with them for the first half, but they were pulling away late in the game. Near the end, with the game still going on, Wooden motioned for me to meet him at the scorer's table. He said, "Tell John Shumate to lay off the rough play on Walton, or I'll put Sven Nater into the game." He was implying that he was going to put Nater into the game to play rough.

I didn't back down. I said, "Go ahead and bring in Nater. I've got three football players at the end of my bench, and I'll put all three in the game and take on your entire team." I just turned and walked away. He was either shocked that I had stood up to him, or he thought I was crazy enough to do it.

The game continued without incident, but after the game, the media wanted to know what we were talking about. I just told the press we were discussing his book, *They Call me Coach*, which had just been published. He wrote me a letter during the off season and apologized.

Still, to say I was motivated for January 19, 1974, would be an understatement.

HOW GOOD WAS UCLA?

Today, 30 years after that game was played, UCLA under John Wooden is still the number-one dynasty in the history of college basketball and among the greatest in sports. When ESPN did a series for *Sports Century* a couple of years ago on dynasties in sports, the two college dynasties they featured were Notre Dame football and UCLA basketball.

Let me throw some numbers at you about UCLA coming into this game.

• UCLA entered the game on an 88-game winning streak, 28 longer than any other streak in men's college basketball history.

• UCLA had won eight of the last nine NCAA Championships, including seven in a row.

• During the 88-game streak they had just two wins by one point, and none in overtime. One of those one-point games had been against Maryland, 65-64 at UCLA in the second game of the 1973-74 season. Their average margin of victory for the 88 games was 23.5 points per game. They had a scoring margin of 26.4 for their first 13 games of this season. In fact, we were tied for first in the nation in that category entering this game.

• UCLA was ranked first in the nation, a position they had held for 45 consecutive Associated Press polls.

• Earlier in the year, in their fourth game of the year, they had faced NC State in St. Louis. NC State was on a 29-game winning streak and had David Thompson. UCLA won by 18 points; it was never close.

• The Bruins were 218-5 entering that game dating to the 1966-67 season.

• Ten players on the 1973-74 UCLA roster would be drafted by the end of their careers and eight made it in the NBA, including Wilkes, Marques Johnson and Walton—who all played at least 10 years in the league. Five players were first-round draft choices and four—Walton, David Meyers, Marques Johnson and Richard Washington—were chosen within the first three selections of the NBA draft.

CUTTING DOWN THE NETS...ON WEDNESDAY AFTERNOON

I always felt the mental part of preparation for a big game was more important than the physical. I even used to have one of my assistants in charge of pregame motivation, some gimmick that would give the players that little extra from a psychological standpoint.

Even though we were 9-0 and had outscored every opponent by 26.4 points per game coming into the UCLA game, I thought it was important to put this team in a positive mindset.

We had lost four straight to UCLA by a total of 128 points, so I had to change that mindset. One of the things I did was show the team film of the first 10 minutes of the two games the previous year when we'd played well and we were in the game. This way they could see themselves playing against Walton and Wilkes and the others, holding their own for a long period of time.

I had a picture hanging in my office from the last time UCLA had lost. Notre Dame was the last team to beat UCLA before it went on its 88-game winning streak, an 89-82 Irish victory on January 23, 1971. Austin Carr had scored 46 points in one of the great individual performances in college basketball history. It was the most points any player ever scored against a John Wooden-coached UCLA team.

After the game the students rushed the court and put Carr on their shoulders so he could cut down the nets. I don't think they had ever done that at Notre Dame before, it was all spontaneous. One of the students who hoisted Carr to his shoulders that day was Shumate, who was a freshman at the time and ineligible to play, like all freshmen in those days.

On Wednesday, it just hit me. Why not practice cutting down the nets? So, that's what we did at the end of practice that day. That's right, still three days prior to the game.

We had a drill where the Blue team (subs) was pressing the gold team, which had a 10-point lead with three minutes left. Ironically, the game situation the following Saturday would be the opposite situation. At the end of that drill I brought the team together and said, "OK, you know what happens know? Shumate, you go to one basket and Goose (Gary Novak), you go to the other. The rest of you split up and lift them up so they can cut down the nets, because that is what we are going to do after we win on Saturday. Someday you will tell your grandchildren about this."

Some of them looked at me like I was crazy, but they did it. We repeated it after Friday's practice. Rich Clarkson, who was covering the game for *Sports Illustrated*, was at Friday's practice and that is how those pictures got in the issue the next week.

Every time Gary Brokaw talks about that game, he talks about cutting down the nets at practice leading into the game. He always said it gave the team confidence.

THE GAME PLAN

Our preparation was rudimentary compared to the way it is done today. We didn't have videotape nor did we exchange film in those days. You scouted a team in person, either an assistant, or the head coach.

We had played UCLA twice the previous year, so we used those films. I got a bonus scouting opportunity when I was asked by Eddie Einhorn, president of TUS, to do the color commentary on the NC State vs. UCLA game back in December. UCLA won by 18, but it did give me another look at Walton and Wilkes. When you look at that today, you would never see an active coach doing color commentary on another game in season. See, even 30 years ago I was planning ahead to my post-coaching career.

I also had the opportunity to scout their game with Iowa on the Thursday prior to our game on Saturday. Can you imagine that today, Coach K going over to North Carolina to scout Wake Forest vs. the Tar Heels?

Scouting UCLA against Iowa didn't do us much good because Walton did not play. He had injured his back against Washington State and had not played against California or Stanford. When I got to Chicago Stadium he was nowhere to be found. He stayed in his hotel room at the Bismark Hotel, resting his back. Ralph Drollinger played the entire game against Iowa and the Bruins, who were struggling at the half, won by 24.

Whether he played or not really didn't affect our strategy. I know I said that then and people were skeptical. But we had decided long ago that we would play them straight up, man to man. I really thought we matched up pretty well with them, even against Walton. If Shumate was on, that could be a draw. Brokaw was a tough assignment for Wilkes because of his quickness. Dantley was young, but he was a better athlete than David Meyers.

And, when we told the team we would play them straight up, it gave them confidence. You couldn't underestimate the importance of confidence when you were playing UCLA.

In Wooden's press conference after the Iowa game at Chicago Stadium he was asked if he had scouted Notre Dame. He said he had not, but he "planed to talk to a friend who had seen Notre Dame play a couple of times." How about that, but he really believed it was all about what his team did, it didn't matter what you did. In those days you could sign 20 guys to scholarships. He had all the good players, so he really didn't have to scout.

THE PEP RALLY

On Friday night, we had a pep rally at Stepan Center, a building on campus about half a mile for the ACC that was used for all kinds of student functions, including football pep rallies. This basketball rally rivaled any football rally, with the exception of a USC football game. Over 3,000 students and fans showed up.

The featured speaker was Sid Catlett, who had been a starter on the last Notre Dame team to beat UCLA three years previously. He read a fictional letter from Bill Walton to John Shumate.

"Dear John,

Sorry I won't be at the game on Saturday. There seems to be a yellow streak running up my back." The place roared.

It was the obvious reference to whether or not Walton would play. Jimmy The Greek had set a double line in Las Vegas. UCLA was favored by four if Walton played, and Notre Dame was favored by four if he didn't.

GAME DAY

John Shumate woke up at 6:30 a.m. in his Fisher Hall dorm room. Considering the party atmosphere the previous evening, he had gotten some sleep. Before he went to bed he personally went to five different parties in the Hall and asked them to keep it down, then appointed a hall monitor on each floor to keep things under control.

As soon as he got up, Shumate called his parents and he prayed over the phone with them. His father was a minister back home in Elizabeth City, NJ. When he finished his phone call, Shumate turned the tables on his dorm mates. He turned his stereo on full blast and went around the halls waking everyone up. "It is Bruin time," he yelled.

At eight a.m. the team met at the Crypt below Sacred Heart Basilica. We had a pregame mass before every game, something all Notre Dame teams did then. All the players attended, whether they were Catholic or not.

Father Edmund P. Joyce, Notre Dame's executive vice president in control of athletics, said the mass. The ACC is now named the Joyce Center after him. Father Joyce's homily that morning was not all about scripture.

"This is not just an ordinary day," said Fr. Joyce. "The chances are good that years from now you will look back on this day as one of the most memorable of your life. Is this melodramatic? I don't think so." He then told the team the most important thing to remember was to do your best to contribute to the success of the team.

Shumate was ever the team leader, and at one point in the locker room started telling everyone within earshot, with his best impersonation of a gospel minister, that he had a dream last night.

"I dreamed I was running from a Big Bear, it was a Bruin!"

"Tell it brother!" responded the team.

"He had me scared for a while."

"We know, we know," said the team.

"I ran into the woods, and there was a leprechaun there."

"Tell it brother!"

"I said, 'Lep, a Bruin is after me. What can I do?'

"The Lep said, 'Lay down a Bear Bryant trap.'"

"Tell it!"

"So I laid down a Bear Bryant trap and the trap said, 'Snap!'"

At 11 a.m. I told everyone to turn off the music, it was time to get to work. Looking back, we were not a tight team... obviously.

Just before the game, the TVS people (the network showing the game) asked me to do an interview at midcourt with Dick Enberg, the play-by-play announcer who has certainly reached legendary status in the profession, Hot Rod Hundley, who would be the color commentator, and Wooden. This would never happen today. Could you see both head coaches doing a simultaneous interview, live, just seven minutes prior to tip-off?

Wooden kept trying to make eye contact, but I ignored him. I just looked at the crowd and they were jacked. This was like a heavyweight prizefight, this was Ali vs. Frazier.

WE MEAN BUSINESS

It was an accident, but just 57 seconds into the game Adrian Dantley was battling for a rebound and hit Walton in the nose, causing it to bleed. UCLA took a timeout because Wooden didn't want to take him out. He was playing the game wearing a corset as it was, now he had cotton stuck in his nose, which would make it hard for him to breathe.

We all waited while they plugged his nose. Wooden didn't want Walton to miss a second of this game, and he didn't, playing all 40, as did Pete Trgovich and Wilkes. Looking back, I am glad that happened because it sent a message that we weren't going to back down from anyone this day. I sure wasn't worried about Adrian's intensity either. Freshman or not, he was ready to play.

As ready as we were emotionally, UCLA was on fire in the first half. They took a 33-16 lead with 6:41 remaining in the first half when Curtis, who had been talking trash all half to Clay, hit a jumper from the corner. I had already called timeout when it was 25-14, so we kept playing, hoping UCLA would miss at some point. Our goal was to get it to nine by halftime to take away their momentum.

Well, they missed eight shots in the first half, but made 19, for 70 percent shooting. Walton was 6-7, so much for him being troubled by an injury. Meyers was 5-5 and Wilkes was 4-7. We were down 43-34 at the half, but I still had hope.

HALFTIME

The first thing I told the team at halftime was to keep confident. We had played hard in the first half, but didn't have anything to show for it. They shot lights out, and they were up by just nine. They could have been up by 20.

It was especially important to keep Shumate confident. He had been outscored by Walton 12-8 and had made just 4-11 from the field. I remember Dwight Clay talking with him at halftime telling him to, "Stick with it, Big Daddy."

I did make a strategy change to start the second half. Wilkes was scoring on Novak, so I went to a three-guard lineup with Ray

Martin in the game, which moved Brokaw to Wilkes. Goose didn't score in the first half and Wilkes had 10, so we had to make a change.

During halftime the fans stayed at a fevered pitch. Ara Parseghian was being presented with the Grantland Rice Trophy, which goes to the national champion of college football. The students were chanting: "Ara change the score; Ara change the score."

It kept everyone in a good frame of mind during the half and it seemed to carry over into the second half. In effect, Ara was changing the score. We went on a 9-2 run to open the second half. A jumper by Brokaw nearly tied the score at 45.

The first 16 minutes of the second half resulted in a series of runs by both teams. After we cut it to 45-43, UCLA went on a 9-0 run to lead 54-43.

With 5:24 left we had cut it back to six, 60-54, when Brokaw got whistled for his fourth personal foul. He then put his arms up in the air and proceeded to disagree with the call to the point that he got

Although Keith Wilkes had a size advantage, Gary Brokaw repeatedly beat him off the dribble to lead us in scoring.

a technical. We were lucky that today's rules were not in effect. Today, he would have fouled out with the technical, but in 1974 a technical was not a personal. I hate to think what would have happened without Brokaw for the final 3:22.

We cut the lead to five at 64–59 with 4:17 left on a three-point play by Shumate. But UCLA then scored six in a row, including a jumper from the corner by Tommy Curtis with 3:32 left to make the score UCLA 70, Notre Dame 59.

I called timeout 10 seconds later. We needed to stop their momentum and change our personnel.

THE FINAL 3:22

The first thing we needed to do was put our pressing team back in the game. That meant putting Ray Martin in for Billy Paterno. "Dice" was the leader of the press and we needed to get some steals if we were going to get back in this game. With Martin in the game we now basically had a three-guard look with Clay and Brokaw. Dantley was the power forward at 6-5 and Shumate the center.

The second thing I did during the timeout was to change the press. We had been pressing previously with Brokaw at the top of the press and Shumate back. All UCLA was doing was bringing Walton into the frontcourt and throwing the ball up high, which meant Brokaw was trying to steal the ball off an-inbounds pass from a player who was eight inches taller than he. So, during the timeout, I moved Shumate to the front and put Brokaw deep.

The third area was pure motivation. I told the team at the end of the timeout that we could still win this game. "If you don't think we can do this, then go to the locker room right now." As we broke the huddle I called for "spurt time."

During the timeout, UCLA was planning its strategy for the rest of the game. Why would they change anything? Walton was sitting on the scorer's table. During the timeout, the TV showed Walton, and Dick Enberg recited his list of accomplishments, including his 139-game winning streak as a player dating back to Helix High School in San Diego, California. Talk about the all-time announcer jinx!

Coming out of the timeout we worked the ball down low to Shumate and he hit a quick jumper over Walton to cut the margin to 70-61. We wanted to go to him for a score, because it would be easier to set up the press with him near Walton. It worked to perfection, as Shumate intercepted the in-bounds pass and went right to the basket for two more. Wilkes, who in-bounded the ball, was expecting Brokaw to be guarding Walton, but instead it was the much taller Shumate. It was now 70-63 with 2:57 left.

Remember, in 1974 there was no shot clock, so UCLA then tried to run some clock after it broke our press, then go to the foul line. With 2:22 left, Dantley stepped into the passing lane and intercepted a pass intended for David Meyers. He is the brother of Ann Meyers, who would be inducted into the Basketball Hall of Fame after her career with UCLA's women's team. She now works for ESPN as an analyst on women's games. Dantley drove in for an uncontested layup to make the score 70-65. As Dick Enberg says on the broadcast, "Pandemonium now!"

We were still in the press. With Shumate covering Walton again, Wilkes tried a long in-bounds pass to Curtis, who was being guarded by Martin. Dice fell down trying to guard Curtis, who only had to catch the ball and drive for an uncontested layup. "I remember thinking that all my family and buddies back in New York had just watched me blow the UCLA game," Ray told me years later. But, as luck would have it, Curtis traveled as he caught the ball, giving us the ball back with 2:16 left.

Gary Brokaw then took over the game for the next three possessions. Dice brought the ball up court and fed Gary. He took Wilkes one on one and hit a 20-foot jumper from the left wing. UCLA 70, Notre Dame 67.

UCLA came down court and they worked a shot for Meyers from the side. After going 5-5 in the first half, Meyers was 0-5 in the second half. He missed with 1:25 left and Shumate got the rebound. Everyone in the building knew Brokaw had it going. Even though he was four inches shorter, Brokaw was a matchup problem for Wilkes. We gave him the ball again and he went one on one, hitting a 17-foot fallaway from just behind the foul line. It was Jordanesque before Jordan. UCLA 70, Notre Dame 69. As Dick Enberg says on the broadcast, "And they are starting to believe that this could be the day at Notre Dame."

As UCLA worked the ball up court, Walton signaled to Wooden asking him if he wanted a timeout, you can see him on the TV tape.

Wooden said no. He never liked to call a timeout, because it was a sign of weakness in his mind.

With the game now in the final minute, UCLA was working the ball and got a mismatch inside. Brokaw was caught down low with Wilkes. He made a move to the basket and scored, but Richard Weiler blew his whistle prior to the score. Wilkes was called for an offensive foul, as he hooked Brokaw on his move to the basket. It was a good call.

For the third straight possession our intention was to get the ball to Brokaw. We accomplished this and Gary drove to the top of the key. Gary saw Clay in the right corner virtually unguarded because

We had converted a game-winning situation just once in 15 attempts in practices the week of the UCLA game, but Dwight Clay's shot swished with 29 seconds left.

Curtis wanted to help out on Brokaw. Gary made the pass and Dwight hit the shot. He made that shot from basically the same place on the court where he had made a jumper to end Marquette's home 81-game winning streak the previous year. It was just Clay's second field goal of the game, his first made field goal of the second half.

Twenty-nine seconds left and the Irish lead, 71-70. As I look back on that last possession, it was incredible that Clay hit that shot. We had practiced last-second game-winning possessions all week. We kept a chart. We had been 1-15 in converting the game-winning play during practice that week.

UCLA called timeout. I am still to this day not sure if Wooden called it or Walton did.

During the timeout the Athletic and Convocation Center was going crazy, it was hard to hear each other. When the team came over I said to Clay, "Great shot, now sit down, we still have 29 seconds left."

Assistant coach Dick DiBiaso made a suggestion immediately. "Why not foul Walton, put him on the line, so we can control our own destiny?" It made some sense because he came into the game shooting just 43 percent (15-35) from the line and he had not attempted a free throw the entire game. But I decided against it, figuring we would play strong defense and rebound.

UCLA in-bounded the ball and early in the possession Shumate took a chance, he jumped out on the passing lane and intercepted, but his momentum carried him toward the sidelines. Instead of throwing the ball upcourt toward the far basket (UCLA had their offense away from their bench in the second half, as they elected not to shoot in front of our students), he threw the ball right back to Curtis, who for some reason panicked. There were still 12 seconds left and he let fly with a 28-footer. Brokaw had the rebound on the weak side, but he lost it out of bounds. He says to this day it went out off a UCLA player.

UCLA then set up out of bounds underneath the basket with six seconds left. But they had to set up to the left of the basket (as the in-bounds passer faces the court). Curtis threw the ball in to Walton, but he was at a disadvantage in that he liked to start from the right black and wheel towards the lane over his left shoulder for a right-handed hook, his favorite shot. Instead he was at the other side of the basket. He got the in-bounds pass and was defended by Shumate. He turned toward the basket over his right shoulder into Shumate and shot immediately and missed, his first miss of the second half and just his second miss of the game in 14 attempts.

With Shumate guarding Walton, he was not in position to rebound, at least initially. Trgovich and Meyers took contested follow-up shots that also missed. It was a wild, intense scramble. Finally Shumate grabbed the rebound, and knowing there was little time left, he just threw the ball toward the ceiling, feeling that the laws of physics would exhaust the final two seconds. Shumate's freshman physics course came in handy.

Final Score: Notre Dame 71, UCLA 70.

POSTGAME EUPHORIA

The postgame scene was electric. The students jumped over the press tables on either side of the court. It was just like it had been after the Austin Carr game nearly 1,000 days previously. Notre Dame had recently beaten Alabama for college football's National Championship. One student paraded a banner that said:

Dear John Wooden,
  God did make Notre Dame #1
  Sincerely,
  Paul "Bear" Bryant

Right on cue, Enberg said on the tape, "Notre Dame No. 1 in football, now No. 1 in basketball." That was just the second and still one of only two times (UCLA, November 1967) a school has been No. 1 in both major sports at the same time.

Just as instructed, Novak went to the basket to the right of our bench, but Shumate was nowhere to be found. After he had thrown the ball in the air, he was undercut by students running on the court and was on the floor. It was the only thing we messed up the whole day.

"Dwight Clay and I seized the moment," remembered Martin, who was underneath the basket when the game ended. "The students put us on their shoulders and we started cutting down the nets.

Since the photographers had been concentrating on that end of the court for the last play, they all came to our end. Dwight and I got in all the pictures that ran on the wire. Poor Gary was cutting down the nets at the other end, but I never have seen a picture of him. The one in the museum at the ACC shows Dwight and me."

While this was going on, DiBiaso and Tony Villani, a friend of mine from New Jersey, picked me up and started carrying me around the court. I still remember how hot it was. I was wearing one of those fashionable two-piece plaid suits of the 1970s and a fresh haircut from Armando.

I started my postgame press conference by saying that this win was for the other 88 coaches who had lost during the streak (I know many coaches, including me, had lost more than once, but you know what I meant). While Wooden was respected, I knew there were a lot of coaches across the country who were glad the streak had been broken. It was good for the game.

Wooden talked about his team beating itself to some degree. He also claimed Walton did not have his normal mobility. All he did was play 40 minutes, shoot 12-14 and get nine rebounds. He looked pretty mobile to me.

"We certainly didn't figure to lose with three minutes left, and we were up by 11 points," Wooden said after the game. "But, they kept at us and they deserve a tremendous amount of credit for the way they played. We lost a little of our drive and played too conservatively at the end, but Notre Dame's man-to-man defense hurt us and their crowd really inspired them."

Then when pressed on the subject of next week's poll, he said, "I am going to vote for Notre Dame, but I think Maryland is the better team. (Maryland had lost 65-64 at Pauley Pavilion back in December). They rallied on our court, and Notre Dame rallied on theirs. If you ask Coach Phelps, he'll tell you it is tougher to come from behind on the road."

Of course, he also talked about the game the following Saturday being a better barometer. The only way we could schedule a home and home with UCLA this particular year was to play them on consecutive Saturdays. That would never happen today with the conference expansions the way they are. We had to go back to Los Angeles on January 26, and had to play Kansas and St. Francis (PA) on

Tuesday and Thursday in between. I must have been crazy to do that schedule.

I never saw Wooden in the commotion after the game because of the chaos after Shumate's rebound. We finally met in between our two press conferences. I told him we weren't coming to Los Angeles the next week because of the energy crisis. He said, "You better be there."

As far as comments about the game from the UCLA players, you won't find many, if any. Wooden would not let the media into the UCLA locker room. He told his team, "Let the winners do the talking." He probably couldn't get away with that today. He was also smart enough to know that he had to play us next Saturday and he knew he had the revenge motive in his favor. The only thing that could blow the intangible advantage would be for Walton or Curtis to say something that would fire up my team.

Some of the postgame stories talked about Walton leaving the dressing room wearing a hooded UCLA sweatshirt, whistling, believe it or not, the "Notre Dame Victory March."

DÉJÀ VU ALL OVER AGAIN

In January of 1971, the year before I came to Notre Dame, Ara upset a No. 1-ranked Texas team in the Cotton Bowl, 24-11. Twenty days later the Notre Dame hockey team upset Denver when it was ranked number one. Then, on January 23, Notre Dame beat No.1 UCLA by an 89-82 score, giving us three wins over number one in three different sports in 23 days.

On New Year's Eve 1973, Ara beat number-one ranked Alabama 24-23 in the Sugar Bowl to win the national championship. The night before we played UCLA, Lefty Smith's hockey team beat No.1-ranked Michigan Tech, 7-1, at the North Dome of the Convocation Center. Then the next day we beat UCLA to end their 88-game winning streak. Three wins over number one in the same three sports in 20 days.

When you think about it that hockey score is a bit spooky....7 to 1 and we scored 71 points to beat UCLA. The ghosts of Knute Rockne and George Gipp were working overtime that weekend.

AN ALL-NIGHT PARTY AT DIGGER'S

We hadn't planned on having a big party that night at my house, but it sure turned out that way. Over the course of Saturday afternoon into wee hours of Sunday morning, over 500 people came by my house on Peashway Street.

The game started at noon local time and ended at 2 pm. Even with all the postgame interviews and well wishers, I was home by 4:30 p.m. People just kept calling, and I just said come on over and bring your friends. I had a lot of guests staying at the house as it was. Dick Harter, my mentor at Pennsylvania who was now the head coach at Oregon, took the red-eye and came in for the game. There were friends I grew up with from Beacon, New York, my parents, my sister... even the governor of Indiana, Otis Bowen, showed up.

I spent half the time on the phone and half the time greeting people at the front door. I remember everyone taking a break at 6:30 p.m. to watch Heywood Hale Broun's report on the game on the *CBS Evening News*. I think I went to bed about 3 a.m. and got up at 7 a.m.

Father Deviney, who was the priest who hired me at St. Gabriel's in Hazleton, Pennsylvania, where I got my start in coaching, stayed with us. He said Mass at our house on Sunday morning. Some of the "congregation" hadn't been to bed yet.

Downtown was up for grabs. I told the players after the game to enjoy themselves, but I didn't want to get any calls at 3 a.m. to come get them out of jail.

No violence or anything like that, but all five bars at the five points intersection near campus were out of beer by 11 p.m. I didn't go by campus, but our players said it was party time all night. The drinking rules at Notre Dame were a lot more relaxed in 1974 than they are today. Shumate went out on a date and he said when he got home at 5 a.m., his phone was still ringing.

One of the most memorable experiences for some of the players took place at the on-campus South Dining Hall that night. Ray Martin, Toby Knight, Billy Drew and some of the others went to dinner there. When the players carried their trays into the dining hall and sat down, everyone stood up and gave the players a five-minute standing ovation.

Ray Martin once told me, "Whenever someone asks me what it was like to play basketball at Notre Dame in the 1970s, and the spirit and support we had from the student body, that standing ovation in the South Dining Hall is what I think of first."

No *SI* Cover

Notre Dame basketball has never been featured on the cover of *Sports Illustrated*. John Shumate was in the background of a photo of Walton after they broke San Francisco's streak in 1973.

After we beat UCLA to end the streak and moved to No. 1 for the first time, and with a writer and photographer on campus for three days, I thought we surely would be on the cover the following week.

Dick DiBiaso and Tony Vilani carry me around the court after we ended UCLA's 88-game winning streak. It was the beginning of a celebration that lasted all night.

I have never been so disappointed to see the *Sports Illustrated* swimsuit issue. When the issue came, there was a young Ann Simonton on the cover. It was a provocative shot of Simonton with her hands behind her head, but I was hoping for a photo of Novak with his hands over his head holding the nets. There was a three-page story on the game and it was very well done, but we all wanted the cover.

Our program had its share of media coverage that week. We had writers from all over the country cover that game. Dick "Hoops" Weiss, still regarded as one of the top college sports writers in the nation with the *New York Daily News*, had quite a day. Bob Levy, a Penn alumnus who owned a plane, and Jim Murphy, one of my former Penn players, flew "Hoops" from Phily to South Bend on Saturday morning.

He covered the game, then even had time to come to the house for an hour or so. Then they flew from South Bend to Columbia, South Carolina for the Pennsylvania vs. South Carolina game, another battle of top-20 teams. They left that game a few minutes early, then got back to Philly in time to catch the final minutes of the second game of a doubleheader at the Palestra.

In those days, Haywood Hale Broun had a segment on the *CBS Evening News* every Saturday night. CBS was number one in the ratings because of Walter Cronkite. He didn't anchor on Saturday night, but the public was used to watching CBS for news. This was the pre-CNN and Fox News era, so the ratings were high.

Broun did a unique sports piece every Saturday night and he picked this week to feature Notre Dame basketball. They still replay his features on *ESPN Classic*. He had cut a piece on Friday with a few seconds reserved to include the UCLA game. We made him do a major rewrite on Saturday afternoon.

CHANGING THE COURSE OF HISTORY

Many basketball historians consider Houston's victory over UCLA in the Astrodome in 1968 as the most important regular-season game in college basketball history. There was a significant impact on television and the popularity of the game. When UCLA and Houston met in the Final Four in March of that year, the game was not on live television, even in Los Angeles.

I am certainly biased, but I still think our UCLA game had the biggest impact. From a television standpoint, that game was televised all over the country on the TVS television network, the brain child of Eddie Einhorn, now co-owner of the Chicago White Sox with Jerry Reinsdorf. He got that game shown in every market in the nation on all kinds of stations, independent and network affiliates.

NBC's contract to televise college basketball came just 18 months later. That game showed the network executives that there was a national demand for college basketball. Once NBC started that contract, college basketball took off. And, we had a lot to do with that because we were the most televised team in the nation in the 1970s.

In addition to the exposure aspect, the ending of UCLA's streak signaled the beginning of parity in college basketball. It had been a west coast game up until that time. Twenty of the first 35 NCAA Champions had come from the west coast. In the 30 years since that game, only six west coast teams have won the championship.

This game was truly an east vs. west game. Our team was composed of players from New Jersey, New York and Washington, D.C. In fact, players from the state of New Jersey scored 33 of our 37 points in the second half. UCLA had all west coast kids, led by Walton, who was from San Diego.

MY BEST TEAM

Your dream as a coach is to get to the Final Four and win the national championship. I had a Final Four team in 1978, and you will read about that team later in this book. But the best team I ever had was this 1973-74 club. The accomplishments of that team lose their impact over time because we lost in a Sweet 16 game in the NCAA Tournament to Michigan. But one off night does not diminish the accomplishments of this team in my mind.

Just look at the results. We beat UCLA, Kansas and Marquette in a 10-day period in January, and all three of those teams went to the Final Four. UCLA ended the season ranked second in the final AP poll with a 26-4 record. Marquette finished third at 26-5, while Kansas finished seventh at 23-7.

In addition to those victories there were wins over Indiana, who finished ninth in the nation at 23-5 and Vanderbilt, who was also 23-5 and ranked 13th in the final poll. We beat them by 30 points on a neutral court. South Carolina finished 22-5 and ranked 19th in the nation. We ended their 34-game home winning streak in February. That is six wins over teams that finished the season in the top 20, including four top-10 teams. No Notre Dame team has done that before or since.

Seven of the coaches we beat that year are in the Basketball Hall of Fame. That list includes Fred Taylor (Ohio State), Bob Knight (Indiana), John Thompson (Georgetown), John Wooden (UCLA), Al McGuire (Marquette), Ray Meyer (DePaul) and Frank McGuire (South Carolina). Four of those coaches were ranked in the top 15 in the nation when we beat them, so it wasn't like they were on a down cycle.

Statistically, we averaged almost 90 points a game and outscored our opponent by 17 points per game, still a Notre Dame record in the modern era. We shot 53 percent from the field even though we were an up-tempo team, and had nearly a +10 rebound margin.

The 26-3 record is a Notre Dame modern record for wins. The 1908-09 Notre Dame team played 40 games and won 33 of them, but that is the only team in the first 99 years of Irish basketball that has more wins.

The road wins that year were also remarkable. In the second game of the year, Dwight (Clay) hit a late jumper to send the game into overtime at Ohio State before we won 76-72. We won at Indiana 73-67. Notre Dame has not won there since. We beat Kentucky in Louisville, 94-79, not to mention the win at Kansas just three days after beating UCLA. If there was an all-time letdown game that should have been it, but we won 76-74.

Later in this book I will reveal my All-Digger teams of my 20 years at Notre Dame. Three of the five first-team selections were on this team. Gary Brokaw, Adrian Dantley and Johns Shumate combined to score nearly 60 points per game and shoot a combined 58 percent from the field. All three shot at least 56 percent. No one does that today.

Shumate was a first-team All-American, while Brokaw made third team. Dantley would have made some All-America teams had he not been a freshman. That was the second year of freshman eligibility, and there was a bias against giving freshmen honors. In fact, in those days there was a lot of controversy about freshman eligibility, and I was one of the coaches against it.

30 Years Later

Last January, on a weekend the current Notre Dame team was playing Kentucky, we had a reunion for the 1973-74 team and to celebrate the ending of UCLA's 88-game streak. Fifteen of the 18 players on the team returned and it was one of the highlight events of my life.

My entire career I preached to my players about the importance of getting your degree from Notre Dame, that it was important to have a life outside of basketball. What are you going to do with the last 40 years of your life?

That weekend made all that preaching seem worthwhile. I know a lot of coaches say that while they are coaching, but I got to experience it. If I had a message to the coaches of today it would be to do more things to prepare your players for life after basketball. We all have a strong impact on the lives of young men, and believe me, that is what is meaningful after you hang up the whistle.

Obviously, Notre Dame is a great institution. Notre Dame people are competitive and it makes student-athletes compete in the classroom. So there is a built-in advantage to Notre Dame when it comes to academic support. All 18 players on that team got their degrees from Notre Dame.

After the luncheon I had all the players and coaches come forward to say a few words about that season and the day we beat UCLA. Hawk Stevens read a poem he had prepared. Dwight Clay had a prepared speech, one he makes when he is asked to speak at banquets back home in Pittsburgh. He had us rolling. He said at one point, "That game was my 15 minutes of fame. It is with me all the time, whether I run into some of the two million who saw it on television, or the one million who were at the game."

Dwight has put on a few pounds since his playing days. I don't think he could get very far off the ground to make that jumper from the right corner today. We were kidding him that we were going to have him reenact that shot at halftime of the Kentucky game later that day.

But I think he enjoyed that reunion more than anyone. He hadn't seen Shumate in 30 years. Shumate, Brokaw and Ray Martin have stayed in touch all these years because they are still in coaching. For the guys who hadn't seen each other in a while, it was certainly special.

I was amazed how many players talked about the preparation for the game and the impact practicing cutting down the nets had on their mental approach to the game. Even the guys who didn't play in that game—such as Ken Wolbeck, Roger Anderson, Myron Schuckman, Greg Schmelzer, and Tom Varga said it just gave everyone a positive outlook.

I went last when it came to making comments and I got choked up in the middle of it. We did something special that day in 1974, special for Notre Dame and for college basketball. But, what stuck out the most was the character this team had 30 years later. These were quality relationships and I felt I had made a positive impact on this team.

It was one of the most rewarding experiences of my life.

Chapter Three

More Wins Over No. 1

I always felt that if you gave me three days of preparation and three tapes against quality opposition, then we had a chance to pull off an upset. Thanks to the hard work of our players and my assistant coaches, we were able to pull off seven upsets of the No. 1-ranked teams during my career at Notre Dame. Heading into the 2004–05 season, no coach had more. In this chapter we will take you behind the scenes in the making of those upsets. We saved one (Marquette in 1978) for Chapter 4, since it took place in that Final Four season.

29... and One

March 5, 1977 • Athletic and Convocation Center • Notre Dame, IN • Pre-game Rankings: ND (unranked), San Francisco (1 AP, 1 UPI) • Notre Dame 93, San Francisco 82

An Unexpected Contender

We spent a lot of time recruiting Bill Cartwright. He was the number-one center in the nation his senior year of high school (1974–75). At 7-1 and 260 pounds, he was agile, and had a great shooting touch. And he was a good kid with solid grades. When we didn't sign Cartwright I decided to schedule him.

We were not in the preseason top 20 of the AP or UPI polls prior to 1976–77, primarily because Adrian Dantley had decided to turn pro after his junior year. He had averaged nearly 30 points a game in each of his last two seasons and was named a first-team All-American both years.

Then we lost Bill Laimbeer, who flunked out of school after his freshman year. With Dantley and Laimbeer gone, the media thought we would be in a rebuilding process. Looking back at what those two accomplished professionally, I should have agreed with them.

But, we had some talented players from Adrian's original freshman class. Billy Paterno, Toby Knight, Ray Martin and Dave Kuzmicz were good senior leaders, and Duck Williams and Dave Batton were experienced juniors. Bruce Flowers was a sophomore, and we added Rich Branning and Bill Hanzlik as freshmen that year.

I also made a change from a strategy standpoint, putting in a matchup zone defense. I had seen Bill Green from Marion High School in Marion, Indiana, use it with great success, so I brought him to campus to teach it to our team during the preseason. We got off to a 7-0 start, including top-20 wins at Maryland and at UCLA, and a victory at home over a top-20 Indiana team that was the defending national champion. We ended UCLA's 156-game home non-conference winning streak. We had gone from unranked to No. 2 in the nation by Christmas Day.

A Change in Schedule

San Francisco was terrorizing the West Coast. They were ranked 11th in the preseason because of Cartwright, Winford Boynes and James Hardy. They had comprised one of the top recruiting classes in the nation, and had added Chubby Cox, a transfer from Villanova who many felt was the missing ingredient needed to make a run at the Final Four. San Francisco was 10-0 on Christmas Day and was ranked third in the nation, just one notch below us.

Someone at NBC took special note of the schedule at some point during the season and noticed that we were supposed to play San Francisco at Notre Dame on Tuesday night, March 1. An NBC executive called Roger Valdiserri and asked about moving the game to the following Saturday, March 5, for a 100-percent national broadcast. The only problem was we were scheduled to play at DePaul on that date.

We really wanted to get the San Francisco game on national TV, so Roger talked to the DePaul people. He called Ray Meyer, a Notre Dame alum, first. But ironically he brokered the deal with Gene Sullivan, Johnny Dee's former assistant who had passionately applied for the Notre Dame job I got in 1971.

Valdiserri was the best at diplomacy and negotiation when it came to these matters. With us agreeing to a 10-year contract to play DePaul home and home, and NBC sweetening the pot financially— plus promising them some added TV exposure—Roger got it done. DePaul agreed to move their home game with us to Monday night, March 7, so we could play San Francisco on NBC on Saturday. It was a strange move because NCAA bids were announced on Sunday, March 6. So we actually played a regular-season game after bid day.

We stumbled over the Christmas holidays when we lost on the road in consecutive games against Kentucky (in Louisville), at Princeton, at Villanova and at Marquette. We rebounded to win 11 of our last 12 entering the San Francisco game, but we were still unranked. In those days only 40 teams went to the NCAA Tournament, so we still needed to beat San Francisco to assure us a bid in the NCAAs as an independent.

The Dons just kept on winning. They didn't play a great schedule, but they did beat Stanford, Houston (twice), Tennessee, Florida State, St. John's and Arizona State before they started league play. They were 29-0 and ranked No. 1 for the eighth straight week coming to South Bend. This had become the national regular-season game of the year. Some executive at NBC was going to get a raise.

Bob Gaillard, the Al McGuire of the West Coast

San Francisco head coach Bob Gaillard brought his team to South Bend on Thursday night prior to the Saturday afternoon game. We met before practice and planned to get together that evening. We had met at a coaching clinic and were good friends.

When I saw him the first thing he said was, "We need a doctor. I have a player who needs some penicillin." At the end of the season Skip Bayless, who is still a nationally renowned columnist, wrote a story about San Francisco's season, which ended with a 29-2 record and a No. 8 final national ranking. It was San Francisco's best record and ranking since the Bill Russell era. But, Gaillard was not a happy man. He had a wild bunch on his team and he never enjoyed the season. In fact, the article quoted Bob as saying, "This team is mentally unbalanced. If something else comes along, I'll consider it."

Bob was a free spirit. There were some pregame features on him in the Midwest papers that referred to him as the "Al McGuire of the West Coast." That was an appropriate comparison because he was flamboyant. When San Francisco came on the court during pregame, our students threw toilet paper streamers, something they always did for big games. Just like McGuire had done, Gaillard picked up the streamers and threw them back at the student body.

After we got a doctor for one of Bob's players, we went to George Kelly's house. Kelly was a longtime assistant coach under Ara Parseghian and Dan Devine, and was a close friend who followed our program closely. So we went to his house for a few beers. I couldn't keep up with Gaillard, so I left about 1 a.m., with Bob still going strong. The next day, we had a press conference. He told the media how I kept him out all night and that I should suspend myself for the first half of Saturday's game for breaking curfew.

Pregame Preparation

On Friday night we had a pep rally at The Pitt, the auxiliary Gym in the Athletic and Convocation Center. I told the students to get to the game a half hour early and remain standing the entire game. I told them to start a rhythmic clap, 29....and one....29....and one.

The students in this era knew what the spirit of Notre Dame was all about, and they knew they had an impact. That was especially the case of the students who were seniors in 1977. They were all freshmen in 1974 when we ended UCLA's 88-game winning streak. They had been a part of something special as freshmen and this was their last home game.

I knew they could really be a factor because San Francisco had not played in front of more than 6,000 people all year, so they just weren't used to this environment. I concluded the pep rally by saying, "I've seen some great games in this building with some great crowds and great emotion. But, tomorrow will be the greatest display of emotion ever. Be there at noon and we will show San Francisco and the nation what Notre Dame spirit is all about."

The place went crazy. I knew we would have the students. Now we just had to figure out a way to stop Cartwright, Boynes and Hardy.

The schedule change actually gave us a full week of preparation. The big question was how to defend Cartwright. After meeting as a staff, we decided to stay behind him and push him away from the basket as much as possible. A key to their success in their first 29 games was his ability to rebound, especially on the offensive boards. We were both ranked in the top three in the country in rebound margin coming into the game, so I knew the boards would be important.

This strategy was not going to be easy because they had a lot of weapons. Coming into the game, Cartwright, Marlon Redmond, Boynes and Hardy all averaged over 14 points per game and they scored 93 points per game as a team, third best in the nation. They were shooting 52.5 percent from the field and 77 percent from the foul line. I thought we could defend Redmond, Boynes and Hardy because they were inconsistent.

Despite all of that, we were a 6.5-point favorite according to the line in Las Vegas. A 6.5-point favorite against an undefeated, number-one team... now that was respect.

Senior Day

San Francisco wanted a game in which both teams scored in the 100s and I was hoping for a score in the 70s. Reality would be somewhere in between.

Billy Paterno was playing in his final home game and he saved us in the first half. He scored 14 points, most on long-range shots in the last 10 minutes of the half. It was his most important performance since the Marquette game his freshman year. He ended the game with 16 points in 20 minutes, ironically, the same point total he had in the Marquette game in 1974.

Paterno and Dave Batton scored 19 of our last 23 points of the first half, including a tip-in by Batton at the buzzer that gave us a 44-42 lead and great momentum. As Dick Enberg described the last tip-in, "Did it count? It counts, but who heard the buzzer?"

San Francisco shot 60 percent (18-30) in the first half of this game. No way they could keep that up, and I told the team that.

Four Corners

The first eight minutes of the second half were more of the same, great up-tempo basketball. With a three-point lead (61-58) and 12 minutes left, I decided to go to the Four Corners offense. We had not used the Four Corners much in my career.

Going into the game, I thought Duck Williams would be tough to handle in this offense, because he had a spin move at the top of the circle that was very effective. San Francisco had great athletes, but they gambled a lot because they wanted a score in the 100s. By holding the ball for periods of time I knew they would get impatient. Duck scored seven points on our first three possessions in Four Corners and gave us a 65-58 lead.

Duck went on to score 17 of his 25 points in the final 11:46, all out of the Four Corners. His floater from the middle of the lane gave us an 87-74 lead and it was over.

Someone had asked Gaillard about Dean Smith and North Carolina's Four Corners offense the previous day at our press conference. He said, "I bet Dean Smith has cost various coaches around the country 1,000 victories because they went to the Four Corners offense at the wrong time with the wrong personnel."

I wasn't one of them, at least on this day.

4,000 MVPs

During the last TV timeout, Enberg and Billy Packer, the NBC announcers for the game, discussed whom they should name as the Gillette Player of the Game, an honor that carried with it a certificate and a $1,000 scholarship for the school. Both had been impressed with the support of the student body.

With a minute to go, Enberg said on the air, "We have decided on our player of the game and we are going to spread that award among a few thousand recipients." He later said he and Billy had decided to give the award to the Notre Dame Student Body.

Rick Valdiserri, Roger's son and a member of the senior class of 1977, was working for NBC and was sitting next to Enberg. When he heard Enberg's MVP choice, he told his dad, who wrote a quick announcement for public address announcer Jack Lloyd. In the final seconds, Lloyd announced to the crowd that the student body had

After winning Player of the Game honors from Dick Enberg and Billy Packer, the student body joined in the celebration with Dave Batton, Duck Williams and Bruce Flowers after we ended San Francisco's 29-game winning streak.

been named Player of the Game and it brought the cheers to a new level.

After the game, the students charged the courts as they had after the UCLA game in 1974. It was quite a Senior Day for our players, and our student body. The next day in the *Chicago Tribune* Paterno's quote put the game in a perspective. "Our students just killed them."

THE GREATEST DEFENSIVE PERFORMANCE

February 26, 1978 • Athletic and Convocation Center • Notre Dame, IN • Pregame rankings: Notre Dame (9 AP, tied for 12 UPI), Marquette (1 AP, 2 UPI) • Notre Dame 65, Marquette 59

This victory over Marquette was a key to the success of our Final Four season of 1977-78. We have a separate chapter on that season so we will review this game in Chapter 4.

THE GREATEST GAME

February 27, 1980 • Athletic and Convocation Center • Notre Dame, IN • Pregame rankings: Notre Dame (14 AP, 10 UPI), DePaul (1 AP, 1 UPI) • Notre Dame 76, DePaul 74 (2OT)

Aguirre Gave Us Some Motivation

Ray Meyer was 66 years old when we played DePaul in February, 1980. He had just taken the Blue Demons to the Final Four the previous season, and now had won his first 25 games of the 1979-80 season and was ranked first in both polls. He had 622 wins under his belt, the winningest active coach in college basketball at the time. He was getting better with age.

One of the reasons for his coaching renaissance was his ability to keep Chicago kids in town. Mark Aguirre was a special player who grew up on the South side. He really reminded me of Adrian Dantley in that he could maneuver inside and get to the foul line. He might have been a better outside shooter than Dantley, but Adrian was a better rebounder and free throw shooter.

And, Adrian kept his mouth shut. Mark liked to talk, and was a little more of a hotdog. After a close win over Wagner in New York, the last game before they were to come to Notre Dame, Aguirre told the media, "Wagner gave us more trouble than Notre Dame will." The Chicago papers made a lot of it. So did our students, and I did mention it to the team before the game.

We had a 21-5 record and were 14th in AP and 15th in UPI entering the game, but we were coming off a last-minute loss to Marquette (77-74). Joey Meyer, Ray's son and assistant coach, scouted that game in person. We should have had a press conference for three coaches after that Marquette game the way the media swarmed around Joey.

It was Senior Night for Rich Branning and Bill Hanzlik, but it would be the three junior frontcourt players, Tracy Jackson, Kelly Tripucka and Orlando Woolridge who would be the key. Jackson had won both the Maryland and Villanova games with last-second shots, and Orlando Woolridge's defense against freshman center Terry Cummings would be important. But I knew this game was going to come down to the matchup between Aguirre and Tripucka.

No one would be disappointed.

We Needed Hesburgh for This One

University president Father Theodore Hesburgh said our pregame Mass for this game. I needed to go straight to the top. Father Ted had said the pregame Mass for the San Francisco game four years earlier. I usually told the priests, "Father, you've got 20 minutes and that includes the homily." But I never said that to Father Hesburgh.

He had a great message. It made the players confident, but at the same time it put prayer in perspective. He talked about having the spirit and strength to do your best and playing to one's potential. When the players did that, they would win. He completed this homily by saying, "Special accomplishments do happen here, because it's Notre Dame."

Believe it or not, we never lost a game when Father Hesburgh said the pregame Mass and sat on the bench, a perfect 7-0. Three of those were wins over No. 1.

25 and One

We didn't have a pep rally for this game because it was played on a Wednesday night. We only did that for weekend games at home. But, we printed "25...and...one" buttons and circulated them through the student body. Just as the seniors at the 1977 San Francisco game had been freshmen at the 1974 UCLA game, the senior students at the 1980 DePaul game were freshmen at the 1977 San Francisco game. They knew how to get inside the opponent's head.

In addition to the buttons, we passed out plastic green New Year's Eve hats. Everyone had them on, even the nuns.

But, the all-time spirit stunt was turned in by the four guys from the Glee Club who sang the national anthem. They had taped to the backs of their sports jacket 2 5 + 1. There was one digit for each guy. They faced the benches so you couldn't see it on TV when they sang the anthem, but the numbers faced the student body when they sang.

No One Wanted It to End

Kelly Tripucka always came to play in big games, especially the games against No. 1 teams, and this was no different. He got us off to a good start by scoring our first six points and 12 of our first 20, giving us a 20-14 lead. It was 28-21 when DePaul starting hitting some outside shots, especially by Clyde Bradshaw and Skip Dillard. Tripucka's 18-footer from the left side gave us a 32-31 lead at intermission.

As Tripucka had done at the beginning of the first half, Aguirre got hot at the beginning of the second. They went on a 12-2 run and took a 43-34 lead with 16:04 left. From there on it was just a back-and-forth game, and was tied six times down the stretch. Tracy Jackson tied the game at 64 with 1:08 left. There was a lot of action in the last minute, but no one scored. Overtime!

There wasn't any shot clock in those days. It was tempting to get the tip and hold the ball. But neither of us did that, because the defenses were too good, especially with Bradshaw, who could pick your pocket or fill the passing lane as fast as anyone.

In the first overtime, the game was tied at 66 and 68. Aguirre hit one of his patented leaners with 1:47 left, giving DePaul a 70-68 lead. We then scored on a tip-in by Woolridge, but it was wiped out because he touched the ball in the cylinder. With a minute left we were down two and DePaul had the ball.

Jim Mitchem, DePaul's starting center, had suffered a broken hand the day before when he slipped on the ice outside his dorm room. The DePaul trainers made a makeshift cast, but he really couldn't shoot. With 36 seconds left Bill Hanzlik fouled him, something that wasn't called by me from the bench, but it was premeditated on Hanzlik's part. He was the smartest player I ever had. If Ray had to coach this game over, he probably would have taken Mitchem out. A 71-percent free throw shooter for the season, Mitchem missed both free throws. The second one didn't hit the rim and we got the ball out of bounds. With seven seconds left, Branning nailed a jumper from the left side to tie the score at 70. DePaul got the ball to Bradshaw, but his 40-footer missed and we went to a second overtime.

After Bradshaw stole the ball at mid-court and made a breakaway layup with three minutes left, DePaul led 74-72. I didn't burn a timeout, but it was time to change strategy. We had to take Bradshaw out of the game from a defensive standpoint, so I inverted the offense. We had practiced this quite a bit, but hadn't used it in a game.

Tripucka, Woolridge and Jackson were excellent ball handlers so we moved them out front and put the guards in the corners, creating an inverted "four corners" offense. With DePaul playing a man for man, this put Bradshaw away from the ball in the corner. After the game Branning was quoted as saying, "It was strange being in that corner. But, it was comforting to see Bradshaw there with me."

We worked the ball around with the big guys penetrating until Hanzlik hit a jumper from the left side to tie the game for the 11th time (74-74). Cummings missed a jumper with 1:53 left and we went back to the same offense with the three big guys on the perimeter. We held the ball, because we were going to go for the last shot if possible. With 39 seconds left DePaul got impatient and fouled Woolridge. There was no double bonus then, so he had a one and one. He made both, giving us a 76-74 lead.

DePaul took its last timeout with 18 seconds left. We didn't want Aguirre to beat us, so we gave Woolridge some help. They took Mitchem away from the basket, but we guarded everyone so well, he ended up with the ball with four seconds left. Broken hand and all, he launched a 20-footer from the left side. It drew iron and bounced right to Bradshaw near the foul line, but his catch-and-shoot attempt missed, and we had a 76-74 double overtime victory.

Postgame Pandemonium

Branning, Hanzlik and Tripucka all went straight to the basket to cut down the nets after the game. Tripucka somehow did all this while holding the game ball. He even took it with him to the postgame press conference. They took it from him during the interviews and he said, "I guess they aren't going to let me sleep with it."

What a great ending for Branning and Hanzlik, who finished their careers 60-5 at home. It was their third win over the No. 1 team at home over their four years. How many college basketball players can make that statement?

After the game Meyer said, "Notre Dame deserved to win, this was no fluke. Hell, I went to school here, it doesn't hurt that bad. Digger and everyone at Notre Dame has always been so good to me." Spoken like a true Domer!

Ironically, the best postgame quote from this game might have come from Aguirre. "The crowd at Notre Dame loves college basketball, and both of these teams showed them some of the best they've ever seen."

THE MASTER OF DISASTER

December 27, 1980 • Freedom Hall • Louisville, KY • Pregame Rankings: Notre Dame (8 AP, 11 UPI), Kentucky (2 AP, 1 UPI) • Notre Dame 67, Kentucky 61

Kelly Tripucka (44) scored 28 in the win over No. 1 DePaul. He held the game ball as he cut down the nets, and did postgame interviews. He would have slept with it had a manager not gotten it from him before he left the Joyce Center.

A "Neutral" Site

Coming into the game, we were only 1-8 against Kentucky since I became the Notre Dame coach. But you have to remember, every game was in Freedom Hall in Louisville. When I first got to Notre Dame, Moose Krause, the legendary athletic director at Notre Dame from 1948-80, told me he had signed a 10-year contract to play Kentucky in Louisville. My first reaction was, "So that means we will be playing them in Elkhart, Indiana, for 10 years after this contract ends?"

Playing Kentucky at that "neutral site" in Louisville actually dated to when Moose was the head basketball coach and athletic director at Notre Dame. In 1948, Notre Dame beat Kentucky and Adolph Rupp in the Old Fieldhouse on campus, 64-55. Kentucky did not lose another game the rest of the year, winning the SEC Championship, the NCAA Championship and the Olympic Gold Medal that summer.

Two years later, Kentucky came back to the Old Fieldhouse and Moose beat a Rupp-coached team that would end the season 25-5 and finish third in the nation. Supposedly, Moose had the Notre Dame band sit right behind the Kentucky bench. Rupp claimed after the game that he had been hit during the game by a trombone.

After the game he wrote Moose a letter and said he was never coming back to South Bend. If he wanted to play Kentucky, Notre Dame would have to come to Lexington or Louisville. Moose wanted to keep playing Kentucky because it added prominence to the schedule, and he thought he could beat them. Kentucky came to Chicago to play Notre Dame twice, but 26 of the next 28 games in the series were in Lexington or Louisville. Kentucky won 25 of the 28. Kentucky didn't come back to South Bend until 1982, my 12th year.

Financially, at least in those days, it was too good a deal for Notre Dame to turn down. But from a competition standpoint, it was brutal. It was always between Christmas and New Year's and the place was filled with Kentucky fans, nearly 18,000 every game. Kentucky would have an open practice the day before the game and it was like going to a Final Four practice. They would have 11,000 Kentucky fans at their practice. I remember a fan had a sign at their shoot around before the 1980 game, "A Kentucky Pervert—a person who likes sex more than basketball."

Christmas Spirit

I usually allowed the team to go home for Christmas for a couple of days, then had them come back Christmas night for an evening practice. But not this year. I didn't let them go home for Christmas at all.

In preparation for the game we were watching a videotape of an earlier Kentucky game. During the tape, a commercial came on for a Christmas show. After it was over I told the players, "OK, that was your Christmas break, now let's get back to work." There were a lot of groans. Kelly Tripucka said, "Coach, you have just drained the last bit of Christmas spirit from my soul."

Tripucka at His Best

Even though we got behind early, 12-6, the tempo was in our favor. Kentucky liked to run, and it was important to play the game at our pace. We thought we could frustrate them by holding the ball at times and working for a good shot after Tripucka, Jackson or Woolridge broke down their defense. It was 24-24 at halftime, thanks to the fact that we had committed just three turnovers at intermission.

Kelly missed a shot at the end of the half and we walked off the court together screaming at each other. We yelled a lot, but that was my way of getting the best out of him. We were much alike in that area, two guys from the New York area, yelling one moment, shaking hands the next.

There were seven lead changes in the second half, but we finally took control with 5:45 left, 56-49 on a basket by Tripucka. We then spread them out, so they had to foul. We just kept knocking down the free throws, led by Kelly, who made 6-6 from the line in the last three minutes.

Digger Can't Coach?

The headline in the *Louisville Courier-Journal* the morning of December 27, 1980, stated, "Digger Digs His Own Grave and UK Fans Dance On It." It was an article by noted columnist Billy Reed, who basically said I couldn't coach. With my record against Kentucky up to that point, Reed had some facts to back up his theory.

After the game, I went straight over to Reed at the press table, pointed my finger at his face and said, "Don't ever say I can't coach again." I was half kidding and half making a point. This was one of the most satisfying wins of my career, because it was the first time we had beaten a No. 1 team away from South Bend.

Better Under Pressure

Tripucka ended the game with 30 points, including 14-15 from the foul line, all in the second half. He played 37 minutes and didn't commit a turnover. If I had to pick one signature performance in his career, this was it. Later in the season *Sports Illustrated* did a story on Kelly and entitled it, "The Master of Disaster." The greater the pressure, the better he played.

Jackson made 6-6 from the field and scored 14, while Woolridge made 5-8 and scored 15. All three seniors enhanced their draft status in this game, as they combined to hit on 19-28 shots from the field and score 59 of our 67 points.

In my interviews prior to the game, I talked about how physical Kentucky was. "Kentucky is a physical team. If Fran Curci (Kentucky's football coach at the time) had some of these guys he would have gone to a bowl game this year." I don't know if the officials (Paul Galvan and Jim Bain) read those quotes or not, but I wanted to create a mindset going in.

It didn't hurt that we were 25-28 from the foul line, all in the second half. Kentucky took just seven free throws and made five, including just two in the second half when we were attempting 28. We were charged with just 10 fouls the entire game.

But, Tripucka's 30 overshadowed what anyone else could accomplish. There were games in his career in which it appeared Kelly could take on an entire team by himself. This was one of them.

WOOLRIDGE AT THE BUZZER

February 22, 1981 • The Horizon • Chicago, IL • Pregame rankings: Notre Dame (11 AP, 11 UPI), Virginia (1 AP, 2 UPI) • Notre Dame 57, Virginia 56

We Owned Chicago

If there was a top high school prospect whom we failed to get, we tried to beat him. I called Terry Holland to schedule a home-and-home series with Virginia after they signed Ralph Sampson. Terry was interested, but he didn't want to come to South Bend.

Holland wanted to play us in Chicago. He gave me the line about a lot of Virginia alumni living in Chicago. I said then let's play your home game in Washington, D.C. I went for that because both towns had a lot of Notre Dame fans, especially Chicago.

I would have preferred a straight home and home, but I really wanted to play them because I knew Sampson was a special player. He was a 7-4 guy who could handle the ball like a guard and run with any small forward. He could catch opponents' shots instead of just blocking them out of bounds.

We owned Chicago that weekend. It was a Sunday afternoon game, but the students started coming to town on Friday night. So by game time it was a zoo in that arena. That was strange in itself because we were playing Virginia at The Horizon, DePaul's home-court. DePaul was ranked second in the nation behind Virginia in the AP poll entering the game. Picture North Carolina playing a number-one ranked Kentucky team in Duke's Cameron Indoor Stadium—that was what we were doing.

Practicing with a Tennis Racket

Entering the game, Virginia was 23-0 for the season and had won 28 in a row over two years. We decided to make someone other than Sampson beat us. Virginia had other guys who could beat you in Jeff Lamp and Lee Raker, because they could both shoot from the outside.

We practiced all week using a 1-3-1 zone concept with Woolridge fronting Sampson, and either Tim Andree or Joe Kleine staying between Sampson and the basket in a most physical style. We had our wings drop to the corners to guard Lamp and Raker, leaving one man to guard their other two guards.

Jeff Jones, who went on to coach Virginia from 1991-97, was a competent floor general, but he preferred to pass. He was scoring just

5.2 points a game and really didn't like to shoot. Our basic plan was to make Jones, Ricky Stokes, and Othel Wilson beat us. If they hit those 18-footers, then so be it.

On offense, we had Cecil Rucker work as the center on our Gold team (reserves) during practice holding a tennis racket. That was about what it would take for Woolridge, or anyone else who drove the lane, to get a shot over Sampson.

I thought we were prepared, and I was pretty confident. On Saturday, we had our shoot around after Virginia's at the Horizon. As we took the court I went up to Terry Holland and exchanged pleasantries. I had never played against him before. At the conclusion of our conversation, I just said, "I don't know how it is going to happen, but it's going to happen."

Electricity was in the air the day before the game and we fed off of that. I knew they would be tight because of their perfect season going and our reputation for ending streaks. I just wanted to get in Terry's head a little.

Another Comeback

We were ranked 11th in the nation in both polls entering this game, and Virginia was No. 1 in the AP and No. 2 in the UPI. But you couldn't tell any difference in the teams over the course of this game. Opening the first half, the game was tied at 2, 4, 6, 8, 10, 12, 14, 16, 18, 20, 22 and 24. I don't think I have seen that at any level before. We finally took a four-point lead at 30-26, but Othel Wilson hit a shot with two seconds left to make it a 30-28 game at intermission.

To start the second half, Virginia took a five-point lead at 40-35, but then Jones took two wide-open shots and missed both. We scored on both possessions to get back to 40-39.

We stayed with our gameplan defensively, and it was working to the extent that Sampson got just one shot in the first 10 minutes of the second half. I still remember Ricky Stokes and Othel Wilson looking at the basket with no one covering them from 18 feet out. But they were afraid to shoot. They looked at Sampson, but he was swarmed over by our interior guys.

With seven minutes left, Jones finally hit a jumper and Virginia was up by six points. We went man to man a couple of times and

Virginia didn't go to Sampson. I couldn't believe it, and fortunately for us, Lamp and Raker missed. Jackson tied the game at 51 with five minutes left.

Virginia had a 56-55 lead with under a minute left when Billy Varner—who I had inserted in the game late to put in our press—stole the ball. He threw the ball ahead to Tripucka, but the pass was a little bit too far. Kelly saved it to himself, went up for a shot, and was hacked. Lenny Wirtz, the lead official of this All-ACC crew, called him for traveling before the foul. I couldn't believe it. We had the ball with 10 seconds left and had blown it.

I called timeout to set up our defense. I decided to guard the four Virginia players on the floor with our five guys. We didn't guard Raker, who was in-bounding the ball. We jammed Jones and fronted Sampson. When the official's count reached four, Raker panicked and threw the ball away by our bench, right by me.

I called another timeout and told the guys to go to the basket, be aggressive. We still had 10 seconds so we had some time. Paxson inbounded the ball to Woolridge, who went right at Sampson with a reverse layup, not exactly what I wanted. But the good thing was at least he started early enough so that we had a chance at a rebound.

Woolridge missed badly, I don't even think the ball touched the rim. But Jackson knocked the ball back outside to Tripucka, who also went right at the hoop. His attempt was blocked at the chest by Wilson, who had no other recourse but to strike from below the belt. The ball caromed over to the right corner where Woolridge picked the ball up with his back to the basket. He turned and shot a fallaway 20-footer, virtually an impossible shot.

It hit nothing but net, giving us a 57-56 victory.

Munich, Munich

When Woolridge's shot went through the hoop there were two seconds left, but in those days the game clock didn't stop after a made field goal with under a minute left. Virginia had a timeout left and they tried to call one.

Lenny Wirtz, a legendary ACC official who would work over 30 years by the end of his career, started running towards the scorer's table with his right hand up. It looked like he was going to give Virginia a timeout. This game was at DePaul's home arena, but we had our game management crew, which meant Mike DeCicco, our academic advisor, was on the game clock. He never stopped the clock after Woolridge's shot, because he never saw a timeout signal, so it hit all zeros and the horn sounded.

When I heard that horn, I didn't want to give Lenny a chance to call the timeout. I shouted to Pete Gillen, my assistant coach who is now the head coach at Virginia, "Munich, Munich!" That was the signal to the players and coaches to get on the court and celebrate with the cheerleaders and students. I headed to the locker room and I wasn't coming back until the National Guard came to get me. The expression came as a result of the ending of the 1972 Olympics when the Russians got three chances to beat the United States in the gold medal game. Had United States coach Hank Iba left the floor immediately, the officials would have awarded the game to the United States. Maybe? But he stayed around and got screwed for doing so.

Our locker room was above the far-end basket balcony. I ran to that balcony and looked back out over the floor. Lenny never knew where I was, but I was watching everything. For Lenny to add time to that clock he was going to have to go find me in a bar down the street. The student body helped out more than they ever knew. Within seconds there were a 1,000 Notre Dame students on the floor, surrounding Tripucka, Woolridge and Jackson. Lenny never could have restored order. After a few seconds at the scorer's table and with the 6-7 Holland and his 6-6 assistant coach Craig Littlepage pleading their case, Wirtz threw his hands in the air and said, "Game over!"

After the game, Holland said in his postgame interviews, "There were definitely two seconds on the clock. I pointed that out to the official (Wirtz) and he told me he had no authority to put time back on the clock. I didn't quite understand that, because I have seen it done dozens of times."

I got a kick out of that quote.

Neutralizing the Giant

Our defensive strategy had worked. We were willing to give Sampson 22 points and 16 rebounds; we just didn't want him to score 40. He ended the game with 10 points and nine rebounds. He only had eight field goal attempts the entire game. You have to give a lot of credit to Woolridge, but Tim Andree and Joe Kleine also made a difference. They had a mindset to be physical, to use their 10 fouls. Actually, they were only called for four between them.

Unlike the win over Kentucky earlier in that season, we had a balanced performance in this game. Tripucka was the leading scorer with 15 points, but Jackson had 14 and Woolridge and John Paxson had 12 apiece.

Epilogue

The 1980-81 season ended in dramatic fashion, Danny Ainge's still-celebrated drive through our entire team to give BYU a 51-50 victory over the Irish in the NCAA Regional in Atlanta. They are still killing me every March at ESPN over that loss.

I was certainly disappointed, plus it was the end of the line for Tripucka, Jackson and Woolridge. Tracy got a concussion at the end of the BYU game, so it just wasn't meant to be. I wasn't devastated after the game, because we would have played Virginia in the regional final. I knew we couldn't beat them on a neutral court in a revenge game. They would have killed us. As it was, Virginia beat BYU 74-60 and went to the Final Four.

V for Victory and Voce

February 1, 1987 • Athletic and Convocation Center • Notre Dame, IN • Pre-game rankings: Notre Dame (Unranked), North Carolina (1 AP, 1 UPI) • Notre Dame 60, North Carolina 58

Reliving January 19, 1974

We were 11-5 and unranked heading into the North Carolina game and we needed a marquis win to get an NCAA Bid. We had gotten off to a slow start that year, including a 17-point loss at home to Western Kentucky to open the season.

North Carolina was 18-1, with its only loss early in the season at UCLA. Dean Smith had his normal list of future pros at every position, including J.R. Reid, then a freshman; Scott Williams, who would go on to win an NBA Championship with the Bulls; and Joe Wolf, another future 10-year NBA veteran. Kenny Smith was the leading scorer and he had just scored a career-high 41 points in just 30 minutes in a game at Clemson.

But Smith tweaked his knee during that game and when he had X-rays in Chapel Hill, the doctors determined he needed surgery, meaning he would not even travel to South Bend. My reaction was that it would not make a difference in our preparation, because they had so many other weapons.

With John Shumate as one of my assistants, I was big on making the preparation of this game just like the 1974 UCLA game. As he did many nights when we were in our war room watching tapes of our oppositions, Roberto Parisi kept us well-supplies with food into the wee hours of the morning. We even practiced cutting down the nets on Saturday afternoon prior to the Sunday game. I had not done that since that 1974 UCLA game.

Before the game, Shumate came in the locker room bringing a tape deck. He broke out his Doobie Brothers collection, the same tapes he had played in the locker room that day 13 years previously. He even got in front of the team and danced to the music, and it really broke the tension, just as he had done for his teammates before the UCLA game.

The students came a half hour prior to tip-off, just as they had in the past. The chant for this game was, "You were...number one."

Just as we fell behind 33-17 in the first half against the Bruins 13 years previously, we trailed 32-16 in the first half of this game. We weren't getting anything started offensively for David Rivers, who didn't even score in the first half. We weren't doing very well with our post defense either, as Reid, Williams and Wolf were killing us inside. Add to that eight turnovers by us and only three offensive rebounds in the first half, and you can see we had some problems at halftime.

Still, I was confident because we had gotten the deficit to 32-23 by the half, the same margin as the 1974 UCLA game. I told the team that very fact and talked at length about the game that ended the streak. Shumate's presence must have helped bring me back to that afternoon, and I could tell the team hung on my every word. Gary Voce, my starting center, commented after the game about my reflections on that game and how it gave him confidence in the second half.

I Ripped My Jacket

It wasn't all serious discussions at the halftime. I had ripped my new blue Hart Schaffner Marx sports jacket during the first half. I was in a crouch and when we turned it over, I got mad. When I stood up I brought my shoulders forward and it ripped. It was a big one, too.

I always wore Hart Schaffner Marx clothes. In fact, they sewed "Digger" on the inside pocket. I was pretty close to Joe Starzec, their rep in Chicago, as well as Kenny Hoffman, the president of the company who was a Fordham Prep graduate. Joe and Kenny's son, David, sat behind our bench for this game. As soon as I ripped it, Joe came up to me behind the bench to tell me...while the game was going on! "Joe, I don't give a damn about my jacket, we are getting our butts kicked by 16 points."

So, he came into the locker room at halftime to try to fix it. Here he was asking our managers for some scissors. Believe it or not, he had thread and pins. I gave him the jacket when I got in, but by the time we had to go back out, he wasn't finished. I told him just to give it to me and I wore the jacket with some pins in it during the second half.

After the game, he took the jacket back and was planning to get it fixed on Monday. He got stopped by a cop for speeding on the way back to Chicago on Sunday afternoon. He told the cop how he had Digger Phelps's sports jacket in the trunk and had to get back to get it fixed. He got out of the car and opened the trunk and showed him the jacket. He took it one step further, showing him "Digger" on the inside pocket. The cop was in stitches and let Joe out of the ticket. Logically, how could you make up such a story?

During the game, NBC showed the rip two or three times. Al McGuire even commented on the broadcast, "Uh oh, Mr. GQ just ripped his sports jacket."

After the game, David called his father, who was overseas and told him the story. When Ken got back to he office, he had calls from all his competitors, joking with him that he had staged the entire jacket episode for the publicity.

Special Day for Rivers

Our game plan on offense was to use Rivers to create and penetrate. We thought Rivers could break down their defense and force Reid to pick him up, then hit Voce for a simple baseline jumper. We sent the rest of the players to the right side of the court to open up the area for Rivers and Voce to operate. Gary was not a great offensive player, but he could hit that baby jumper from the left side. He had been hitting that shot in practice consistently.

Rivers took just three shots in the first half because he was trying to let the game come to him and not force shots. But he wasn't penetrating enough, so I told him to be more aggressive, even if it meant going one on one.

With 6:07 left we were still down by nine, 53-44. This was a special day for David Rivers because his father, Willie Rivers, was seeing David play his first game at Notre Dame. David had made quite a comeback from an August automobile accident that nearly took his life.

He took over the last five minutes of this game. Rivers hit a jumper from the foul line with 4:12 left to bring us within seven. On the next possession he knocked down the same shot to make it 53-48. He penetrated on the next possession and fed Voce, who got fouled and made two free throws.

Two minutes later he fed Voce again and he connected from the right baseline, cutting the lead to one. With 1:06 left Rivers nailed a jumper from the foul line again to give us our first lead of the second half. He was fouled with 16 seconds left and made both ends of a one and one to give us a 58-55 lead.

North Carolina then came down court and missed a possible game-tying three-point goal attempt. Voce got the rebound with five seconds left. We had the game in the bag if Voce could make just one free throw. Only something out of the ordinary was going to take this game from us now.

Monograms in Orbit

We passed out 10,000 navy blue and bright yellow (not the mustard gold they are using today) 12x12 cardboard ND monograms prior to the game. The intent was for the crowd to hold them up when

Gary Voce (54) was an unlikely hero in the upset of No. 1 ranked North Carolina in 1987. He had just three double-doubles in his Notre Dame career, but one of them came against J.R. Reid and Dean Smith's Tar Heels, when he had 15 points and 10 rebounds.

the lineups were introduced prior to the game, or when North Carolina was shooting a free throw.

Unfortunately, we also didn't realize they were perfect frisbees, capable of traveling large distances in varying directions. When Voce was fouled with five seconds left, the fans started to celebrate a bit early. One fan threw a monogram on the floor, then two, then five. ...They went crazy. After we had scored the first basket of the game, the students threw toilet paper and streamers on the floor, a tradition I had brought to Notre Dame for big games from my days coaching in the Palestra. I had to get on the PA and warn them that another outburst would be a technical.

When this outburst happened at the end of the game, I knew we were in trouble. It was a no-brainer for official Gerry Donaghy, and a technical foul was called.

I went bananas, stomping my foot like I was Lefty Driesell. I wasn't mad at the officials, I was upset at our crowd. Everything had gone according to plan, just like the UCLA game of 13 years ago. Now our crowd, who had helped us win so many times previously, was going to mess it up for us. Gary was a 70-percent free throw shooter, but he hadn't been in this situation.

After we calmed everyone down, Voce went to the foul line. It was as quiet as Sacred Heart Church on a Sunday morning. He made both free throws, giving us a five-point lead, 60-55.

Now Jeff Lebo went to the foul line to shoot the technical. This was one more flashback to the 1974 UCLA game. Remember in chapter two, I talked about Gary Brokaw getting his fourth foul, plus a technical with six minutes left? By today's rules he would have fouled out and never would have been on the floor when he made those clutch jumpers in the final 3:22. By today's rules, Lebo would have gotten two technical foul shots and a chance to cut the lead to three. But in 1987 it was just one shot. Lebo made the technical, then he hit a 15-foot jumper at the buzzer to make the final score 60-58.

THE ONE THAT DIDN'T COUNT

March 3, 1990 • Athletic and Convocation Center • Notre Dame, IN • Notre Dame 98, Missouri 67

I always felt I had eight wins over No. 1 teams instead of seven. On March 3, 1990 we played Missouri in South Bend. Norm Stewart's team was ranked second by the coach's poll on the previous Monday of this Saturday afternoon game that was televised nationally by NBC.

On Wednesday, Kansas, who had been number one, lost to Oklahoma. Had there been a poll on Friday, Missouri would have been number one, at least by the coaches and probably by AP. UNLV was second in the AP heading into the week, but they also lost.

We had to have this game to get a bid. In fact, we had to win this game and against Rick Pitino's first Kentucky team on the following Monday night. We had lost our last two games, a heartbreaker in overtime to a Georgia Tech team that would go to the Final Four that year, and our bi-annual loss at Dayton. We led at the half, then gave up 57 points in the second half to Dayton and lost by 18.

We were not on a high coming into this Missouri game and the students were starting to get on me. We entered the season as a top-20 team, but did not have Laphonso Ellis for the first semester, and that cost us some losses. My daughter Karen wrote a letter to *The Observer*, the student newspaper, urging the students to stay with us. I didn't know anything about it until it was published.

Perhaps that letter had an impact, because the students were behind us from the outset. But we were so great that day that their true loyalty was never tested. We were on our game from the beginning and played with great emotion. This was a Missouri team with Doug Smith, who would be named an All-American at the end of the season; Anthony Peeler, who played in the NBA with the Lakers; and Travis Ford, who would later transfer to Kentucky.

We led 46-33 at halftime, then got the margin to 30 early in the second half. No one saw that run because NBC did a long investigative report on NCAA problems at NC State during halftime, a feature that spilled into the first three minutes of the second half. At one point Stewart benched all his starters to try to give them a jolt, but it didn't matter. During the run, Dick Enberg said of our team, "Who are these guys?"

It was like coaching an all-star game. We had five guys in double figures and three more who scored nine. I had decided to start Kevin Ellery to try to give us some scoring burst from the outside, and he scored 11 and was named Player of the Game by NBC. Every move I made worked.

Monty Williams, then a freshman, actually led us in scoring with 14 points, while Scott Paddock had a career-high 11 points on five-for-five shooting. In most games Paddock couldn't have gone five-for-five in the backyard by himself. But on this day he looked like an NBA prospect.

I cleared the bench with a couple minutes left and we were still up 30. I gave each player a bear hug as they came off the bench. It was an emotional victory because it meant we were going to the NCAA Tournament. But it had been an emotional season for me. For the first time in my 19 years at Notre Dame I wasn't sure if the administration, even the students were behind me. But all of that was forgotten on this day.

The final score was 98-67, the largest margin of victory I had in my Notre Dame career over a top-20 team, never mind a team that would have been No. 1 had there been a fresh poll.

Tim Bourret, my co-author on this book, did some research and discovered that this victory over Missouri was the 50th win of my Notre Dame career against a top-20 team, my 30th over a top-10 team and my 20th over a top-five team.

It was my last great victory at Notre Dame.

Chapter Four

A FINAL FOUR SEASON

"WE WERE LIKE NOAH'S ARK"

My outlook for the season printed in the 1977-78 Notre Dame media guide was conservative. "Our goal, as always, is to earn a place in the NCAA Tournament," I was quoted.

But, with four returning starters, plus the reinstatement of Bill Laimbeer, plus the best recruiting class of my career, I really thought we could go to the Final Four and win the National Championship.

We brought in a freshman class that included Kelly Tripucka, Tracy Jackson and Orlando Woolridge. Gilbert Salinas, a 6-11 center from San Antonio, was a top-40 national recruit, and I thought Stan Wilcox would be the second coming of Ray Martin, a point guard who wouldn't score much, but could run the show and play defense.

When I look back at that team now, we really were a Noah's Ark team...we had two of everything. We had Bruce Flowers and Bill Laimbeer at center, Kelly Tripucka and Bill Hanzlik at small forward, Dave Batton and Orlando Woolridge at power forward, Rich Branning and Stan Wilcox at the point, and Duck Williams and Tracy Jackson at the second guard. Eight of those 10 later played in the NBA.

We sold them on the team concept and they bought into it. Batton was the leading scorer on the team with just a 14.0 average, and no player had a 25-point game all season. No one averaged more than seven rebounds per game, yet we had a +6.3 rebound margin, among the best in the country. Six different players shot at least 50

Our 1977-78 Final Four team had seven players who scored at least 1,000 points over their careers, a first in NCAA history. Front row, from left: Randy Haefner, Gilbert Salinas, Dave Batton, Bill Laimbeer, Bruce Flowers, Orlando Woolridge, Bill Hanzlik, Tracy Jackson, Kelly Tripucka. Back row, from left: trainer Arno Zoske, assistant coach Scott Thompson, assistant coach Danny Nee, Tim Healy, Chris Fabian, Stan Wilcox, Rich Branning, Duck Williams, Jeff Carpenter, assistant coach Dick Kuchen, head coach Digger Phelps, head manager Rick Gabbianelli.

percent from the field and we shot 51.5 percent as a team for the year. And, we shot free throws pretty well, hitting 71.5 percent for the year.

By the end of their respective careers, seven different players, Tripucka (1,719), Williams (1,433), Jackson (1,293), Branning (1,232), Batton (1,205), Woolridge (1,160) and Flowers (1,029) all had exceeded 1,000 career points. According to research by Mike Douchant, a writer for the *Sporting News* and other basketball publications over the years, this 1977-78 Notre Dame team was the first in college basketball history to have seven different players on its roster who would finish their careers with at least 1,000 career points.

SCOUTING WITH A VCR

We were ranked fourth in the AP preseason poll that year and rose to a No. 3 ranking in both polls by the time we went to UCLA for a December 10 showdown with a Bruins team that was ranked fifth in both polls. The Notre Dame vs. UCLA rivalry was in high gear by now.

We had taken it to another level the previous year by beating UCLA at Pauley Pavilion for the first time. In fact, it ended a 156-game winning streak for UCLA against non-conference opponents in Pauley. But they had beaten us in South Bend in January the previous year, meaning we had a reversed split in 1976-77 (both teams won on opponents' home floors), the first time that had happened in the series.

This was our first big game of the 1977-78 season, and we wanted to do everything we could to prepare for UCLA from a strategy standpoint. Julian Lobosky (who passed away in early August 2004) was a friend of mine in California whose son went to Notre Dame. In 1977, he was one of the first people I knew who had a home Betamax video recorder (same function as a VCR today).

Frank McLaughlin, one of my assistants, went to UCLA over Thanksgiving to scout the Bruins. He went over to Lobo's house and showed Frank the Betamax machine and how it taped games in his living room.

UCLA had three games on local TV prior to our game in December, so Lobo taped them for us and shipped them to South Bend. In those days the Betamax machine must have cost $2,500 and the tapes were $25 a pop, so we were very appreciative.

The only Betamax machine in South Bend was at a local electronics store, so Frank and I spent all Monday morning and afternoon in this store watching these tapes and taking notes. We sold some televisions for the owner while we were at it.

In those days no one had tapes, so you scouted teams in person. But, that was obviously hard to do when you were playing a school 2,000 miles from your campus. To have these extra game tapes was a huge advantage.

When we went to UCLA to play the game, I decided to have some fun with Gary Cunningham, a former John Wooden assistant who was in his first year as head coach. I went up to him before practice the day before the game and said, "That [Kurt] Rambis kid from Santa Clara, was something against you guys. How about the move he made on the baseline in the closing minutes? I thought that was a bad call on Roy Hamilton at the end of the Colorado game."

Gary stared at me because he knew we didn't have a scout at those games. Coaches checked on who scouted a game very closely in those days. Then I said, "Hey Gary, your tie didn't match your suit the other night against Seattle."

I had him now; he didn't know where I was coming from. We were in his head the entire night, and our players knew UCLA's offensive and defensive tendencies. We were able to get one of those tape machines for our office just before we left, so we could show the players. We even showed UCLA's plays in slow motion.

We shot 56 percent from the field and beat UCLA at Pauley for the second straight year, 69-66. Batton hit 9-11 shots in the first half and had 22 points for the game. Laimbeer had 10 points, nine rebounds and six blocks. He was always motivated to play at UCLA because he grew up in the area. But for some reason he hated them. It was just UCLA's sixth lost in Pauley in 13 years and the first time anyone had ever beaten them at Pauley in consecutive years. We would increase that streak to four straight.

Before we left Los Angeles, we bought one of those Betamax machines and took it home with us on the plane. It cost $2,500, but I was sold on its value. We would have paid $5,000 for it after the way we played against UCLA. We eventually contacted other alums around the country that had them and set up a network of people who would send us tapes of future opponents.

We eventually taped our own games at home and would put together a highlight package at halftime to show our team. It was just a two-minute tape, but it was more effective than chalk on a blackboard.

It also served as a motivation for the players. They couldn't deny when they got beat on defense, we had it on tape.

WE WERE TRULY A BLESSED TEAM

After we won at UCLA on Saturday, our next game was at Indiana on Wednesday night, December 14. As the head coach at Notre Dame, especially in the winter, you are always concerned about the weather and its effect on travel. You can drive from South Bend to Bloomington in four hours, but for a midweek night game the Wednesday before finals week I wanted to fly so the players would not miss class on Tuesday and would be back to at least a semi-coherent state for 8 a.m. classes on Thursday.

We chartered DC3 airplanes out of Indianapolis in those days. The same company serviced Valparaiso, Purdue, Evansville and us. We were supposed to fly to Bloomington late in the day after practice, but the weather around the Midwest was awful. Valparaiso flew to Missouri on Tuesday, then that plane was supposed to come back to South Bend and take us to Bloomington. But there were weather problems, so they couldn't take off from Columbia, Missouri. The company then decided to fly a different plane out of Indianapolis to South Bend to pick us up and bring us to Bloomington.

During the afternoon that got scratched because of bad weather in South Bend. I told my manager who was in charge of travel to make sure that plane was in Bloomington after the game to take us back to South Bend.

Instead of coming to South Bend, the company sent that plane to Evansville to pick up Bobby Watson's team and take Evansville to Nashville, the closest airport to Murfreesboro, Tennessee, where they would play a game against Middle Tennessee.

It was foggy, windy, and rainy, but not snowing, when the Evansville team got on board for the 7:20 p.m. departure of Air Indiana Flight 216. When they loaded the plane at the Dress Regional Airport, the president of the airline, the pilot and the co-pilot got everything ready for the trip. There were 29 passengers on board, including the crew of three. The crew did not do a good job of calculating the weight on board and there was too much weight in the tail. Someone also forgot to remove the rudder lock, which, combined with the improper weight distribution, caused the tail of the plane to spin out of control shortly after takeoff. Ninety seconds after takeoff the plane crashed into the side of a hill on airport property, killing everyone on board.

Our bus arrived at the hotel in Bloomington about 11 p.m. and the first thing they told us when we arrived was that the entire Evansville team and coaches had been killed in a plane crash. Dick Kuchen, one of my assistants, was a good friend of head coach Bobby Watson and immediately broke down and cried. That plane was the same plane that was supposed to take us back to South Bend on Wednesday night after the Indiana game.

The entire incident made for an unusual atmosphere when we played Indiana the next night. Bob Knight had a moment of silence prior to the game. Some of the Indiana players had known the Evansville players who had been killed. We were a much better team than Indiana that year, but they beat us, 67-66. We shot 39.7 percent from the field, the only game all year we didn't shoot at least 40 percent. We missed 11 shots inside 10 feet in the second half.

It was a long, ambivalent ride home. We were disappointed we had lost, but we were alive. I wondered how Jerry Sloan must have felt. Sloan had accepted the Evansville job the previous February (1977) while playing his final season with the Chicago Bulls. He was a former Evansville player and had taken them to an NAIA National Championship as a player in the 1960s. But six days after taking the job he changed his mind and backed out.

Two weeks later, I picked up the newspaper and read about the fate of David Furr, who was the only Evansville player who did not make the trip to Nashville. He was a walk-on so he was left behind. Just a couple days after Christmas, he was killed in an automobile accident.

40 INCHES OF SNOW IN 48 HOURS

We had a revenge game on January 25, 1978 against West Virginia at the Convocation Center. It was a big game for us because West Virginia had upset us in Morgantown the previous year. West Virginia had a guard named Lowes Moore, who was very quick, could shoot it on the run and draw fouls because of his ability to break down opposing defenses. He scored 37 in a West Virginia win over Duquesne, six days earlier.

Moore was on his game that night, scoring 40 points, the most ever against one of my teams by an opposing player. It was still the opponent record for the building entering the 2004–05 season.

But our balance overcame his one-man show, as we had five guys in double figures and two more with eight in a 103–82 win. As I left the ACC after the game, the snow was coming down in buckets. West Virginia could not get out and returned to the Holiday Inn on Route 31, just a few miles from campus.

Mother Nature turned her wrath on South Bend overnight, and when I woke up the next morning I could barely open our front door. It was snowing at an incredible rate even for South Bend, and the forecast didn't see an end in sight until Saturday.

All the roads were closed, so we had to walk to the ACC to practice for our next game against Maryland. Thank goodness I lived (and still do) just a few blocks from campus. Dick Kuchen had a house east of campus, but four miles away, so he just stayed at my house. Arno Zoske, our head trainer, was also stranded, so another neighbor, Gene Paszkiet, the football trainer, had to pinch hit during practice.

By late Friday afternoon, 40 inches of snow had fallen in a 48-hour period. It was a fine sugar snow. You really had to fight your way through it just to walk. School had been closed on Thursday and Friday, the second time since 1960 that Notre Dame had cancelled class due to weather.

We had to make a call as to whether or not to play the Maryland game, scheduled for Sunday afternoon, by Friday. It was scheduled for national TV on NBC and they really wanted us to play it because there was no backup game. It wasn't like the baseball Game of the Week when they always had a backup game for weather.

Maryland took a prop plane from College Park to South Bend on Saturday afternoon. The South Bend Airport agreed to clear off one runway and let the plane land. That plane and a private plane with the NBC announcers were the only planes to land at the South Bend Airport in a four-day period.

West Virginia had been sequestered in the Holiday Inn since Tuesday and had spent the last three days doing walkthrough practices in the hotel ballroom for its next game. A snowplow met the

West Virginia bus at the Holiday Inn on Saturday afternoon and the bus followed the plow to the airport runway.

When the Maryland team landed, West Virginia got on the plane and flew to Morgantown, where they played Penn State on Monday night. Amazingly, they won that game, 78-68. That was a good test for the importance of mental preparation vs. physical preparation.

Maryland's team bus then followed the same plow to the Holiday Inn where it checked into the same rooms the West Virginia team had held. Maryland had been told there was a bread and milk shortage in South Bend, so the team was seen carrying two five-gallon cans of milk when they checked into the hotel.

We had a bit of a dilemma with the local authorities over the playing of this game. The city had basically told everyone to stay off the streets. There was a $150 fine for anyone seen driving a car downtown.

But once Maryland got to South Bend and it appeared we could play the game, Father Joyce decided to open the Convocation Center to anyone who could walk to the game, whether they had a ticket or not. The parking lots were not going to be plowed and we made that very clear. Don't drive!

Father Joyce figured a couple of thousand fans, including students, would make it to the game. He didn't take into account two things, the level of cabin fever in the surrounding community, and the spirit of the Notre Dame and St. Mary's student body.

This was a big day for the careers of the students who worked for Roger Valdiserri in the sports information department. With the exception of Betty Cuniberti of the *Washington Post*, who had flown in with the Maryland team, none of the national writers could make the game. As a result, many of the newspapers, including the *New York Times* and the *Philadelphia Enquirer*, hired Roger's students to serve as stringers for the game. They all had by-lined stories in major newspapers for their résumés. Roger's students, including Ted Robinson, now the voice of Wimbledon for NBC and the New York Mets, ran the preparation for the game from a media standpoint, because Roger and his assistant, Bob Best, couldn't get to the office until Sunday. Both walked three miles to the game.

It was a 4 p.m. tip-off and we had people everywhere. NBC opened the broadcast by showing the fans walking to the game. They had a camera shot from the top floor of the library and it looked like thousands of ants walking on white sand.

We averaged 4,000 students per game in those days, which was impressive for a student body of 8,750. I think every student at Notre Dame and St. Mary's came to this game. It was the wildest crowd we ever had. When Lefty Driesell (the Maryland coach) came out before the game, he asked me, "Where are you going to put all these people?" I just told him Father Joyce didn't think anyone would come. Father Joyce said anyone who could get here could come whether they had a ticket or not. I just shrugged and walked off with a big grin on my face.

My daughter, Karen, had broken her leg while skiing over the Christmas Holidays in Vail, Colorado, but she was bound and determined to go to this game. The McFadden family, who also lived on our street, put her on a toboggan and dragged her all the way to the ACC from our house.

Maryland had a talented team that featured Albert King, who had been the national high school player of the year the previous season. It also had Greg Manning in the backcourt with Lawrence Boston and Larry Gibson up front. They stayed with us during the first half and we walked off the court with a narrow 31-28 lead.

Once in a while an SID can have an effect on the outcome of a game. Roger had been told that Notre Dame had decided to cancel classes for Monday, but he held the announcement until just before the opening tip of the second half. When the announcement was made it was like New Year's Eve. We went on a 16-3 run over the first 6:34 of the second half. Lefty took three timeouts during that run. By the time he called his third, we had a 47-31 lead. We went on to a 69-54 victory.

I remember a follow-up story by the local media on September 25, 1978, nine months to the day after the blizzard. The birthrate for that date was 500 percent higher than the normal birthrate for any date in the city that year. There are different ways to deal with cabin fever.

BOTTLING UP BUTCH

February 26, 1978 • Athletic and Convocation Center • Notre Dame, IN • Notre Dame 65, Marquette 59

A Guest Speaker at the Pep Rally

Al McGuire had retired as Marquette's coach after winning the 1977 national championship. He rode off into the sunset, something I would have done if I had ever won it at Notre Dame. Yes, even if we had won it all in this Final Four season, I would have quit at age 37.

In Al's first year of retirement, NBC hired him to be the third announcer on their crew with Dick Enberg and Billy Packer. That broadcast team was assigned to our game with No. 1-ranked Marquette, so I asked Al to speak at our pep rally the night before the game.

I know that sounds odd, but we had a special relationship. While Notre Dame was Marquette's top rival at the time, Al had respect for Notre Dame. Somewhere inside I always thought he might have wanted to be the coach at Notre Dame. When we would play in South Bend, he would go to the Morris Inn (hotel on campus across the street from Notre Dame Stadium) before the game and have a drink with Notre Dame administrators, including a lot of the priests. He'd stay there until 7:30 p.m. for an 8 p.m. game. Hank Raymonds ran the team, Al was just the ringmaster.

I wasn't really sure what he would say at the pep rally. When he was introduced, the crowd was half booing and half cheering. He started by saying, "Quiet down, if you don't let me talk, I'll go back to Marquette and start a football team." He was very entertaining. He complimented the Notre Dame student body, but still made it clear he was the old coach from Marquette. "You are the greatest sixth man in the country and don't forget that… but you might need a seventh and eighth man to beat Marquette tomorrow."

I then took the microphone and gave the students the theme for the game. Al's best player, the MVP of the NCAA Tournament the previous year, was Butch Lee. When it came time for a basket, Al made sure his team got the ball to Butch. He referred to it in his postgame press conferences as BLT, Butch Lee Time. I told the students that the pregame chant would be, "Butch Lee...No Time." Just as they had with 29...and one, for the San Francisco game the previous year, they showed up a half hour early and taunted Lee with that cheer.

Green Socks

You will read later in this book about the story of the Green Jerseys. After three years of badgering, I finally convinced Dan Devine to wear green jerseys for the Southern California football game the previous fall. The result was a convincing 49-19 victory.

I didn't want to change our jersey color, but I did bring in special solid kelly green knee socks for the Marquette basketball game. Hank Raymonds's first Marquette team was 22-2 entering the game, losing only twice, to Louisville and Loyola (Chicago). Not only was Marquette No. 1 in the nation, they were defending national champions and had beaten us three straight years.

I handled it the same way we did with the green jerseys. We warmed up in white socks, then had the managers lay them out for the team when they came in for their final instructions.

When the players came in the locker room they laughed. They had all gone to the football game the previous fall, so they knew what it was all about.

"Are you serious?" said Dave Batton, who was one of the co-captains.

"You are unbelievable," Bruce Flowers said.

Jeff Carpenter, a reserve with a lot of personality said, "Look, I can jump higher."

Tripucka went right to the point and probably spoke for the entire team. "These are the ugliest things in the world."

After the game the media asked the Marquette players and coaches about the socks. "I thought those were their regular socks," said Raymonds in all honesty. Jimmy Boylan, one of their starting guards said, "I didn't know they were special, but they sure were ugly. They looked like a baseball team."

Ok, so maybe they didn't have the dramatic impact the green jerseys did, but we won the game. And we kept on wearing them all the way to the Final Four.

A Bad Start... What Else Is New?

Going into the game our objective was to stop Butch Lee. Lee was the leader and he came in on a hot streak. He had shot 64 percent from the field, 94 percent from the line and had averaged 20.6 points a game over the last seven Marquette games, all Warrior (their nickname then) victories.

With the crowd going crazy from the opening tip, the green socks, and a sound game plan to stop Butch Lee... we were awful in the first half. Hank Raymonds had prepared for this game by playing a recording of a locomotive over the PA at their practice gym, and it didn't appear anything was going to distract them.

Lee scored just six points on 3-7 shooting in the first half, but Ulice Payne killed us, hitting 3-4 from the field and scoring 10 points. Payne was a high school basketball teammate of Joe Montana back in Pennsylvania. Joe spoke with Payne outside their locker room before the game. Maybe I should have suited up Joe to guard him because our perimeter people weren't doing the job. Payne was a talented person. He once sang the national anthem prior to a Marquette home game and became the president of the Milwaukee Brewers 20 years later.

Just as had been the case in our first two wins over No. 1 teams, Marquette shot the lights out in the first half, hitting 17-28 shots from the field for 60.7 percent. We had hit on 9-22 for 40.9 and trailed 39-25. It could have been worse, we were down 34-17 with 3:20 left in the half.

At halftime I listed six things on the blackboard we had to do to win: "don't foul," "make free throws," "box out," "contain Lee," "run when you can," and "we are only down seven baskets." Seven baskets seemed a lot less than 14 points.

Father Hesburgh had said the team Mass prior to the game and sat on the bench during the game. He had been very positive about the team's ability to win this game. As we walked out to the court after halftime, I was looking to him for some divine inspiration.

Hanzlik and Tripucka Took Over

I substituted frequently in the first half. When you watch the game tape, the announcers, including Al, got on me about that, but I thought we would be the fresher team in the second half. Hank never substituted that much, and his bench would play only 16 minutes on this day, compared to 58 minutes by our bench. But I did sub less in the second half, because we got on a roll with a specific lineup.

Thanks to great defense by Bill Hanzlik and 15 second-half points from Kelly Tripucka, we overcame a 14-point halftime deficit and beat No. 1-ranked, defending national champion Marquette.

Bill Hanzlik entered the game with 6:18 left in the first half with us down, 28-14. He was the 10th player I subbed into the game, but he was the most important. Bill was not much of a scorer (he averaged just 3.2 points a game in 1977-78), but he could defend. At 6-7, he had incredible range and the arms of a seven-footer. That really helped against Lee. He said after the game that he had spent the first 10 minutes of the game watching only Lee from the bench so he could get a read on him. His strategy was to stay off of him in the open court by a step or two, then force him to his teammates where he could get some help when he drove to the basket.

Lee was just 3-11 from the field against Hanzlik and scored just seven points in each half. Bill even contributed a jumper to open the second half, and it seemed to step up his tempo defensively. At one point he blocked one of Lee's shots then clapped his hands in Lee's face. He was lucky he didn't get a technical for taunting. Lee had gotten one in the first half, and a lot of officials like to balance out technicals. But Richard Weiler and George Solomon let it go.

On the offensive end, Kelly Tripucka was taking over as only Kelly could, even as a freshman. He was my best clutch player over the course of a game in my 20 years at Notre Dame. (I still wouldn't trade Dwight Clay for a last-second shot.) Kelly had started the game and was 0-2 in the first half, a non-factor, and had scored just one basket in the last two games combined. But he was 5-6 in the second half against Marquette and scored 11 of our first 17 points of the second half.

We finally took the lead with 2:48 left on a jumper by Duck Williams. We went to the Four Corners, just as we had against San Francisco the year before, with Williams controlling the ball. With 51 seconds left, Duck was fouled, but he made just one free throw to give us a two-point lead.

Tripucka then turned in two great defensive plays in the last minute when he drew two charges, one from Boylan and one from Lee. We made 15-22 shots from the field in the second half and outscored Marquette 40-20 to win by six, 65-59. Tripucka scored all 15 of his points in the second half and was named the MVP of the Game by NBC.

I still would have given the MVP award to Hanzlik, who had entered the game averaging just 10 minutes of playing time a game. Lee ended the game with 14 points, but he shot just 6-19 from the field and had five turnovers and just three assists while playing all 40 minutes. Hanzlik finished with four points, a team best six assists and two steals in 25 minutes.

But, most importantly he took Butch Lee out of his game. As Al McGuire would say, "Lee was the brains of that team. You cut off the head, and the body dies."

GETTING REVENGE AGAINST DEPAUL

We began our NCAA Tournament run by beating Houston in the first round, 100-77, in Tulsa. Guy Lewis played a 1-3-1 trap press against us the entire game. We literally sliced right through it and with Laimbeer hitting shots from the wings, we just torched them.

In the next round, at Allen Fieldhouse in Lawrence, Kansas we beat a Utah team coached by Jerry Pimm, 69-56. Utah had two great players in Jeff Judkins and Danny Vranes. They got 30 between them, but the rest of the team scored just 26. Kelly had another great game with 20 on eight-of-11 shooting in just 29 minutes. Again, our defense was sound, forcing 23 turnovers. We broke it open in the second half behind Tripucka and Branning.

Kelly was really coming along as a freshman. At this point he was shooting 67 percent from the field and getting 11 points a game in just 20 minutes a game.

The win over Utah put us in the Midwest Regional Final against DePaul, who had won its 14th straight game with an overtime victory against Louisville.

I was big on revenge games. Most coaches, especially today, don't talk about getting revenge when they preview a future game. I guess that isn't politically correct today, but when I coached it was a big factor, something I certainly used to motivate my players, and to get the students fired up. Why not be a risk taker?

DePaul had beaten us during the regular season by a 69-68 score on a buzzer shot by Gary Garland. Ray Meyer had Dave Corzine, the modern day George Mikan of DePaul basketball. They were an excellent team and reached number three in the final AP poll prior to the NCAA Tournament. He had 46 points in the win over Louisville.

It was a close game for the first 32 minutes. We were up 37-33 at the half because we were holding down Corzine. He got just four shots in the first half and had just six points. Flowers, Batton and Laimbeer were doing a job on him. Flowers had three fouls in the first half, but we had 15 fouls to give. I figured we could wear him down.

It was 56-54 with eight minutes left when our depth took over. We went on an 11-0 run over the next 2:47 to take a 67-54 lead on a jumper by Laimbeer. They cut it to 71-62 with 2:29 left, but we outscored them 13-2 the rest of the game to win by 20, 84-64. Ray might have said it best after the game. "Notre Dame turned into a cash register in the last five minutes, they just kept ringing up the points."

Tripucka finished the game with 18 points and 11 rebounds, while Laimbeer had a double-double (12 and 10) in just 28 minutes off the bench. Kelly was named the MVP of the regional as a freshman. Branning was the player of the game, as he had 15 points, seven assists and just one turnover in 37 minutes. Corzine ended the game with 17 points, but our inside guys had neutralized him.

When the clock in Phog Allen Fieldhouse hit all zeros, I just hugged players, coaches, anyone. When I talked with Dick Enberg on NBC after the game I had to pause before I could get my thoughts together. Yes, I was virtually speechless. Can you believe it?

As we road the bus from Lawrence to Topeka, I was sitting in the front seat with Roger Valdiserri. We were talking about going to the Final Four. I remember telling him, "It is finally here," and I started to get tears in my eyes. You go to the Final Four every year and sit in the stands facing the teams during the games and you wonder what it would be like to be on the bench on that side of the court. I was finally going to experience it.

The back page of the *Chicago Tribune* on Monday morning was a full-page picture of Laimbeer holding his arms in the air in victory. I will never forget that picture. For the first time ever, Notre Dame was going to the Final Four, and that picture told the story.

The Final Four Experience

There are so many distractions, and they must be 10 times as great today. The 1978 Final Four was in St. Louis, at the Checkerdome, a facility that was the home of the St. Louis Blues hockey team in that era. It has since been imploded.

We stayed at the Roadway Inn in St. Louis, and of course everybody and their brother wanted to stay at the team hotel, ride the team bus to practice and the game. I remember standing in line to get on the bus for practice, and there were about 20 people waiting to get on. I said sarcastically, "Can we get the team on the bus for practice? It would be nice to let them on since they are playing in the games."

Our semifinal opponent was Duke. In a way it was fitting that we were playing a team coached by Bill Foster, because our relationship had gone back to my start in coaching when I was at St. Gabriel's. He used to run a camp in the Pocono Mountains for four weeks in the summer. I spent a lot of time learning from the coaches at that camp and I have Bill to thank for that opportunity.

We remained friends over the years and I watched how successful his teams were at Rutgers, Utah and now Duke. He did it the right way at every stop. Before that season we were actually at a banquet together and talked about what it would be like to coach against each other now (we had competed when I was at Fordham and he was at Rutgers). Not only was it going to happen, it was going to happen in the Final Four.

Duke was a three-headed monster in that they had three players capable of going for 20 on any given night. Mike Gminski, now a rising star in the broadcasting business for Fox Sports Net and CBS, was a sophomore center. He graduated from Monroe high school in Connecticut a year early and started at Duke as a freshman when he was 16. He took his lumps as a freshman against veteran ACC centers like Tree Rollins, but he had learned from the experience to make a dramatic improvement in 1977-78.

What worried me about Gminski was his ability to shoot from outside. I knew Laimbeer, Batton and Flowers could push him around inside, but when he was bumped outside and hit that jumper, we were in trouble.

Gene Banks was just a freshman but was a force on the boards and could score from anywhere because he was quick and strong. Jim Spanarkel, who is also in broadcasting today, was a great two-guard who was a terrific athlete. The previous spring he pitched one game for the Duke baseball team and threw a one-hitter against a Clemson team that went on to the College World Series.

We had a lot of confidence going into the Final Four because we had won the first three games of the tournament by an average of 20 points a game. We also had this aura going at Notre Dame that had carried over from the football season.

The football team had won the National Championship the previous fall and now the basketball team was in the Final Four. No team had ever won the national championship in football and in basketball in the same year at the Division I level, and that was a great motivation for our team. As it was, we were the first and still only school in the history of college athletics to win the national championship in football and go to the Final Four in basketball in the same academic year.

"I Thought, This Is Going To Happen"

The game was even (14-14) for the first 10 minutes until Gminski and Banks started getting inside for easy buckets. At one point, Bob Bender threw a lob pass for Banks for a diving dunk that had the place rocking. Gminski had 14 points in the first half and Banks had 10 rebounds, leading to a 43-29 halftime lead for Duke.

Duke kept the tempo in its favor to open the second half. This was a young Duke team that played two freshmen, two sophomores and a junior in its starting lineup. They had no fear, they didn't know any better.

It was still 80-66 in favor of Duke with four minutes to play when we started hitting some outside shots. Flowers hit a basket, and then Hanzlik got a bucket and two free throws to cut the lead to 80-72.

Then Tracy Jackson and Duck Williams hit three long jumpers apiece and Batton made two free throws. All of a sudden it was 88-86 with 27 seconds left. After Batton's free throws I called timeout to set up our press. I had subbed Wilcox to lead the press, just as I had with Ray Martin for the 1974 UCLA game.

Precocious freshman Orlando Woolridge was one of eight future NBA players on the 1977-78 team.

The Duke in-bounds pass was intended for Banks, but he let it go right through his hands and it went right to Wilcox. When he made that steal, I thought, this is going to happen. We are going to beat Duke and then have another revenge game with Kentucky, who had beaten Arkansas in the other semifinal. Kentucky had beaten us by two over Christmas break in Louisville.

Wilcox got the ball to Williams with 16 seconds left. Duck was about 20 feet from the basket at the left elbow, but was wide open. He had just made three in a row, but his arching shot bounced off the front of the rim into the right corner. Bender got the rebound and threw ahead to Johnny Harrell, who was fouled with nine seconds left by Branning. He made both free throws and when we missed our last attempt, Duke had a 90-86 victory.

Duke came into the tournament ranked number one in the nation in free-throw shooting, and they won that game at the foul line, hitting 32-37 overall. Just as I had feared, Duke's three-headed monster beat us. Gminski shot 13-17 from the field and scored 29 points. Banks had 22 points and a dozen rebounds and Spanarkel had 20 points and five assists. Duke's spacing on offense had been outstanding.

Prior to 1981, you had to play a national third-place game. We faced Arkansas, coached by Eddie Sutton, who took Oklahoma State to the Final Four in 2004. That Arkansas team was very athletic and they were led by The Triplets, Marvin Delph, Sidney Moncrief and Ron Brewer. They were all in the 6-4 to 6-6 range and played the same style of ball. It was a second straight game we were playing a team with three strong weapons. Again, we fell behind, then made a comeback behind Tracy Jackson, only to lose at the buzzer on a jumper by Ron Brewer.

I hated the third-place game. I suggested during the press conference the day before that they move the NABC All-Star game to Monday night and use that as a preliminary game. When you lose in the Final Four it's over, the last thing you want to do is get ready for a game that really has no meaning.

We had gone 0 for the Final Four. But, at least we had finally gotten there. As I left the Checkerdome I told myself that this had been a great learning experience. I would be better prepared for my next trip to the Final Four. Surely we would get back before Jackson, Tripucka and Woolridge graduated.

Chapter Five

THE PLAYERS OF
THE 1970S

DAVE BATTON, 1974-78

In 1988 I went to a Cubs vs. Dodgers game in Chicago as the guest of Tommy Lasorda. I went on the field during batting practice and then Dodger and current Anaheim Angels Manager Mike Scioscia approached me.

"I remember the day you came to my high school to recruit Dave Batton!" he said. Scioscia went to Springfield High in Springfield, Pennsylvania, which is near Philadelphia, around the same time Batton was the star of the basketball team.

Batton was the subject of quite a recruiting war between us and Kentucky. He visited Notre Dame with classmate Duck Williams on the Southern Cal weekend in 1973 when Eric Penick had the 85-yard run in our 23-14 win. It was a great atmosphere, so we thought we had him cold. But as the year progressed, he went back and forth on his decision, and at one point told us he was going to Kentucky. When he said that, Frank McLaughlin, my assistant, got on a plane and went to Philadelphia and got him back.

It was a worthwhile trip, because Dave became one of the co-captains of our Final Four team. He is the answer to a great trivia question: Who led our Final Four team in scoring? Despite having four guys on the roster who played 10 years in the NBA, the answer is Dave Batton (14.0 points per game). He and Laimbeer changed the image of big men because of their ability to hit the outside shot from the elbow against a 2-3 zone. He was one of the most coachable players I had at Notre Dame.

Batton did have problems with allergies and asthma. He was allergic to about 60 things, and at one point in his career we had to put him in the hospital because we thought he had some serious illness, something similar to what Shumate had. When he was a sophomore we had to put him in the hospital for three days just before the first round of the NCAA Tournament. But he got well and scored 18 points in that first-round win over Kansas.

Batton might have been the best Bookstore Basketball player ever. Those games could get a little rough. He once said in an article in the student paper that the most physical game he ever had in college was not against UCLA, San Francisco or Marquette, it was in a Bookstore game against a priest. He went head to head with Father Don McNeill, who was the son of the famous radio personality.

"He came out knocking me around," said Batton. "I think he was doing it because he knew I wasn't Catholic. I told him, 'Father, I'll convert.'"

RICH BRANNING, 1976-80

My first five Notre Dame teams were dominated by players from the east coast. But with the victories over UCLA in 1974, 1975 and 1976, and three straight NCAA Sweet 16 berths, I thought it was time we went into California and took some of the guys UCLA was getting.

We had signed Bill Laimbeer for the 1975-76 season, but his parents were moving to Toledo and he had grown up hating UCLA. Rich Branning had strong roots on the west coast, but I went after him. UCLA had plenty of good guards already on its roster.

I told Branning that Notre Dame was the place for him because he could come in and make a difference right away. The wins over UCLA had made an impression on him, so he signed with us.

Branning was one of the first players I had who was significantly involved in Fellowship of Christian Athletes, and he had the respect of the other players. Bill Hanzlik called him Cunningham because he looked like and acted like Richie Cunningham on *Happy Days*, and he had that same wholesome personality trait.

Branning was a consistent, efficient player, but he bumped up his production about three notches when we played UCLA, especially in Pauley Pavilion. In his four years at Notre Dame we became the first team to beat them four years in a row at Pauley. Rich's freshman year he scored our last four points, including a diving shot with 46 seconds left that gave us the lead for good. His junior year he scored a career-high 21 points, and his senior year he made eight of nine from the field and scored 20. Branning had just two 20-point games in his career and both were at Pauley Pavilion.

Rich started all four years, the first Notre Dame player to make that claim since Kevin O'Shea from 1946-50. He was the best player I ever had who never made it in the NBA. He just didn't have the body to take the pounding at the next level.

Branning's senior year we lost a heartbreaker in the NCAA Tournament to Missouri in the second round. Rich's father had moved from California to South Bend to be closer to his son during his Notre Dame career. As the bus drove off from the University of Nebraska's basketball facility after that NCAA loss, I remember a very sad Mr. Branning waving to us. Soon after, Mr. Branning died after a bout with cancer.

We had the basketball banquet the next week and we were all still feeling the effects of that loss to Missouri. Rich was the last player to speak and he gave a soft-spoken, but positive speech about his time at Notre Dame that ended with a poem.

> *"Talent is God-given, be humble;*
> *Fame is man-given, be thankful;*
> *And, concede the self-given, be careful.*
> *Thank You Notre Dame.*

That was the last of many standing ovations for Rich Branning at the Convocation Center.

Last year, Rich's 12-year-old son was writing a paper for grammar school and I was the subject. At the end of our conversion I told him, "Young man, your dad is probably too modest, so let me tell you something. Your dad was a great basketball player at Notre Dame. He did things against UCLA no one had ever done before and hasn't done since."

GARY BROKAW, 1972-74
See Assistant Coaches Chapter

JEFF CARPENTER, 1974-78

Jeff Carpenter was the leader of the S.W.A.T team. In 1976-77 we used to bring the S.W.A.T team in as a unit and their job was to give the starters a rest, but also provide a spark off the bench. S.W.A.T. was a popular TV show at the time, so we dressed the five guys (Carpenter, Chris Fabian, Billy Sahm, Randy Haefner, and Tim Healy) in helmets and clubs for a photo that we used on a game program.

"Carp" started five games as a freshman, including three NCAA Tournament games. I also remember him clinching a win over South Carolina that year when he made three clutch free throws in overtime. He was a tough, Chicago Catholic League player who suffered a separated shoulder in the Bookstore Tournament after his junior year when he crashed into a pole holding up one of the baskets. That was Carp; he even played all out in the Bookstore Tournament. That injury did a great service for the rest of the campus. The injury got a lot of publicity and it forced the tournament commissioners to make sure all of the basket supports were padded in the future.

The next spring, the spring after his senior year when he helped us to the Final Four, Carp might have played his best basketball at Notre Dame when he led his team to the Bookstore Championship. I am not being sarcastic. His team, called Leo's Last, beat a team led by Batton and Joe Montana. Carp's team was the underdog and Batton's was the evil empire, because they hadn't lost in three years before Carp's team beat them. That was the year the tournament was featured in *Sports Illustrated*.

DWIGHT CLAY, 1972-75

Dwight Clay averaged just 9.2 points per game and barely shot 40 percent from the field for his three years on the varsity. But if I needed a last-second shot to win a game, he was the guy I turned to. We have already talked about his shot that ended UCLA's winning streak in 1974.

There were three other games in which he hit a jumper with under 30 seconds left to win a game or send it into overtime. As a sophomore in 1972-73, he nailed a jumper with three seconds left to beat third-ranked Marquette, 71-69. That was my first win over Al McGuire, and it ended Marquette's 81-game home court winning streak. The very next game, in South Bend against Pittsburgh, Clay hit a jumper to send the game into overtime. We finally won that game, 85-76. The next year, in the second game of the season, he sent the Ohio State game in Columbus into overtime before we won, 76-72.

Of all the players who came back to Notre Dame last January for the 30-year reunion of our 1974 team, Dwight might have gotten the most out of it. It had been his moment, he made the shot. He never played any professional basketball and returned to Pittsburgh to enter the business world after he graduated in 1975. While he had been back to Notre Dame, he had never been back with all the players from that team. It had been 30 years since he had seen John Shumate.

Dwight got to the luncheon early and was doing an interview with Jack Nolan from WNDU when Shumate, Brokaw and Ray Martin came into the monogram room. Those three had gone into the coaching world and had stayed in touch consistently because of their common profession. They all came over to Dwight and started giving him a hard time while he was doing a taped interview. Finally they all just hugged him. Dwight has put on a few pounds since his playing days so there is plenty to hug.

PETER CROTTY, 1972-75

On May 3, 1971, the day I got the phone call from Moose Krause offering me the head coaching position at Notre Dame, Peter Crotty was celebrating his 17th birthday on a fishing trip near his home of Rockville Center, NY.

I had signed Peter to play at Fordham on April Fool's Day, but when I took the Notre Dame job, he said he wanted to follow me. He said he had signed with Fordham because of me, not because of the school. I tried to convince him to stay at Fordham because he was a New York kid, and I already was making the Fordham people mad by leaving after a 26-3 season. But in August of 1971, just a few weeks prior to the beginning of the semester, Peter got his acceptance.

Crotty was one of the most highly recruited players on the east coast and would have been a star had he stayed at Fordham. He started every game his sophomore year and made four huge free throws when we beat North Carolina (and Dean Smith) in the NIT. In the championship game against Virginia Tech Gary Brokaw made a late free throw, but it was wiped out when they said Peter stepped in the lane too early. On the film, looking at it 30 years later, it sure looked like Allen Bristow of Virginia Tech stepped in first. We lost by one point. Some people unjustifiably blamed that loss on Peter.

When we signed Adrian Dantley the next year, Peter lost his starting job. That was a tough situation because I knew he had come to Notre Dame because of me and now I was benching him. But, looking back, most forwards would have lost their starting job to Adrian Dantley.

Out of high school Peter Crotty picked a coach instead of a school. Notre Dame certainly had a positive impact on him in his four years in school and beyond. This past year he had a son graduate from Notre Dame and there is another on the way.

ADRIAN DANTLEY, 1973-76

I remember when I went to Adrian Dantley's home in Washington, DC for an in-home visit. I took Austin Carr with me because I knew Dantley could be a difference maker. Austin was in the NBA by this time with Cleveland and was Notre Dame's greatest player and a Washington, D.C. native.

Austin met me at Adrian's home, just a few miles from DeMatha High School where Adrian played for the legendary coach Morgan Wooten. We knocked on the door and this beautiful woman answered the door. Austin and I both figured Adrian had a very attractive older sister. It turned out to be Virginia, Adrian's mom. She worked for the Department of the Interior, and her sister, Muriel Jenkins (known as Aunt Rose), was a school librarian. It didn't take us long to figure out that Aunt Rose was the force of the family. That was a plus for us, because she was big on Adrian getting a good education and she was aware of the graduation rate of the past players we had had from Washington, D.C. Fran Collins, a friend of Johnny Dee's from his days in the navy, helped recruit Carr, Collis Jones and Sid Catlett before I got to Notre Dame. Even though he was a Georgetown graduate, he continued to help me with players from the Washington, D.C. area.

We had a lot going for us in recruiting during this period, but our biggest plus was John Shumate. When I look at the great players we signed during this period, Shumate was the guy who served as their host. He was the best salesman Notre Dame had. He got Brokaw and Clay to take an interest in recruiting Adrian also. When Dantley came on his visit he had planned on staying for just one day, but after Shumate got a hold of him, he stayed the full 48 hours.

He finally signed with us in June of 1973. He called a press conference at DeMatha and carried a basketball with him into the press conference. He announced his decision by turning the ball around to the crowd, and it had Notre Dame spelled on it.

•••

Adrian came to Notre Dame at 230 pounds, so he battled criticism that he was out of shape all year. He was a quiet kid and it bothered him more than we knew. At one point in February he started fasting in an attempt to lose weight. He had been struggling a bit but finally broke the spell with a 23-point, 15-rebound game against DePaul, a game we won, 101-72.

I took him out with a couple minutes left. Shortly after play resumed, one of the players grabbed me and said that Adrian had passed out. He had gotten dehydrated from not eating and was out cold. We stopped the game and the ACC became totally silent. The trainers couldn't revive him, they actually had to carry him out on a stretcher. Fortunately, they got some fluids in him at the infirmary and he was back two games later.

After that incident he decided that he wasn't going to go on any more crash diets. He had a terrific freshman year, averaging 18.3 points a game, second only to Shumate's 24.2 that 1973-74 season. He lost 20 pounds over the summer when he had his wisdom teeth removed.

He did struggle in the NCAA Tournament game against Michigan that year. He made just one of seven shots from the field and scored just two points, his career low. Adrian was not the most quotable guy in the world, but he captured the feeling in our locker room after that loss. "My legs felt like log cabins," was his explanation for his poor performance.

He was a dedicated player who loved the game. Back in South Bend that next Sunday, Dantley knocked on Shumate's door in Fisher Hall. He told Shumate he wanted to go play a pickup game right now. "I need to score," he told Shu.

•••

Adrian was the best one-on-one player I ever had, and no one was better at getting to the foul line. When we beat Kansas in the 1975 NCAA Tournament he personally fouled out three guys and shot 21 free throws for the game. In his 15-year NBA career he made 6,832 free throws, still fifth in NBA history. And he was an incredible rebounder at 6-5. He had a big backside and knew how to use it to his advantage. He averaged almost 10 rebounds a game for his career. He was Charles Barkley before Charles Barkley.

•••

Adrian had a lot of great games, but a few stand out. His freshman year he scored 41 points against West Virginia in a game at the ACC. He made 18-23 shots from the field, and scored those 41 points in just 29 minutes, still the most points scored by a Notre Dame player in less than 30 minutes.

Adrian's career-high scoring game was 49 points against Air Force in 1974–75, his sophomore year. But, what I remember most about that game was that he drew seven charging fouls. With everything else he did, he was also the best player I ever had in terms of drawing the charge.

Adrian finished his sophomore year second in the nation in scoring, and his junior year he was fourth. He shot over 55 percent from the field, averaged over 28 points a game, and 80 percent from the line both years. I never had another player close to those figures. We

Adrian Dantley was a two-time, first-team All-American, but his most memorable day at Notre Dame took place two years after his last game, when he became the first "hardship case" at any school to earn his degree.

ran special plays for Adrian, something we called the A.D. Blue offense.

He turned pro after his junior year but remained an amateur so he could play for the United States Olympic team. Even Dean Smith couldn't hold him back. He scored 30 points in the Gold Medal Game against the Yugoslavians. That year he and Scott May were neck and neck for National Player of the Year. Indiana went 32-0, so May won all the awards. But when they both played on that Olympic team in 1976, Dantley showed everyone who was the top player, and he continued to do that in his NBA career. He finished with 23,177 points as an NBA player, still ninth in the history of the league.

•••

Dantley holds one more distinction in basketball history. He became the first hardship case to come back to school and get his degree. In the 1970s, you just couldn't declare for the NBA draft, you had to file a "hardship" application with the league that basically stated that your family's financial situation required it.

Adrian got his undergrad degree on August 4, 1978. With diploma in hand, I went with him to the Golden Dome after the graduation exercises, and we had our picture taken together. I remember how proud his mother and Aunt Rose were. I also thought about all those opposing coaches who said he would never get his degree. He spent his career proving everyone wrong. He had been an All-American, an Olympian and the NBA Rookie of the Year. But, what I will always remember was what he told me the day he graduated. "Nobody can ever take this away from me. I earned it."

I coached a lot of great players, but if I had to pick one who deserved to be in the Basketball Hall of Fame, it would be Adrian.

BRUCE FLOWERS, 1975-79

Bruce Flowers was one of the most efficient big men I ever coached. For his career he shot 57.4 percent from the field, including two separate years in which he shot at least 60 percent. His senior year, 1978-79, he shot 65.6 percent from the field, 83.3 percent from the line and scored 9.5 points per game.

I always believed in a strong inside game, and he was one of the reasons we had that power game. We led the nation in rebound margin two of his four years. Against West Virginia his freshman year he made 13-16 shots from the field and scored 27 points, which was the high game of his career. It was one of just two games during the 1975-76 season that Adrian Dantley didn't lead us in scoring.

Bruce had a reputation for being aggressive, one that was enhanced because he was called for two of the most famous fouls of my Notre Dame career. Ironically, both plays took place in the same building, Cole Fieldhouse in College Park, Maryland.

In 1976-77 we were playing North Carolina in the Sweet 16 NCAA Tournament. The score was tied at 77 and the Tar Heels had the ball with under a minute left. As was the case in every North Carolina game in that era, Phil Ford had the ball and was running the "Four Corners Offense." With the seconds winding down, Ford broke down our defense and drove to the basket. Flowers left his man, and came over to defend Ford at the foul line. Flowers deflected his shot, but a foul was called. Ford made both free throws and we lost by two points.

My co-author, Tim Bourret, is the SID at Clemson and saw Ford quite often when he was an assistant coach and fundraiser at North Carolina. One day, Bourret said, "Phil, you ruined my senior year at Notre Dame when you made those two free throws. Did Bruce really foul you?" Every time, Ford answered the same way. "Great block, but they called a foul."

Two years later, we were playing Maryland in Cole Fieldhouse. We were ranked number one in the nation at the time and had a 66-64 lead with 10 seconds left. Lawrence Boston, Maryland's center got the ball on the left baseline and drove on Bruce. Boston made a great move at the last minute, scored the basket and Bruce fouled him. Boston converted the three-point play, and Maryland beat us by a point.

RANDY HAEFNER, 1974-78

Randy Haefner was a Cincinnati kid who could shoot the ball, but he was average in the other areas of the game because of a lack of quickness. He played in 44 games and scored 66 points over four seasons. Coaches would love to have him today because he would have been a terrific three-point shooter.

When I went to work at ESPN, I met Dan Patrick, who was a pretty good high school basketball player in Cincinnati in the 1970s. In fact, I sent him two letters while he was in high school, one in the summer to tell him we were checking him out, and another in the winter to tell him we weren't.

When I got to ESPN he told me about the letters. He said, "You gave my scholarship to Randy Haefner! Randy has my four NCAA Tournament watches!" That just killed him. He used to go on and on in the newsroom when I was there on how I gave Randy Haefner his scholarship.

Finally, I decided to bust Patrick. One day, at 4 p.m., the busiest time of the day in the ESPN *SportsCenter* newsroom, I called everyone together because I wanted to make a presentation.

"I wish to make a special presentation to Dan Patrick. He wanted to go to Notre Dame and play basketball, but I took Randy Haefner instead. Dan, on behalf of the University of Notre Dame, here is your NCAA Tournament watch 25 years later." I then gave him one of my NCAA Tournament watches. Dan was stunned while the entire newsroom broke up.

BILL HANZLIK, 1976-80

If I had to pick the smartest player in my coaching career it would be Bill Hanzlik. He was amazing on the floor, especially when it came to setting our defense. I just signaled to him what we wanted, and he got everyone in the right place. One of the reasons our match-up zone worked so well was because of Hanzlik in the 1970s and Jim Dolan in the 1980s.

Hanzlik was also a great team leader. One of the most important contributions he made to the Final Four team in 1977-78 was to serve as a mentor for Bill Laimbeer. Laimbeer had flunked out of school after the 1975-76 season and was not at Notre Dame for Hanzlik's freshman year (1976-77).

Hanzlik could guard anyone, and he proved that with Notre Dame and later in the NBA. In the NBA he guarded guys at all five positions. I remember someone sending me an article after he guarded Karem Abdul Jabbar. After the game Jabbar praised Hanzlik's defense.

Hanzlik made me look good with Lenny Wilkens, who was coaching the Seattle Supersonics when Hanzlik was a senior. He was trying to decide between Hawkeye Whitney of NC State and Hanzlik for his first-round pick. Hawkeye was an All-American and averaged nearly 19 points a game his senior year. Hanzlik didn't even average double figures (8.5), but he was a great defender, he could rebound and play every position.

Lenny called me and asked me about both players. I went through all of Hanzlik's attributes as a defender, capable scorer, and team leader. Then, he asked me, "Did he graduate?" I said, "On time, in engineering. You can't go wrong with Hanzlik."

Wilkens took Hanzlik in the first round, the 20th pick of the entire draft. It was only the third time an NBA first-round pick had failed to score in double figures at the college level the year he was drafted. Hanzlik went on to play 10 years and 748 games in the NBA, while Whitney, who was taken four picks earlier, played two years and 70 games.

Tracy Jackson, 1977-81

According to *Chicago Sun-Times* writer Brian Hewitt (now an in-studio analyst for the Golf Channel), Lefty Driesell wanted Tracy Jackson to come to Maryland so much that he changed churches so he could sit next to him during Sunday services his senior year of high school. Jackson went to Paint Branch High School in Silver Spring, Maryland, just a few miles from the Maryland campus. Lefty was a master recruiter, but he might have outfoxed himself when it came to Jackson.

Danny Nee recruited Jackson and determined that the soft-sell approach was best because Jackson's father had passed away during his senior year. He needed some time to himself. We told him we wanted him, went to some of his games, but basically took the low-key approach.

Fortunately, this approach worked, because I wouldn't have won nearly as many games at Notre Dame without him. I can tell you two games off the top of my head that I wouldn't have won, and they came just 12 days apart. Tracy was the top clutch shooter I had this side of Dwight Clay.

Tracy Jackson was my all-time sixth man. Soon after his playing career ended, he was elected to the Notre Dame Board of Trustees, my only former player who can make that claim.

In the 1979-80 season, we were struggling in a game with Villanova at home. Villanova, then coached by Rollie Massimino with assistant coach Pete Gillen (now at Virginia and one of my future assistants) had scored with three seconds left to take a 69-68 lead. We called timeout and we had to go the length of the court.

We didn't design a set play for Tracy. We just said whoever gets open at halfcourt, take the ball as far as you can and let it go. We got the ball to Tracy and he let go with a 30-footer from the left wing. I don't think he ever squared up, but he swished the shot as the buzzer sounded, giving us a 70-69 victory. It gave us momentum going into that weekend's game at UCLA, a game we won 80-73.

Just 11 days later, on January 26, 1980, we were playing a 15th-ranked Maryland team that would go on to win the regular-season ACC championship. We had a comfortable lead until Albert King got hot. He drove and scored to put the Terps within a point at 62-61, then stole the in-bounds pass and scored again with 15 seconds left to put Maryland up 63-62.

We didn't take a timeout; we just got the ball to Tracy again. This time he had more time and drove all the way to the baseline and hit a short jumper with five seconds left. Maryland got the ball to King, who tried a long, off-balanced shot that missed, and we had stolen a 64-63 victory.

It was quite a victory for Tracy, who genuinely liked Lefty. But, he knew this would create quite a splash back in Maryland. It was an especially gratifying victory for us because we had beaten Maryland without Tripucka, who was in the hospital with a back ailment. In the locker room after the game I pulled the team together for a final cheer, and said, "and someone please take Kelly a six-pack." It was also a nice way to get my 200th win at Notre Dame.

Tracy was the best sixth man in college basketball his freshman and sophomore years. He was our leading scorer in 1979-80 as a junior and was a second-round pick of the Boston Celtics in the 1981 draft, the 25th pick overall. He played just three years in the league, then went into private business. He had made a strong impression with the administration at Notre Dame when he was a student-athlete, especially with Father Hesburgh and Father Joyce. Soon after his playing days ended he was elected to the Notre Dame Board of Trustees, one of the youngest members of the board in its history.

TOBY KNIGHT, 1973-77

When Toby Knight came to Notre Dame he wouldn't work on weights, and he just didn't practice hard. He had John Shumate ahead of him when he was a freshman and he knew there was no way he was going to beat him out. He got better as his career went along. In the 1976 NCAA Tournament against Cincinnati, he scored a tip-in at the buzzer to win the game.

Prior to his senior year the lights came on when it came to working out, and it paid off. The dunk was back in college basketball for his senior year and he became more aggressive, and this helped his overall game. He had the first memorable dunk of that year at home in a win over Indiana, who was the defending national champion. He went from averaging 2.7 points a game as a freshman to averaging a double-double (15.2 PPG and 10.6 RPG) as a senior. He also shot 59 percent from the field and 71 percent from the line. Willis Reed made him a first-round pick of the Knicks after his senior year.

When he was negotiating a contract with Eddie Donovan, the Knicks GM, I called Eddie and asked him what he was going to get. He told me they were talking $40,000 the first year, $50,000 the second year and $60,000 for the third year. I said, "Eddie, his family is on welfare, you can't do that to him." I called Larry Fleischer, who was one of the top agents at the time and got him to take on Toby's negotiations. Larry got him 70-80-90 for his first contract, plus a bonus.

In his third year, Toby averaged 19.1 points a game and shot 53 percent from the field. He was one of the rising stars of the NBA. He negotiated a second contract through Fleischer and got $900,000 a year for three years, guaranteed.

As it turned out, Toby was fortunate he got a guaranteed contract. In an exhibition game in Portland, ME prior to the 1980-81 season he blew out his knee. There wasn't any contact on the play, he just turned the wrong way and twisted the knee. He sat out a year, then tried to come back in 1981-82, but he was never the same and called it a career at the end of that season.

He has made good use of his Notre Dame degree. He is now a salesman for a company that makes portable basketball hoops in Pittsburgh.

Dave Kuzmicz, 1973-77

Dave Kuzmicz was a 6-3 guard from South Bend St. Joe High School, one of only three players from St. Joe High that I gave a scholarship to in my 20 years at Notre Dame (Tom Varga and Michael Smith were the others). That school is right across the street from the old Notre Dame golf course.

Kuzmicz came in with Dantley's class in the fall of 1973. He had one game that stood out in his four years, a game at the Convocation Center against Holy Cross in January of 1975, his sophomore year. We had just lost consecutive games to Pittsburgh and Marquette, so we had to have this home game against Holy Cross. But, Ronnie Perry, who was the best player the Crusaders had in years, was filling it up from everywhere. They were playing a zone defense and we were cold. Dantley was scoring inside, but that was about all we were getting offensively.

I decided to put Kuzmicz in the game and he started hitting everything he threw up. He shot eight of eleven from the field and scored 20 points. He would have had 25 had there been a three-point goal then.

Dave's nickname was "Kuz", but we pronounced it "Cooze" as in Bob Cousy, the former Celtic great. Ironically, Holy Cross was the college Bob Cousy had attended. Kuz only scored 51 points the entire season, but 20 came in that game against Holy Cross. I started Kuzmicz the next game against UCLA and we beat John Wooden's last team, 84-78. That was a thrill of a lifetime to start for Kuz.

Bill Laimbeer, 1975-79

The smartest frontcourt player I ever had (Hanzlik is the smartest overall) also flunked out of Notre Dame. Fortunately, he came back... and graduated on time with his class.

Bill Laimbeer had scored over 1100 on the SAT coming out of Palos Verdes High School in Los Angeles, CA. But, when he came to Notre Dame he didn't think going to class was that important. He enjoyed going to the pool hall and the golf course more than to class. At the end of the semester he had a GPA between the 1.6 that would have allowed him to keep playing under NCAA rules, but not at the 2.0 needed to be eligible at Notre Dame. We checked class attendance, but I was not of the opinion that we should go over to the dorm and walk him to class. He had to learn to be responsible, even if he flunked out.

It was a shame, because he was our third leading scorer and second leading rebounder at the time he became ineligible. He scored 15 points and had 14 rebounds against Manhattan in his last game that season (1975-76). With the games taken away from him we figured he would get his act together in the second semester and be ready to go for the 1976-77 season. We were wrong, as he did the same thing, scoring a GPA between the 1.6 and 2.0 levels.

With two consecutive probation semesters, he was dismissed from school. But when he left he told me he wanted to come back to Notre Dame. He transferred to Owens Technical School in Toledo, which was near his family's home. His dad was very successful in the business world, as he owned a corrugated box company. In fact, when Bill went to the NBA he was the only player in the league whose father made more money than he did.

I went to bat for Bill with Father Hesburgh. He said he needed to get a 3.0 at Owens and then he would consider it. Bill made the 3.0. Hesburgh then said he needed to come to summer school at Notre Dame and get two A's. Bill did that, and in August of 1977 he was readmitted.

That year we went to the Final Four for the only time in history, and his last year we went to the Regional Finals before we ran into Magic Johnson and Michigan State. He scored 509 points and had 433 rebounds in his 69 games at Notre Dame. I thought he could make it in the NBA as a center, but I never dreamed he would lead Detroit to two World Championships.

•••

We called Bill "Lamb" at Notre Dame because of the pronunciation of his last name. That nickname certainly became ironic in light of his reputation as the "bad boy" of the NBA. He was a physical player at Notre Dame, but he never got into any fights or thrown out of a game. But, that all changed when he got into the league.

He might not have gotten a chance to play in the NBA had he not gone with us on a trip to Yugoslavia in the summer of 1979. He graduated in May of 1979 and still had another year of eligibility, but he had decided he was ready for professional basketball. He was drafted by the Cleveland Cavaliers in the third round, a full round behind Bruce Flowers.

It was questionable at best as to whether or not he would make the Cavaliers as a rookie. So, even though he was not going to play for us the next winter, we let him play with us in the games in Yugoslavia to give him some exposure in Europe. I contacted some scouts from the Italian pro league and they came to Yugoslavia to see him play. They were impressed, and "Lamb" liked the idea of playing in Italy. He had just gotten married, and his wife liked the idea of spending their first year of marriage in Italy.

Bill scored 22 points a game and was one of the top players in Italy. The NBA took note and he came back to the NBA for the 1980-81 season with Cleveland, the first of his 14 years in the league. He was traded to Detroit, and finished his career as a four-time All-Star and scored over 10,000 points and grabbed over 10,000 rebounds, just the 19th player in NBA history to reach both levels. He missed just eight games in 14 years and, despite his reputation, only two were due to suspensions.

•••

After Bill finished playing in December of 1993, he went into business with his father. But, he still had the urge to stay involved in basketball, so he coached his daughter's AAU team. That has since led to his current occupation as head coach of the Detroit Shock of the WNBA. One of the first moves he made was to sign Ruth Riley, who had led Notre Dame to the NCAA Championship of women's basketball in 2001.

In their first season together, the Shock won the WNBA Championship in an upset of Los Angeles and Lisa Leslie. Laimbeer was named the Coach of the Year, and Riley was named the MVP of the Finals. At the championship celebration one fan had brought an appropriate sign: "15 Good Girls and 1 Bad Boy = WNBA Championship".

I have no explanation, but I am apparently the cradle for WNBA coaches. Laimbeer, Shumate, and Orlando Woolridge have all coached in that league.

Ray Martin, 1973-77

Ray Martin was one of the best defensive players and one of the smartest players I ever had. He grew up in New York, so I knew he was tough when I recruited him. It was easy for him to follow our team his senior year because we played four games in the 1973 NIT and I think he went to every game.

He was another player whom Shumate helped recruit. But when he came to Notre Dame, Shumate used to ride him about his shooting. Ray was not a big scorer and he had an unusual shot. In fact, Shumate gave him the nickname Arthur. He said Ray shot the ball like he had Arthur-itis.

I used to kid him that he was one of the smartest players I ever had, because he was smart enough not to shoot the ball during any possession we had over the last 3:22 of the 1974 UCLA game. I used to tell him that if he had taken a shot, the streak would have reached 89.

Ray was one of my favorite players, and we are still close today because he is in the coaching profession. In fact, he is the only Notre Dame grad with a men's basketball National Championship ring. He was one of Jim Valvano's assistants at NC State in 1983.

I still remember how quiet it got in the Convocation Center when he broke his ankle against Indiana his senior year (1976-77). It happened in the sixth game of the season, just one game above the cut line to get a medical redshirt year. He was off to a great start. We were undefeated and he was one of the main reasons. It was a 90-degree break, and I knew it was over when it happened. They had to put a pin in it. It was such a bad break, getting another year probably would not have mattered.

Bob Knight knew it was over for Ray also. Just before they wheeled Ray off on a stretcher, Knight went over to Ray and shook his hand and told him to hang in there. We won that game over an Indiana team that had won the national championship the previous year, but I had an empty feeling after the game. The toughest part was calling his parents in New York that night and telling him he was going to have to have surgery and that his basketball career was over.

GARY "GOOSE" NOVAK, 1971-74

Coaches take great pride when they say that their former players have gone on to become doctors and lawyers. Gary "Goose" Novak is my former player who has gone on to become a doctor, as he is a GP in Illinois.

He wanted to be a doctor from day one. He took his books with him on road trips and was always studying. When we had the reunion for the 1974 team that ended UCLA's 88-game winning streak, Gary came back. We talked about how I told the team that day in 1974 that this day would be something they could tell their grandchildren. Gary now has a daughter who has graduated from Notre Dame. Some day soon she will probably have a child and Gary will tell that grandchild about the day he cut down the nets after ending that streak.

•••

What does a coach say to a team when you are down 44-13 at Indiana at halftime? That was my challenge during my first year when we were the dedication game at Assembly Hall in Bloomington. I didn't have a "Gipper Speech", because there are none for a 30-point halftime deficit. I remember talking to the team through Gary during that halftime. I said, to Gary, "Some day you are going to be a doctor and be responsible for someone's life in front of you on an operating table. Are you going to lose that life, or are you going to give it everything you have to try to save it?"

My message to Gary and the rest of the team was to not give up, because if you give up now, you might do the same in more important situations after you left school. It sounded good, and Gary is a very respected doctor.

But we did go on to lose that game at Indiana by 65.

•••

Gary was a popular guy on campus. He had survived the 1971-72 season, a year in which he actually averaged a double-double (19 points and 10 rebounds). Thank goodness he did, or we might not have scored 50 points a game that season.

Gary was the subject of the most unusual Senior Day presentation ever. Known all over campus as "Goose" some of his teammates arranged to have the cheerleaders bring a live goose (in a cage) out to center court when he was introduced for the last time.

BILL PATERNO, 1973-77

Billy Paterno came in with Dantley and Toby Knight. He had over 1,000 points and 500 rebounds and shot at least 70 percent from the foul line each of his four years. He might have scored 1,200 points had there been a three-point goal in those days. He could shoot from long range. He had some game-winners in his career, one at Michigan State his freshman year that comes to mind and he had a great game that same year when we beat Marquette.

While he could shoot from the outside, nothing will top what he did against Pittsburgh his senior year. The half was running down and there were just a couple of seconds left. After a Pittsburgh score he took the ball out of bounds and attempted to throw the ball the length of the court to Toby Knight for a possible tip-in. He overthrew Knight, but the ball went into the hoop, a clear swish from 94 feet.

Everyone went bananas, but then came the reality. It didn't count for any points because he had thrown it in from out of bounds. This past March, I was in the ESPN studios when Greg Bosl—a walk-on for Notre Dame—hit a half-court shot at the final buzzer against Purdue in an NIT game in South Bend. Some of the guys at ESPN asked me if I could remember a made field goal longer than that at the Convocation Center. I said, "Yes, I saw one twice as far, and it didn't even count."

GIL SALINAS, 1977-81

Gilbert Salinas was 6-11 and 175 pounds when we signed him in the spring of 1977 out of San Antonio, Texas. He was the world's tallest Mexican, but we needed to put some meat on him if he was going to battle underneath with his own teammates in practice, never mind the regular games. When he took a shower we needed to have a lifeguard on duty to make sure he didn't go down the drain. Today, he goes about 300 pounds and could play the defensive line for the Dallas Cowboys.

His father grew up a big Notre Dame fan and used to listen to Bill Stern broadcast the football games on the radio in the 1940s.

One of his heroes was Frank Tripucka, a Notre Dame quarterback during that time who went on to play with the Denver Broncos. When we signed Gilbert, one of his classmates was Kelly Tripucka, Frank's father. Gilbert and Kelly lived together in Morrissey Hall their freshman year. Gilbert's dad was thrilled when he finally met Frank Tripucka the day the two sons moved into the dorm.

•••

We had a national recruiting base so we had players from all over the country. I always tried to schedule a homecoming game for each player and we did that with Gilbert when we scheduled a game against Texas Christian in San Antonio his junior year. When we got to the San Antonio Airport, we were met by his high school's band, all 12 of them. It was one of the more off-key renditions of the Notre Dame Victory March ever, but it meant everything to Gilbert.

Gilbert had a solid career, a backup to Orlando Woolridge most of the time, but he did start five games as a junior in 1979-80. In December of that year he made four of six shots and scored eight points off the bench in a win over a UCLA team that would play in the national championship game at the end of the year.

•••

Unfortunately, Gilbert's Notre Dame career had a very sad ending. His entire family drove to South Bend from San Antonio for his graduation in May of 1981. We had a party at the Rockne Lake house during graduation week for all the seniors and Gilbert's entire family was there. I couldn't go to graduation because I had committed to speak at a clinic in Yugoslavia.

The next week, I got a call with some bad news. Minus Gilbert, the Salinas family was traveling back to San Antonio in two cars. At 4 a.m. on a road just outside of Austin, Texas, Gilbert's mother had fallen asleep at the wheel and crashed into a parked truck.

Gilbert's mother survived, but Gilbert's father, sister-in-law and her daughter, Gilbert's one-year-old niece were killed. The next time I went to the lake house I walked in the backdoor and noticed the little girl's fingerprints on the living room window. I have had to deal with death all my life, but that was difficult to accept. I can't imagine how hard it must have been for Gilbert.

JOHN SHUMATE, 1972-74
(See Assistant Coaches chapter)

HAWK STEVENS, 1971-74

Hawk Stevens was a forward on my first three Notre Dame teams. He was a starter in my first game against Michigan in December of 1971. He could mimic me better than anyone. Even when he didn't play that much as a senior on the 1974 team, he was a big asset because of his ability to keep everyone loose. When we had the 30-year reunion this past January I had every player speak at the luncheon. Hawk came prepared with a 50-line poem. It was classic Hawk Stevens.

He was one of the most popular guys on campus because he had his own show on the campus radio station. He should have been on Johnny Carson.

Every year we had a Jocks vs. Girls game in conjunction with Antostal weekend, a celebration of spring at Notre Dame. It was a game in which the varsity would play a basketball game on the Bookstore Courts against a team of co-eds (there wasn't a varsity women's team then). The only catch was that the men had to play with boxing gloves. Hawk played in the game every year and he would dress up as a girl, complete with false breasts. He took great delight in imitating a girl named Bonita Bradshaw, who was an African-American who was the best female athlete at Notre Dame during the time. People came to that game just to see what Hawk would do.

KELLY TRIPUCKA, 1977-81

Kelly Tripucka was the most charismatic player I ever coached. He had an engaging personality. He was like the pied piper, people just liked to be with him. He lived in Morrissey Hall on campus and he thrived on living with the general student population. He always told me how schools that had "jock dorms" were missing the boat. He engaged in the Notre Dame experience.

Kelly used to get over 400 letters a year from Notre Dame fans from all 50 states and overseas. I can't imagine what it would be like with e-mail today. A secretary in the SID office spent half her time answering Kelly's fan mail. We were like the Rolling Stones in those days, because we were on TV so much and Kelly was like Mick Jaggar. In his four years we were on national TV over 20 times, probably double any other school. ESPN did not start until September of 1979, so there weren't many outlets for a national broadcast. It was NBC, WGN or nothing.

In the 112 games of Kelly's career, we played before a sellout crowd 75 times, including 34 sellouts away from home. People either loved us or hated us, and Kelly was usually the lightning rod for that interest. We went to West Virginia Kelly's sophomore year and a student approached him before the game and asked him for his autograph. Kelly signed and gave it back to the student, who then ripped it up and threw it in his face. We won the game, but we had a lot of other problems at West Virginia that day. After the game I told Gale Catlett we would never come back. . .and we didn't.

•••

Kelly was a natural fit at Notre Dame because his father, Frank, was an All-America quarterback under Frank Leahy at Notre Dame in 1948. He led the Irish to an undefeated season, then played professionally for many years in the NFL. He was the first Denver Bronco to have his number retired.

When we were recruiting Kelly, I kept in touch with Frank, who was also very close to Angelo Bertelli, Notre Dame's first Heisman Trophy winner. Angelo lived close by and Kelly used to refer to Bertelli as uncle Angelo. Kelly talked about Angelo using his Heisman as a doorstop. Another close friend of the family was Yogi Berra, who lived nearby.

Kelly's senior year of high school he visited Notre Dame, Duke, Maryland and South Carolina. On his visit to Notre Dame he went out with Rich Branning and Bill Hanzlik the first night, then tagged along with Dave Batton and Jeff Carpenter the second night. Branning and Hanzlik were more conservative, while Batton and Carpenter were the life of the party. He later said that the first night of his visit was like going out with Phyllis Diller and the second night was like going out with Raquel Welch. Kelly could fit in with anyone.

During his senior year of high school I kept calling Frank and asking him if we were OK. I was worried when Kelly went on visits to other schools. Frank kept telling me not to worry and in the end he was right.

•••

Kelly grew up in an athletic family. Frank was a distributor for a beer company in New Jersey. Randy, Kelly's mother, didn't breast feed him when he was a baby, Kelly grew up on Budweiser.

Kelly was one of six sons, and there was a sister, Heather, who graduated from Saint Mary's College, the school across the street from Notre Dame in 1972. She even once scored 56 points in a high school game.

Kelly was a great all-around athlete. He didn't play football, but I bet he would have been a terrific quarterback. He was a national semifinalist for the Ford Punt, Pass and Kick contest as a youngster.

Kelly Tripucka was the most charismatic player I ever coached. When we went on the road in the late 1970s we were like the Rolling Stones and Kelly was Mick Jaggar.

He led the state of New Jersey in goals scored as a soccer player his senior year of high school.

Kelly's brother, Mark, was a quarterback at UMass. Todd was an All-American and career scoring leader at Lafayette, while another brother, T.K., was starting forward at Fordham. In 1977-78, Kelly's freshman year, we played Fordham in the garden on Kelly's birthday and he played against T.K. There were some very physical plays in that game, probably the most physical since pickup games in the Tripucka driveway. Kelly's older brother, Tracy, was the head coach at Fordham that year at the age of 29. Kelly had 15 points and we won that game. The entire town of Essex Fells, New Jersey must have been at The Garden that night.

Randy was very enthusiastic in her support of her boys, so much so that Frank wouldn't sit with her at games. She had quite a voice and you could hear her whether she was behind the bench or in the upper deck. For the 1980 UCLA game at Notre Dame she brought a cowbell and two or three times she went behind Larry Brown to ring that cowbell. During a timeout Randy was yelling at the officials, and Kelly said as we broke the huddle, "Hey, does anyone know who that woman is?"

STAN WILCOX, 1977-81

Stan Wilcox was a backup point guard on the Final Four team who went on to get his law degree. He now works in NCAA compliance for the Big East Conference. He is the type of former student-athlete Notre Dame needs to hire in its administration.

One day before practice near the end of my career I told the team that Stan Wilcox had just passed the bar in the state of New York. I asked one of the players what that meant. "He can open a bar in New York?" Another player said, "No, it means he can practice law."

That made me think that we needed a daily lesson in current events on this team. So, every day I put the front page of the *Chicago Tribune* at a place near the front door of the locker room. I told them they had to read the front page every day before practice because I was going to ask them a current events question before practice.

DUCK WILLIAMS, 1974-78

It didn't take much recruiting to get Duck Williams to come to Notre Dame. He had grown up watching Austin Carr play at Notre Dame because Carr had attended the same high school, Mackin High, in Washington, D.C. The day he signed he told the media he had been dreaming of this day since the sixth grade.

Williams scored 1,433 career points from 1974-78, second behind David Rivers among guards I coached at Notre Dame. He had a good two-handed jumper and could make free throws, but he made his mark when we went to a Four Corners attack. We ran that in special situations, and Duck responded. He scored 25 in the win over San Francisco and then 26 the very next game at DePaul.

Duck played just one year with Utah in the NBA. He played in 77 games and scored over 500 points, but he was one and done. A few years after he finished his playing career, he went into business back in Washington, D.C. We were playing a game at Cole Field house, so he and Tracy Jackson came to the shootaround the night before the game. As soon as he got to the floor he took off his jacket and tie and went to the ball rack. He said, "Watch this coach, I still have it." He then drained a 25-footer. He was one of the best offensive players I ever had.

ORLANDO WOOLRIDGE, 1977-81

Willis Reed and Orlando Woolridge's mother were first cousins. During the 1976-77 season I was at a Knicks game and I ran into Reed. He said, "Are you going to recruit my cousin?" I said, "Who is your cousin?" He started telling me about Orlando and the fact that I had already met him. A few years back, when Orlando was 14, I was giving a lecture at a camp at The New York Military Academy and asked for volunteers for a passing drill. Orlando was the guinea pig.

I sent an assistant down to Mansfield, Louisiana, to check him out, and sure enough, he could play. Willis and I actually made a trade by the end of that year. We signed Orlando in April and he drafted

Toby Knight for the Knicks in the first round. It worked well for both of us.

Orlando had as much pure talent as any player I ever coached. He played 14 years in the NBA, the most of any of my former players, and he was by far the best dunker I ever had. We went to Yugoslavia in the summer of 1979 to play a series of games against their national teams. Before one of the games we were warming up and Orlando was putting on a show for the home fans. They hadn't seen anything like Orlando. He could jump from a standing start and touch his head on the rim.

He came down one time and threw one down so hard that he shattered the backboard. The Yugoslavian players looked at him like he was someone from another planet. The gym didn't have a back-up basket, so we had to go outside on an adjacent court to play the game. The Yugoslavians thought they were going to have a big advantage, but I didn't worry. All my players had taken part in the Bookstore Tournament, so they were used to playing outside. We won by 50.

Above: I first suggested to Dan Devine that the Irish wear green jerseys in 1975. Two years later he finally took my advice and the ploy worked to perfection. The game was over before it began; just look at John Robinson's reaction (in front with his hands on his hips and mouth open) as the Irish take the field. *Courtesy of Digger Phelps*

Below: The pep rally in Stepan Center the night before the 1974 UCLA game rivaled any Notre Dame football assembly. *Courtesy of Digger Phelps*

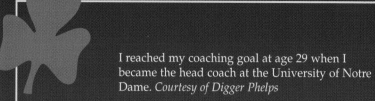

I reached my coaching goal at age 29 when I became the head coach at the University of Notre Dame. *Courtesy of Digger Phelps*

Above: Today I spend March Madness with Chris Fowler and Dick Vitale at ESPN in Bristol, Connecticut. The hours are long, as we tape a battery of segments for various programs on ESPN's family of channels. Sometimes we get carried away and have way too much fun. © *ESPN*

Right: The 1974 win over UCLA had great historical significance, but the first time we won at UCLA (December 1976) also holds a special place in my career. The 66-63 victory ended UCLA's 156-game home non-conference winning streak. *Courtesy of Digger Phelps*

Above: Art is one of my true passions. This is my impression of Vincent Van Gogh's "The Red Vineyard," which I did in October 2003, in my home. Van Gogh had just one painting (out of 903) that sold during his lifetime. It was "The Red Vineyard." After visiting my son Rick in Amsterdam this summer, I did four new paintings in South France. *Courtesy of Digger Phelps*

Left: "Naked Stems in a Vase." I painted this on June 3, 2001, at an art supply show at Navy Pier in Chicago. *Courtesy of Digger Phelps*

Chapter Six

THE PLAYERS OF THE 1980S

TIM ANDREE, 1979-83

We recruited Tim Andree, Billy Varner, and John Paxson the same year. Andree and Paxson both played in the McDonald's All-American game, so with Tripucka, Woolridge and Jackson graduating in 1981, we needed Andree to lead our frontcourt.

Tim was from a large, devout Catholic family in Michigan. Among his 11 brothers and sisters were a priest and a nun.

His freshman year we were ranked 10th in the nation and had just won four in a row. Marquette came in as an unranked team, but a late field goal by Sam Worthen gave the Warriors a 77-74 victory. With the outcome obvious in the final seconds, I looked down the bench and noticed that Andree was crying. I knew it was a tough loss, but he hadn't even played.

I said, "What's wrong with you?" He said in a cracking voice, "This was the first game I haven't played in since I was in the fifth grade." I looked back at him and said, "Get used to it." He didn't even play the next game against DePaul when we ended their 25-game winning streak.

I had four years to get my players ready for manhood. I had a different approach depending on the type of upbringing. Some guys you needed to toughen up.

Andree matured over his career, as a player and as a person. He had a hand in both of our wins the next season over No. 1-ranked Kentucky and Virginia, when he had to face Sam Bowie and Ralph Sampson. He had one of his best games on his Senior Night against

Northern Iowa when he had 20 points on eight-for-10 shooting and 12 rebounds.

After his senior year, he wanted to continue to play professional basketball. He came to me and said he had an opportunity to play in Israel. The only catch was that he had to go to Las Vegas and marry a Jewish girl. I said facetiously, "OK, let's call your mother right now and tell her. Are you going to call her in between her first, second or third rosary of the day?"

Tim is one of the guys who really benefited from the Notre Dame experience and he has been very successful. After he graduated, he played pro ball in Japan and learned the language. He went to work for Toyota and became a chief spokesman for Toyota USA in New York City. He now works for David Stern as a vice president for communications for the NBA.

KEN BARLOW, 1983-86

Ken Barlow was a starter for most his 120 games over four years at Notre Dame. He scored 1,342 points, had 649 rebounds and shot 53 percent for his career. Ken's senior year, he averaged nearly 15 points a game and shot 88.7 percent from the foul line, the best ever by one of my frontcourt players.

Many times in those 120 games Barlow was a hero in a Notre Dame victory. But he was never more heroic than he was a few months after his Notre Dame career ended.

On August 24, 1986, Barlow was driving David Rivers in a van near Elkhart. They had been working all summer at Port-O-Pit, a catering agency, and were returning to campus to help David move into his room in Howard Hall.

In August, the corn in Indiana can grow as tall as 14 feet, so on some rural two-lane highways it can grow taller than a stop sign. On the trip back to campus, Barlow thought a car coming from another street was going to miss a stop sign, so he tried to avoid the car and ran onto the shoulder and loose gravel pavement. The van skidded and he lost control of the car, forcing the car to turn over.

Neither Barlow nor Rivers had his seat belt on, but Barlow stayed in the van because of the steering wheel and the fact that he was six foot 10. Rivers, who was just six feet, was thrown through the shattered windshield and came to rest 90 feet beyond the van. During his exit from the car, Rivers stomach was sliced in two, a 15-inch gash, by the broken glass.

Despite a deep cut to his leg, Barlow sprinted to a nearby home and called for help. He then went back to the scene of the accident where he found Rivers in a ditch, bleeding profusely. Later, paramedics said they could see David's aorta. Barlow fought back the nausea of the moment and wrapped his shirt around David's stomach to at least cover the wound. David would lose three pints of blood before he got to the hospital.

Throughout this time, Barlow and Rivers had the presence of mind to talk to each other, giving each other positive thoughts, telling each other they were going to make it. They prayed together until the ambulance arrived.

When I arrived at Elkhart General Hospital at 4:30 a.m., they were taking David into the recovery room, while Barlow was in another area of the hospital getting treatment for his less severe injuries. He had his head down and told me he was sorry. "You have nothing to be sorry about," I said. "You saved David's life tonight."

ELMER BENNETT, 1988-92

I was sitting at home watching a World Series game between the Cardinals and the Twins on the night of October 15, 1987 when Elmer Bennett called the house to tell me he was coming to Notre Dame. He had visited the weekend of the Michigan State football game in September, the game when Tim Brown had two punt returns for touchdowns. Brown gave Notre Dame Stadium an electric atmosphere that night, and I knew it had to be a positive experience for Elmer.

Elmer went on to score 1,488 career points, still in the top 15 in Notre Dame history. But three of those points stand out in my mind.

During his sophomore year (1989-90) we were 13-8 heading into a huge game at third-ranked Syracuse. We needed this game and a couple of more down the stretch if we were going to go to the NCAA Tournament for the sixth straight year. It had been a disappointing season to this point, because we were coming off a 21-9 record in 1988-89 and we were ranked 19th in the preseason AP poll. We had some injuries, and LaPhonso Ellis had been ruled ineligible for the first seven games after summer school.

The Syracuse game was tight throughout, and when Billy Owens, their star player, scored with just a few seconds left, it looked bleak. We called timeout after Owens's shot and the scoreboard read two seconds.

We had a set play for Bennett in a game-ending situation that took three seconds to run. As I've said, at the time the clock didn't stop after a made field goal inside the last minute.

After we called the timeout I went straight to Gerry Donaghy, the same official who had given our crowd a technical at the end of the North Carolina game in 1987 (see chapter 3), and said, "Four seconds, we called timeout with four seconds." I knew the clock had gone under four seconds, but I knew if I asked for four, I would have a shot at getting three, which is what we needed to run this play for Bennett. Gerry gave us the three seconds and I went to our huddle where assistant coach Matt Kilcullen had already drawn up the play.

We had been practicing this play at the end of some practices all season. Keith Robinson in-bounded the ball. It was his job to long pass to Ellis, who started at our foul line. It was Phonz's job to go get it, just like a football receiver going up for a long pass in a crowd of defenders.

The other three players—Elmer, Joe Fredrick and Jamere Jackson—started at midcourt and ran toward our basket. Fredrick was on the wing near our bench, Bennett in the middle and Jackson on Ellis's left. The play was not designed to go to a specific player, it was Ellis's job to find an open man. When he caught the ball, he saw Elmer was open and he hit him with a perfect pass. From the top of the key and with his front toe an inch from the three-point line, he buried the jumper as the horn sounded. All 32,747 fans were in stunned silence.

The only noise you could hear were our players rejoicing and the sound of my shoes hitting the floor as I did an Irish Jig to mid-court for a "drive-by" handshake with Jim Boeheim.

They must have replayed the finish 10 times on *SportsCenter* that night. I was excited because it was a top-five win on the road, the kind that gets you into the NCAA Tournament.

It was quite a clutch shot by Elmer on an unlikely play. Fredrick, a 47-percent three-point shooter that year, didn't take that last shot, as Syracuse probably figured. Elmer hadn't made a three-point goal in his last five games and had made just 11 in 51 career games entering that game. For LaPhonso, it was his only assist of the game and he had just 33 assists all year.

But the play worked, just as we had practiced it.

JIM DOLAN, 1983-86

Jim Dolan was Bill Laimbeer lite. He would rank right up there with Laimbeer as being a smart player who played in the frontcourt. And he would mix it up on the inside when needed. He would smack an opponent around when it was warranted, but like Laimbeer he was smart. He knew the tricks of the trade when it came to playing defense and getting position for a rebound. After he finished playing he was an assistant coach with us for three years and got his master's degree in the process.

Just like Hanzlik did in the 1970s, Dolan was my coach on the floor when it came to calling defenses. He knew where all five players were supposed to be at all times. I communicated with the team through Dolan when it came to calling defenses.

When John Paxson was a senior, Dolan was a freshman and he learned a lot about the game from Pax. In 1982-83, Dolan's freshman year, we were trailing Marquette in Milwaukee, 57-49. But we scored the last 10 points to win by two, and Dolan scored the tying basket and the game-winner. We wanted to get the ball to Paxson, but he was covered, so Dolan went to the basket and scored.

Dolan was one of the best all-around players I ever had. He was named our top defensive player three of his four years. His sophomore year he started all 33 games and led us in assists, steals and rebounds. Now think about that combination! He is still the only player in Notre Dame history to lead an Irish team in those three areas in the same year, and was the only forward I ever had who led the team in assists.

He was not going to score a lot, but he could shoot at a high percentage from the field (.574 from the field as a senior). His senior year he scored 22 against Marquette when he made 10 of 11 from the field. He was a great fit with Barlow and Kempton on the front line. We won 84 games in four years with those guys.

KEVIN ELLERY, 1987-91

Kevin Ellery was known as the "Pit Bull." He was 6-5 and 235 pounds and could back an opponent down close to the basket or hit an outside jumper. He made 30 three-point goals my last year and he averaged 11 points a game. When we signed him, a lot of people compared him to Adrian Dantley, which wasn't fair, but he certainly had the physical comparison.

His most memorable game was against Missouri in 1990. They were ranked second in the nation coming into the game, and the No. 1 team (Kansas) had lost earlier in the week. So, Missouri would be No. 1 if they beat us. We needed a spark, so I started Kevin for the first time in his career. This was his junior year. He hadn't even played the two previous games. Sometimes you have to go with your gut, and it paid off. Kevin scored 11 points and was named MVP of the game by NBC.

LAPHONSO ELLIS, 1989-91

I first saw LaPhonso Ellis at the Nike camp in Princeton, New Jersey in the summer of 1986. He was from the combat zone in East St. Louis, so we wondered about his academic background. His high school was near a river that was filled with chemicals from local industrial plants.

We checked him out and he was fine academically. He told us then, as a junior, that he wanted to go to Notre Dame. I said to my assistants, "Let's see what he says when he is a senior."

He had a great junior year and everyone in the world was recruiting him. David Rivers loved him, and by the time he was a senior he probably wished he had red-shirted because of that auto accident. Then he would have played with Phonz in 1988-89. John Shumate was an assistant coach that year and also had a major bearing on Phonz's decision to come to Notre Dame.

Ellis didn't want the daily grind of recruiting to continue through his senior year, so he called a press conference at his home on November 17, 1987, the last day of the early signing period. If he didn't sign on this day we were going to have to go through the process until April. I wanted to get it done—who knows what can happen over a six-month period.

He had a table set up in his living room with three letters of intent on top of the table. There was one each from Notre Dame, Illinois and UCLA. I really didn't know what he would do. I was in South Bend waiting by the phone. After a dramatic couple of minutes, he picked up the Notre Dame letter of intent and signed it.

One of the statements he said in his press conference was that even though Illinois was closer to his home than South Bend, he thought his mother would see him play more as a Notre Dame player because we were on TV much more than Illinois.

There were a lot of rumors about illegal payments to LaPhonso from other schools during the recruiting process and LaPhonso did talk with the NCAA after he came to Notre Dame, but no one ever went on probation as a result of his recruitment.

He played well his freshman year with us, averaging 13.5 points and 9.4 rebounds a game. In the NCAA Tournament victory against Vanderbilt he had 17 points and 18 rebounds. After the game he stayed at the Providence Civic Center until 1 a.m. because he had been selected by the NCAA to be drug tested, but he couldn't pee because he was too dehydrated.

Phonz is still one of just three players in Notre Dame history with 1,500 points and 1,000 rebounds (Tom Hawkins and Bob Whitmore are the others). But he missed two semesters due to academic probation. Think of the numbers he would have had if he hadn't missed those 20 games.

LaPhonso was bound and determined to get his degree in business administration. We could have put him in an easier major, but we didn't do it. He thought about turning pro after I left, but I urged him to stay. He had put so much effort into getting that degree, and another year was going to make him a lottery pick. He ended up getting drafted No. 5 by Denver after his senior year.

In 1992, the year after I left, he got his degree. He missed the NBA's predraft camp in Orlando to concentrate on his studies. He said in an article published later that summer, "That degree is a momento of my life. I look at it every morning when I wake up because I know all the trials and tribulations I had to go through to get it."

JOE FREDRICK, 1986-90

Joe Fredrick was the first player I had who committed to us publicly before his junior year. Charles Fredrick, his father, was a former Notre Dame football player who had played with Paul Hornung, so Joe probably would have committed when he was 10. He was from Ohio, the same area as John Paxson, so he grew up following Notre Dame and Pax.

When Joe was a kid his dad used to take him to the Kentucky game in Louisville every year. He would get autographs from Dantley, Tripucka, Paxson, all of them. The players wrote their uniform numbers next to their autograph. When he would get home after the game, he would write his name and No. 4 (his number as a kid and in high school) next to their names, like he was already imagining he was part of the Notre Dame team.

People gave me a hard time about taking him because he wasn't that highly recruited. But when someone commits early, they fall off the radar screen of some of these recruiting services. He didn't get a lot of respect from anyone. Even when he signed with us, all of the articles spelled his name wrong (Frederick). But I knew Joe was an outstanding shooter and that he would be a team leader.

His freshman year he scored just 31 points, but he hit a field goal and two free throws in the last three minutes to help us beat Duke in the only game I ever beat Coach K. By his junior year he was becoming one of the best outside shooters I ever had. He had five straight 20-point scoring games at one point and scored 24 in a win over LaSalle when he hit the game winner at the buzzer.

When you look at his career numbers, especially from three-point range, I have to ask myself why he didn't shoot the three even more. He made 49 percent from three for his career, still seven percent better than anyone else in Notre Dame history. And he shot 54 percent overall for his 103-game career. No guards do that today.

SCOTT HICKS, 1983-87

Scott Hicks had a great senior year and was a big reason we went to the Sweet 16 (1986-87). Every time I see Jamie Dixon, the current coach at Pittsburgh, I remind him of the 1987 NCAA Tournament game in Charlotte when we beat his TCU team by a point (58-57). That Notre Dame victory ended his college career.

People remember David Rivers hitting the game-winning free throw with four seconds left, but it was Hicks who put us in that position. We were down by seven with seven minutes left. Scott scored on a drive and was fouled, leading to a three-point play. Then, with three minutes left he hit a three to tie the score at 53-53. Then, after David's free throw, Hicks stole the in-bounds pass to ice the game.

Hicks was 2-2 on threes in that game and made just three threes all year. That was the first year of the three-point goal. Scott was my starting wing guard in all 30 games and took just 10 the entire year. Today wing guards do that in a game. But, I was like a lot of coaches who thought taking a lot of threes would take you away from the power game and take you out of your offense.

Scott played professionally in Europe for four years, and then went to work at Butler as an Assistant AD. In 2000 he became the head coach at his high school alma mater, Cathedral High School in Indianapolis.

JOE HOWARD, 1983-84

The toughest player and the best athlete I ever coached didn't come to Notre Dame on a basketball scholarship. Joe "Small Wonder" Howard was a 5-9 football player who came to Notre Dame in the fall of 1981. In his freshman year he used his 9.8 speed to catch a 96-yard touchdown pass against Georgia Tech, still the longest pass reception in Notre Dame football history. He led Notre Dame in receiving yards in each of his first three years.

We were going to have to find a replacement for John Paxson at point guard when we started the 1983-84 season, but we had candidates in Dan Duff, a returning letterman, and Jo Jo Buchanon, a freshman who had been one of the most highly recruited point guards in the country.

But by Christmas break, Buchanon had a bad case of tendinitis and Duff was ruled academically ineligible for the second semester. I was aware of Howard out of high school because he had been one of the best players in Washington, D.C., and had been recruited by

Maryland and North Carolina for basketball. He played football for Moss Collins at Carroll, and then led Carroll to a win at DeMatha in basketball. At the end of the year he played in the McDonald's Capital Classic, one of the top high school all-star games of the era.

The best all-around athlete I coached in my 20 years at Notre Dame was not on a basketball scholarship and played just half a season. Joe Howard didn't join the 1983-84 team until January, but we never would have reached the NIT finals without him.

It was a game Patrick Ewing had played in, so that should give you an idea of Howard's competency as a basketball player.

After clearing it with football coach Gerry Faust, I contacted Howard in Memphis where he was preparing for the 1983 Liberty Bowl against Boston College. He was really excited when we talked. He said his mother had told him he would play both sports at Notre Dame by the time he was a junior, and now that was coming true.

After helping Notre Dame to a 19-18 win in the Liberty Bowl, he flew from Memphis to Philadelphia and practiced with us one time before a game with LaSalle. I didn't play him in that game, but after one more practice, he was ready for our next game at Holy Cross.

The afternoon of that game, I got a call that Gene Paszkiet, our longtime football trainer, had passed away. He had been fighting cancer and was close to all the football players. I told Joe about it before the game and he started to cry. I thought about holding him out another game, but I then changed my mind. He had a resolve about him, and it seemed like he wanted to play this game for Gene.

We put him in Duff's No. 22 jersey for the Holy Cross game before we ordered a No. 24, his football number. He was so small that half the number disappeared into his shorts.

What an athlete! That night in Worcester, Massachusetts, he made six of seven shots from the field, had four assists, two steals and scored 14 points in a 73-61 win. Less than two weeks after playing in a bowl game, he was our best player on the floor that night. We went on to win nine of our next 11, including a nationally televised victory over Villanova when he made nine free throws down the stretch. That Villanova team was led by Ed Pinckney and would win the national championship the next season.

We also beat a fifth-ranked Maryland team that featured Len Bias. With Joe at the point, we finished the regular season 17-11, and he was our leader during the run to the NIT finals. He drew a charge in a game at Pittsburgh and I thought we were going to have to peel him off the court. But he bounced up like nothing had happened.

Joe played his senior year of football and had the option to play basketball, but he wanted to work out for the NFL scouts. At 5-9, he thought his future was in football. Plus, David Rivers was a freshman and the starter from day one, so he knew he wasn't going to get that much playing time. He went on to play in the NFL with the

Redskins. He finished his football career at Notre Dame with a 19.6 yards-per-reception average on 85 catches, still a Notre Dame record given a minimum of 75 receptions. That's right, even better than Tim Brown.

JAMERE JACKSON, 1986-90

Jamere Jackson was one of the strongest guards I ever had. He was 6-2 and almost 210 pounds and could score on the drive, or could hit the outside shot. His junior year he and Joe Fredrick made quite a combination at guard and we won 21 games. Joe shot 52 percent on threes and Jamere made 43 percent and we shot 45 percent as a team, eighth in the nation. It is still the best three-point shooting team in Notre Dame history. The way teams shoot threes today, that record will probably stand forever.

Jamere made steady improvement each of his first three years. In fact he more than doubled his scoring output each of his first three years until he scored 13.5 points a game as a junior, second on the team. That year he had 23 points and 12 rebounds in a win over Marquette. A 6-2 guard—and he got 12 rebounds.

But his senior year he started the season 10-35 from the field and lost his confidence. Elmer Bennett and Tim Singleton were playing well, so he lost his starting job and never got it back. Slumps are a strange occurrence in all sports, and that was the case with Jackson.

MARC KELLY, 1978-82

Marc Kelly was a walk-on from Los Angeles who used to collect our players' sweatbands after our games at Pauley Pavilion. We saw him play at Crescenta Valley High School when we were recruiting Greg Goorjian, who was one of the top guards in the nation. We didn't get Greg (he went to Southern Cal), but Marc had always dreamed of coming to Notre Dame, so we told him he could walk on.

The summer before he came to Notre Dame, Marc got a call from Jim Harrick, then an assistant coach at UCLA who would lead the Bruins to the NCAA Championship in 1995. Jim was involved as a technical advisor for the movie *Fast Break*, which stared Robbie Benson. The movie centered around a high school team that won a championship behind the play of a girl, who was disguised as a guy. Harrick needed some extras to fill out the opposing basketball team. Among the other basketball notables in the movie was Bernard King.

Kelly got paid $512 for his role in the film, which included one scene where he spoke two lines. When the movie came out in South Bend he went to the theatre with his buddies to see how the movie turned out. At the end of the movie, his friends carried him out of the theatre on their shoulders. Word got out on campus and in town, leading to some interviews in the *South Bend Tribune* and on local radio shows.

One of those articles was sent to NCAA Headquarters in Shawnee Mission, Kansas. Two days before we were to leave for Indianapolis, Indiana, and our second-round NCAA game with Toledo, I got a call from our administration telling me that Marc was ineligible.

At first I laughed, but then it really pissed me off. I never traveled non-senior walk-ons during the regular season, but I brought them to the NCAA Tournament as a reward. The NCAA said I couldn't even take him on the bus. With all the cheating going on in college athletics, they were worried about one of my walk-ons who made $500 for a bit part in a movie. That same year, Kirk Gibson, then a wide receiver on Michigan State's football team, made $200,000 during the summer playing in the Detroit Tigers organization. That was OK, but my 5-9 freshman walk-on couldn't make a dime.

I remember telling Marc he was on probation. He thought I was kidding. We asked the NCAA to review the matter, but they said they couldn't do that until the following week, so we left Marc at home. He still drove to the game on his own. In the end, he had to pay the $512 back to the movie company, and when he did he was reinstated.

Marc was one of my best walk-ons, he stuck it out all four years and played in 45 games, second only to the 57 Tim Healy played (1976-80) among walk-ons in my career. He is now a Circuit Court Judge in Los Angeles.

Two years ago he was reviewing a drug case involving a 20-year-old high school player. Marc wanted to put this kid in his place in more ways than one. He told the kid he would take him outside for a little one-on-one game. At 42 years of age, he beat the kid, 10-2. He told the kid, "If I hear about you getting in trouble again, I'll put you in jail."

Tim Kempton, 1982-86

When someone asks me, "Which one of your players had the most guts," I have a quick answer. "Tim Kempton, because he dated my daughter Karen."

Think about it, would you date my daughter if I were your coach? But I really didn't care, because when kids are that young, they date a lot of different people. My son, Rick, used to tell Karen when she was in high school that she used to look in the *South Bend Tribune* and date whoever was the High School Athlete of the Week. Karen has done well in marriage, as she and Seattle Mariners pitcher Jamie Moyer are the proud parents of six children.

Kempton was a strong kid who was from Oyster Bay, New York. His mother was a cop in New York who chased down drug traffic in the streets. He came from a great family, but he did some things that made me shake my head. At the 1986 basketball banquet, Kempton's senior year, he ended his senior speech by saying I love you to Karen in French. I gave him a John McEnroe look that said, "You cannot be serious."

Before the junior prom, he went to the Rockne Memorial and stole Rockne's bust from the lobby. I don't know how he did it, but he took it right off the pedestal. He brought Rock to the dance. At the after prom someone saw him with Rock in his room. The next week I got a call. Student affairs wasn't thrilled that he had taken Rock to the dance, so I had to strip him of his captaincy his senior year. That's the price you pay for taking Rock to the prom.

Joe Kleine, 1980-81

On the 1980-81 Notre Dame team that won 23 games and featured a roster that included three of the top 25 players in the NBA draft,

Tim Kempton, who dated my daughter Karen, stole Knute Rockne's bust from the Rockne Memorial and brought it to the Notre Dame junior prom. The prank cost him his team captaincy for his senior season (1985-86).

Joe Kleine played in all 29 games and started 11 as a freshman. He played 10 minutes per game, shot 64 percent from the field, 75 percent from the foul line, scored 76 points and pulled in 80 rebounds.

With the graduation of Kelly Tripucka, Orlando Woolridge, Gil Salinas and Tracy Jackson, the sky was the limit for Kleine in his sophomore year. When we met in the War Room after the season to evaluate our personnel, we had Kleine and Tim Andree marked in ink as the front line for 1981-82 and beyond.

In early May I was relaxing on a Saturday afternoon at the Rockne Lake House and I got a call from Danny Nee. It was the last day of finals and Danny was with Kleine's father. He said that Mr. Kleine was here to pick up Joe and bring him back to Slater, Missouri, and he wanted to see me before they left. Danny then repeated himself, "You really need to come and meet with Mr. Kleine."

So, I drove to the Holiday Inn on route 31 and met Mr. Kleine, Joe and Danny. Mr. Kleine had come to see me after the Valparaiso game early in the season. Like a lot of parents, he was complaining about his son's playing time. But, I told him, it wasn't Joe's time yet, we had a lot of upperclassmen ahead of him. Still, he had started 11 games and had a significant role in our two wins over No. 1 that year, Virginia and Kentucky.

There was some discussion, but the bottom line was that Mr. Kleine wanted Joe to transfer. It was obvious to me that Joe had fit in very well at Notre Dame in general and with our team. The conversation ended when Mr. Kleine told his son, "Joe, you can stay at Notre Dame, but I will never speak to you the rest of your life if you do."

That was it. Joe transfered to Arkansas, where he started for three years, just as he would have here. He went on to play 15 years in the NBA. He is the best player I ever had that transferred out of the program.

Some other players who benefited by the Notre Dame experience before transferring during my years at Notre Dame were Keith Adkins, John Bowen, Bill Drew (who still came to our 1974 team reunion last year), Tony Jackson, Bernard Rencher, Ron Rowan and Mark Stevenson.

Mike Mitchell, 1978-82

Mike Mitchell got interested in basketball at an early age. When he was four, his dad coached the eighth grade team at a local Catholic school, so Mike used to tag along and carry the ball bag. When he got older, his dad wanted him to play against good competition because he thought that was the way to get better. So Mike always played against kids one year ahead of his current class.

When Mike was attending Capuchino High School (you can imagine the jokes about the nicknames for that school) the Golden State Warriors used to practice at the nearby San Bruno Recreation Center. Mike was always hanging around, and in the off season Warriors coach Al Attles let Mike scrimmage now and then with the Warriors. Mike even had a key to the gym.

Mike was one of the top players in California coming out of high school. By now we had a California connection going and Rich Branning's success had a positive effect on Mitchell.

After a solid freshman year at Notre Dame, Mike developed knee problems. He suffered a knee injury his sophomore year that required surgery. Then, while playing in a pickup game prior to his junior year, he hurt the same knee. At one point the doctors told him to just give up playing basketball at this level.

Not knowing how much the knee would hold up his senior year, I made him team captain. He worked hard in the off season to get the knee back in shape, and he was a starter most of the 1981-82 season.

Mike had one magic game his senior year and it was against San Francisco, the school near his hometown of San Bruno. We had quite a rivalry with the Dons at that time, a carryover from our win over a 29-0 and No. 1-ranked San Francisco team in 1977. This San Francisco team was just about as good and came into this February 2, 1982 game with a 19-2 record and a number-seven national ranking.

Mike hit six of seven shots in the first half, leading us to a 37-29 advantage at the half. San Francisco's gameplan was to sluff off on Mitchell and double-team John Paxson. Mike entered the game with a 5.6 scoring average, lowest among our five starters.

Mike Mitchell was never a star, but he is the only player in my 20 years at Notre Dame who got a game ball.

In the second half, Mitchell continued the onslaught, mostly from the foul line, where he would make seven of eight in the second half. He ended the game with 19 points, his career high, and we had a 75–66 victory.

After the game in the locker room, I gave Mike the game ball. It was the only time I gave a game ball to a player in my 20 years at Notre Dame. He is now the president of Nestles USA in Los Angeles.

STEVE NICGORSKI, 1985-88

Steve Nicgorski was a walk-on from South Bend St. Joe's High School. His father taught Russian Literature at Notre Dame and Steve grew up just a few blocks from my house. He had a 3.5 GPA and now works for the CIA.

We saw him play in the Bookstore Basketball Tournament in the spring of 1985 and invited him to try out as a walk-on for the 1985-86 season. He was a practice player, but he became one of the most popular practice players we ever had because of his free throw shooting style. He was an aggressive player when he got in the game and had a knack for drawing fouls. His first year he played just 10 minutes but took six free throws. He missed them all.

While we were scouting Kansas during the 1986-87 season we noticed Henry Carr of Wichita State, who was a good free throw shooter. He had this routine where he held the ball up in the air with his right palm facing the basket. It looked like he was offering up the ball before he shot it.

I stopped Nicgorski before practice one day and showed him the tape. "You are going to shoot free throws this way." He practiced it and liked it. The first time he did it in a game, the students went crazy. Before long they copied his entire routine, holding their right arm straight out like they also had the ball in their hands.

He used that routine his junior and senior years. He still wasn't that successful—he made just seven of 16 from the line over his last two years. He missed his last five, including a couple on Senior Night. After the game I let the seniors speak to the crowd. He said a few words, and then said, "I am going to make one more free throw before I leave Notre Dame." With the crowd standing and cheering, he put the microphone down and walked to the foul line. He went through the routine with the students imitating his every move. He missed his first, but made the second, much to the delight of the crowd.

In addition to Nicgorski, other walk-ons who contributed to our program were Tom McGraw, Kevin Hawkins (son of former Notre Dame All-American Tom Hawkins), Gary Grassey, Karl Love, Casey Newell, Chris Nanni, Tim Crawford and Matt Adamson. All the walk-ons were Rudy stories.

SCOTT PADDOCK, 1986-90

I always kid Scott Paddock that he was the third best redheaded center and the 16th best center overall in my 20 years at Notre Dame. He was one of my 6-10 physical guys on the inside. I just wanted him to rebound, set screens and play defense. He never averaged more than three points a game in any season, but he was a very good team leader. Today he is a national salesman for Gatorade.

He was naive when he first came to Notre Dame from Plantation, Florida, in 1986. He had never seen snow before he came to South Bend. We were on a road trip to Omaha to play Wichita State. We were on the bus during the trip and passed a frozen lake and there were guys ice fishing. He had never seen anything like that in Florida. He yelled out in the bus, "How do they do that?" I said, "What you do is take a worm and put it on a hook and just throw in on the ice. The fish are so hungry they just come right through the ice." "Really?" he said. The entire bus broke up.

We have continued to stay close over the years. In fact, he came to the 30-year reunion luncheon this past year just to hear the speeches. He had heard so much about that game he wanted to meet those guys.

I used to give Paddock a hard time in practice because I knew he could take it. I remember Professor John Houck, who used to come to our practices once in a while. He used to call me Richard. I was giving Paddock a hard time in practice. Afterwards, Professor Houck came up to me and said, "Richard, you gave Paddock a new first name today. I thought his first name was Scott, not Jesus Christ."

But, Paddock was one of the few players who would give it back to me when we kidded each other. One day I was jogging, slowly to the point where it was more like a fast walk, over at the North Dome of the ACC. Paddock saw me and came down stairs and said, "Coach I am going to time you." He was holding a calendar, turning the months from January to February to March.

I got him back at practice that day.

JOHN PAXSON, 1979-83

John Paxson had the best all-around personality of any player I ever coached. He knew the game, had the passion for the game, and had compassion for other people. He had no ego. He just blended in with the other students. He had a letter jacket but never wore it because he just wanted to be another student at Notre Dame. He didn't live with basketball players his junior and senior year. His roommate was Rick Chryst, now the Commissioner of the Mid-American Conference. Rick was the captain of the baseball team and Pax was the captain of the basketball team.

John came by his stable nature naturally. His father was a star player at Dayton who later played two years in the NBA. His brother Jim was a four-year starter at Dayton from 1975-79 who later went on to a great career in the NBA with Portland and Boston and is now the General Manager of the Cleveland Cavaliers. John was never an NBA All-Star, but he got three NBA Championship rings.

When Jim was coming along we recruited him and he strongly considered coming to Notre Dame, but we had Dantley and Paterno at his position already. I told him he should go somewhere else where he could play for four years. Plus, Mickey Donoher, the Dayton coach, was his godfather! He went to Dayton.

We still had a good relationship, even when he was playing at Dayton. He would work my camp in the summers. We beat Dayton three of the four years he was there. Ironically, the only year we lost was 1977-78 when we went to the Final Four. His senior year we won at Notre Dame, but Jim scored 32 points.

The way we handled Jim's recruitment helped us with John, because we had credibility with John's parents. We were recruiting four guards when John was a senior in high school. In addition to John we were talking to Leon Wood, who went to Arizona State and later became a referee in the NBA, Quentin Dailey, who went to San Francisco, and Isiah Thomas who went to Indiana to play for Bob Knight. Every time I see Isiah he tells me how his mother wanted him to go to Notre Dame.

I thought they were all very good players and could help us right away because whoever came would learn behind Rich Branning for one year, then become the starting point guard in 1980-81.

John Paxson had no ego and had the best all-around personality of any player I ever coached. If I had to pick a player who was the most respected by the Notre Dame community it would be Pax.

John didn't really like the recruiting process, so he called us on January 10 and said he wanted to come to Notre Dame. He said publicly that he didn't want to go to the same school as his brother. He had all the admiration in the world for Jim, and he even switched from No. 23 to No. 4, Jim's number, for his senior year at Notre Dame, but he also wanted to make a name for himself.

•••

John went on to become a two-time All-American and two-time Academic All-American. He stands alone in Notre Dame history as far as that double-double is concerned. He was one of the most respected players I ever had, especially from the administration on the other side of campus. Near the end of his career, his sister Maggie, who was seven at the time, had her first Holy Communion at Notre Dame in the Log Chapel. Who do you think said the Mass? Father Hesburgh not only said the Mass, he gave Maggie a rosary that had been blessed by Pope John Paul II.

•••

John was a first-round draft choice of the San Antonio Spurs, and then went to the Bulls in 1985. He played alongside Michael Jordan for eight years. He was the perfect complement to Jordan, and Jordan knew it. Near the end of John's career I was playing in a golf tournament at Lake Tahoe and Jordan was there. Pax was negotiating a new contract and Michael was worried that it wasn't going to get done. "They better not screw it up," Michael told me. He even let John use David Falk for the negotiations.

Michael experienced firsthand how good Paxson was in the clutch. In Game 5 against the Lakers in 1991, the Bulls' first championship, Paxon scored 20 points, including 10 in the last four minutes. Two years later it was Pax who hit the game-winning three-point shot with 3.9 seconds left in the championship-clinching sixth game. There was great irony in that game winner, because the opposing Phoenix player assigned to Pax on the last possession was Danny Ainge, who had driven past Pax (and our entire team for that matter) on a last-second shot for BYU in an NCAA Tournament loss in 1981.

Today Pax is the general manager of the Chicago Bulls. For him to be successful he is going to have to pull off some deals like the one Jerry Krause executed to get him to the Bulls in 1985. San Antonio owed the Bulls $100,000 from a deal that had taken place two years previously that sent Artis Gilmore from Chicago to San Antonio. Krause said just give us John Paxson and we will call it even.

I ran into John in New York at the beginning of the 2003-04 season when I was at Madison Square Garden for the Coaches vs. Cancer games. I had seen him in an interview the week before and he was all over the Bulls players for not producing. When I saw him later that day, I said, "We are starting to see some of the Digger kick in."

JOSEPH PRICE, 1982-86

I mentioned Bill Green, the head coach at Marion High School in Marion, Indiana, earlier. He was the coach I brought to campus prior to the 1976-77 season to teach our team the match-up zone. Bill also made a contribution to our program by sending us Joseph Price, an off-and-on starter at a wing position from 1982-86.

Price played over 2,000 minutes in 115 games during that period, and we won 84 of them. He was a part of a rebirth of our program during that time. Starting with his junior year we went to six straight NCAA Tournaments.

He was another guy who would have benefited from the three-point shot. It became a part of college basketball the year after he graduated. He began his senior year on fire, making 38 of 59 shots from the field to open the season. For some reason, Joseph played well against teams from Oregon. As a junior he had the most important game of his career when he shot seven of nine and scored 16 points in an NCAA Tournament win over Oregon State. The following December he scored 20 points, his career high, on 10-of-13 shooting against Oregon.

Joseph was a seventh-round NBA draft choice, but he never made it, because he just had too many problems guarding the ball. He is now an assistant coach at IUPUI, and he helped that team to the NCAA Tournament in 2003. They were playing at Notre Dame that year and I walked into practice and said, imitating Price's high-pitched voice, "OK, I'm here to run the shooting drills." They all stopped and started laughing. Joseph came across the court and we hugged. I am proud of what Joseph has accomplished.

DAVID RIVERS, 1984-88

I first met hockey legend Wayne Gretzky at Mario Lemieux's celebrity golf tournament in Pittsburgh. In our initial conversation, he started telling me how he used to watch our teams play on Saturday afternoons in his hotel room while waiting to play a road night game. He told me his favorite player was David Rivers, because he could control the other nine guys on the court at once. He could appreciate that, because that is basically what he used to do when he played hockey. Gretzky really did follow Notre Dame and he stayed at my house for the Southern Cal weekend in 1997. He even spoke at the pep rally.

David Rivers was my best player in my 20 years at Notre Dame. That might surprise some people, but when you take into account all aspects of the game on the court, plus leadership qualities, he is at the top of the list. Another reason I feel this way is the comments of the players who played before him at Notre Dame. Whenever I talked with the older players, they always would tell me how they wish they had played with David Rivers.

•••

Rivers was from a large family. In fact, it was so large he rarely lived at home. Sometimes when I called there would be 20 people in the house, and one of his brothers would tell me, "You better call back later Coach, he is number four for the shower. If he gets out of line he will have to go back to number 10."

David was one of 14 kids born to Mamie and Willie Rivers of Jersey City, New Jersey. When he was nine years old, two brothers were killed 45 days apart, one the result of a stabbing and one was run over by a truck.

Because of the constant crowd at his home, David occasionally stayed with Bob Hurley, the head coach of David's high school team, St. Anthony's. Two of the youngsters who played basketball in the driveway with David were Bob's son, Bobby, who would go on to lead Duke to two NCAA Championships and Danny, who later played at Seton Hall. When I watched Bobby play at Duke I saw many of the same moves David used at Notre Dame. David taught Bobby a lot about basketball in those pickup games.

David Rivers was the best player I had over my Notre Dame career. He was the most exciting player I ever had...even Wayne Gretsky took notice.

I detailed David's automobile accident under my entry for Ken Barlow earlier in this chapter. David's recovery from this near fatal accident spoke volumes about his character.

He had to undergo many hours of surgery just to clean out the debris in his stomach. He remained in the Elkhart General Hospital until September 2, when he was moved to the campus infirmary.

We received an academic waiver from the NCAA in which they said he could take just six hours in the first semester and still be eligible. But, David wanted to try to pass 12 hours and keep on track for graduation. The first couple of weeks of the semester he stayed in the infirmary and tutors came to his room.

He was back in class by September 15 and held a press conference in which he stated that he planned to be back at practice on November 1 and be ready for the season opener against Western Kentucky on November 22. He had no intentions of red-shirting.

Skip Meyer, our trainer, and Dr. Fred Ferlic, our team doctor, did a great job getting David ready for the season. By September 29 he was jogging in shallow water in the pool at the Athletic and Convocation Center. We even put a little plastic hoop at one end of the pool so he could shoot a nerf ball. On November 1 he shot his first jumper in the ACC and went through walk-through portions of practice. He was full go at practice by November 16. He didn't start the opener but played 34 minutes.

On December 6 he scored 22 points, had eight rebounds and eight assists in a victory over BYU. It was the closest any of my players had come to a triple double. On February 1, with his father watching him play at Notre Dame for the first time, he scored 14 points in the win over No. 1-ranked North Carolina.

David took us to the Sweet 16 of the NCAA Tournament that year, scoring 74 points in the three NCAA games. We lost to North Carolina in a revenge game in the Meadowlands.

We certainly had hoped to go to the Final Four, but had we done that we wouldn't have had David. On March 26, the week of the Final Four, he was having severe stomach pains and was vomiting. He had emergency surgery at St. Joseph's Hospital because he had bands of scar tissue that were twisting his bowel.

On March 29 he was honored at the Final Four by the U.S. Basketball Writers as the Most Courageous Athlete of 1987. Fittingly, he accepted the award from his hospital room over the phone.

Keith Robinson, 1985-89

Keith Robinson's high school basketball coach was Art Serotte who was one of the best high school football coaches in the country. He won many city football championships in Buffalo at Grover Cleveland High School and never had a practice field. They used to practice on the grass in front of the school. No goal posts, no blocking dummies, but he still won.

Art also coached the basketball team, so I got to know him when we were recruiting Robinson. When I was recruiting Keith I used to stay at his house, and he was the only coach I ever stayed with in my 21 years as a head coach.

Keith was an agile 6-9 power forward who could really shoot it from 15 feet and in. His senior year he ranked in the top 20 in the nation in field goal percentage (.607) and free throw shooting (.870). He was the only player I ever had who ranked in the top 20 in the nation in both categories in the same year.

•••

We lost to DePaul in January of 1988 when Keith didn't block out on a late shot, and DePaul scored on an offensive rebound. After the game I threw all the managers, media, and administrators, out of the locker room. We went back to the coach's room and got the tape of the last play and replayed it to the team six times. I ripped into Keith because it was a lack of hustle on his part and it cost us.

I know I must have embarrassed him in that situation. But he was a tough kid who could take criticism, and a lot of times I got on his case to make a point to the rest of the team. I had firmly ingrained to Keith and the rest of our players how important it was to box out and rebound, especially in crunch time.

The following Saturday we beat Kansas and Danny Manning, who would go on to win the National Championship at the end of that season. With Robinson leading us in rebounding with 10, we topped Kansas in rebounds, 34-23. At the end of the season we led the nation in rebound margin.

DONALD ROYAL, 1983-87

Gary Brokaw and I had as much fun recruiting Donald Royal as anyone. Donald was from New Orleans, so that meant some great eating. We used to go to Dooky Chase, the best restaurant in New Orleans. Leah Chase still freezes Gumbo for me to take back to South Bend when I am in New Orleans.

One day after lunch at Dooky Chase we went to see Royal at his high school, St. Augustine. All of a sudden there was a big crowd in front of the school. The St. Augustine Band was about to practice and the entire school came out to watch them practice. We went outside too, and they were just as good as Southern, Grambling, Jackson State, or any of those bands you see today. They have performed at the Super Dome for New Orleans Saints games many times.

Donald had a great first step. He was a lot like Woolridge in that regard. It was a very effective move for him because he could draw free throws and he made a living at the line, in college and the NBA. His sophomore year we beat Marquette at the end of the season, a big reason we got in the NCAA Tournament that year. The next year we beat Syracuse in the Carrier Dome and he was three for seven from the field and 14-17 from the line.

He went on to play eight years in the NBA. He only started one of those eight (for Orlando in 1994-95), but he got a nice pension. He went on to play in Europe after his NBA career and unfortunately had to battle colon cancer. But he has beaten that and is now back in New Orleans.

Donald Royal was one of my best players and one of my favorite players.

CECIL RUCKER, 1980-84

Cecil Rucker missed a game due to injury for the most unusual reason in my 20 years at Notre Dame. We had a game the night before and Cecil had barely played. The next day I came by the training room and there was Cecil with both knees in ice. He was hurting.

"When did you get hurt?" I asked Cecil. He had an unusual reaction, just saying he had hurt his knees. I wasn't getting a straight answer so I went to our trainer, Skip Meyer. He started to laugh, then explained to me that Cecil had fallen from the top bunk during an amorous moment with his girlfriend and had landed on both knees.

Try explaining that one to the media.

TIM SINGLETON, 1987-91

Tim Singleton was a point guard from New Orleans, the same area as Donald Royal. He was a good student who didn't shoot much from the outside. In fact he played 112 games for me, 70 as the starting point guard, and never made a three-point goal. But he didn't turn the ball over and had the respect of his teammates. He was the captain of my last team at Notre Dame.

Tim was 6-1 and just over 170 pounds, but he was quick and didn't back down from anyone. The players called him "the mouse." He had a dunk against DePaul his sophomore year and Billy Moor of the *South Bend Tribune* referred to him as, "the mouse that soared."

There was only one occasion that Timmy was intimidated. It happened his freshman year when we were playing at Duke, and the intimidation didn't come from another player. We got to Cameron Indoor Stadium a little early and he was excited to play at Duke as a freshman. He got dressed in a hurry and decided he was going to be the first player on the floor for warmups.

Knowing the reputation of the Duke students, I asked him, "Are you sure you are ready to go out now?" He had watched games from Duke when he was in high school, but wasn't aware of the circus atmosphere the students create prior to a game.

When Tim got to the court the place was already packed and they were throwing tennis balls back and forth across the court. The place was typical Duke crazy. He was the only Notre Dame player on the court for about 10 minutes and the Duke students were all over him. They were shouting, "One-man team, one-man team." He told me after the game he wanted to retreat to the locker room and wait on his teammates, but that would have looked obvious, so he stuck it out until the rest of the team got there.

Tim had a bad back his senior year and missed six games in the heart of the season. That was a big factor in us having a losing season in 1990-91.

TOM SLUBY, 1980-84

In the sixth game of the 1983-84 season we lost a heartbreaking overtime game at Northwestern, 40-36, to fall to 3-3 for the year. I could sense on the bus ride back to South Bend that this team was feeling sorry for itself. It was not a good way to start the year. We had gone 19-9 in the regular season the previous year and won seven of our last eight games with the only loss by two points to DePaul. Even with Gene Corrigan, our athletic director at the time, on the NCAA Committee, we still didn't get in.

On that bus ride home I decided to do two things to try to turn our season around. The next day I took the team to Logan Center, a center for the mentally handicapped, and had the entire team watch their Special Olympics basketball team practice. After watching them practice for an hour, I asked my team if they still felt sorry for themselves.

I then told the team that we needed Tom Sluby to take more shots. At this level of basketball you rarely have to tell someone to shoot more, but that was the case with Sluby. I told the team he had to take at least 16 shots for us to win. If I had told that to Kelly Tripucka he would have taken 32 shots and then told me he thought I meant 16 shots a half.

It was a radical decision when you look at what his stats were at this point in his career. He was built like Adrian Dantley and was from Washington, D.C., so he had been saddled with those comparisons when he arrived at Notre Dame. He had struggled with injury and missed a semester due to academic probation. He averaged a little under 5.0 points a game his first three years.

Sluby had shown me something the previous spring in our trip to Yugoslavia. Twice during that trip he had come off the bench to have big games (22 and 18), so I thought he had it in him. John Paxson had just graduated, so we needed a leader.

After that Northwestern game, Sluby started taking over, and we started winning. We had a seven-game winning streak at one point, including a 52-47 win over a ranked Maryland team. Sluby scored what proved to be the game-winner on a three-point play.

He had 15 games of at least 20 points over the last 23 games, including 30 in a win over Marquette. We didn't make the NCAAs, but he took us to the finals of the NIT. By the end of the season he had averaged 18.7 points per game, a 13.7-point improvement over his previous year. That was the biggest scoring improvement by any player in my 20 years at Notre Dame. He scored 616 points that year, exactly double his total from his first three years combined.

Sluby was a second-round pick of the Dallas Mavericks after his senior year and played a year in the NBA. He got cut after that first year and asked me about going to play in Ireland. I said, "Let's call your mother (Barbara) and tell her you want to go to Ireland. I don't think so. You need to come back to Notre Dame and be my graduate assistant coach and get a master's degree. Then we will see about Ireland."

I knew at 6-4 he was a good player, but he wasn't Adrian Dantley. He came back to graduate school and got his MBA.

BARRY SPENCER, 1980-85

Barry Spencer was one of the top high school players in the country in 1979-80. When we signed him, Joe Kleine and Billy Varner to be freshmen for the 1980-81 season, we thought we would be set for the early 1980s. But Kleine transferred and Barry got injured his freshman year.

Barry had a 3.7 GPA in high school and he wanted to be an architect. A lot of schools wanted him, but it came down to Notre Dame and Virginia. Terry Holland had Ralph Sampson then, and it looked like they were going to challenge for the National Championship. They needed a small forward to replace Jeff Lamp and Holland thought Barry would be the answer.

We told him Barry it would take five years, but he could get an architecture degree from Notre Dame. Terry Holland tried to steer him away from that major because it was too time-consuming, and he didn't think he could graduate from Virginia in architecture and play basketball.

Barry was on academic probation a couple of times and he missed an entire year, but in May of 1985, he got his architecture degree. When he came into my office graduation week, I said, "Let's get on the phone and call Terry Holland." It was a struggle, but Barry was the only scholarship player I ever had who got a degree in architecture.

DAIMON SWEET, 1988-91

Daimon Sweet and Elmer Bennett were known as the Texas Express. They were both from Texas and combined on many an alley-oop play in the three years they played for me. Daimon was the leading scorer on my last team with a 16.5 average and he shot 56.5 percent from the field. In fact, when you look at the Notre Dame record book today, his 54-percent career field goal percentage is still the best in school history by a wing player.

With a name like Sweet and with his consistent jumper, it was a free for all when it came to a nickname. The student newspaper, *The Observer*, solicited candidates and ran a top 10-list. Al McGuire called him "Nutra" during an NBC broadcast. Jack Lloyd called him that on the PA after a field goal one night, and I still remember Daimon jerking his head back in the direction of the scorer's table. He got a kick out of it.

There was a bit of irony in Sweet's recruitment. He originally committed to SMU in the fall of his senior year of high school (1987-88). Matt Kilcullen recruited him, but Shumate was on my staff at Notre Dame at the time. Sweet finally signed with us in April. A few weeks later, Shumate became the head coach at SMU.

KEITH TOWER, 1988-92

Coaches have to plan a couple of years ahead in the recruiting process. During the 1986-87 season we were planning our freshman class for 1988-89, and we determined we needed to sign two big guys. Our early evaluation concluded that the top four big guys who had a chance to get in school were LaPhonso Ellis, Eric Anderson, Keith Tower and Christian Laettner.

Even though there was some anxiety on signing day the next year, Ellis had told us all along that he was coming, so we needed another big guy. Laettner was from upstate New York, but his sister played basketball for Valparaiso. So he and his family came to the North Carolina game (February 1, 1987) on the same weekend they came to see the sister play at Valpo.

We beat No. 1 North Carolina, 60-58. It couldn't have been a more exciting atmosphere. After the game, Laettner and his family came to my office and Christian's body language was, "I don't care about being here one bit." He slumped on the couch in my office and barely looked at me the entire time I was talking to him. It was the only downer of the entire day.

After he left, I called the staff together in the war room and told them we weren't going to get that kid. If Notre Dame didn't interest him on that day, it never would. We had an idea that Anderson was going to go to Indiana, so we put our efforts on Tower.

Keith started 29 of our 32 games my final year, when he was a junior. He was the Dayton killer. I wish I had him for some of those games we lost to Dayton in the 1970s. He had just two 20-point scoring games in his career, and they were both in my final year against Dayton. In my final game at the Convocation Center, my final victory at Notre Dame, Keith was the star. We beat Dayton in overtime, 92-87, and he had 21 points and 17 rebounds.

BILLY VARNER, 1980-84

Billy Varner was a highly recruited player out of the Pittsburgh area. He was a good kid, but his father had a very high opinion of his abilities. We were in Yugoslavia in the spring of 1979 and I got a call from Danny Nee, who had stayed behind to recruit Varner. Marquette was making a late push for Billy, so Danny stayed behind.

Danny called me and said he had just talked with Billy's father. Mr. Varner was excited because Magic Johnson had just announced that he was leaving Michigan State to turn pro. He said that means Billy could now be the next Magic Johnson. I said to Danny, "Just tell his dad we just want him to be Billy Varner."

He had a solid career for us. He averaged double figures each of his last two years and even shot 60 percent from the field as a senior. He was the same class as John Paxson and we won 19 games his last year.

Billy played in Belgium for many years, and he was a legend over there. After I left Notre Dame I went with my wife to Europe where she was running Notre Dame's Law School program. We took a side trip to Belgium one weekend. This country was famous for having over 400 different brands of beer, and I wanted to test at least half of them.

We went into the lobby of the hotel and who do you think was checking in with his team? "Varner!" I barked, just like I used to at practice. He couldn't believe it. We talked for a while. He was about 30 by then. He said, "Coach, I was a pain in the ass back then, how did you put up with me?" It was all part of the maturing process.

Today, Billy works at Nestles for Mike Mitchell in Los Angeles. The Notre Dame family network is something that lasts a lifetime.

Gary Voce, 1984-88

Of all the postgame celebrations we had on the court after beating a No. 1 team, the most unusual situation happened to Gary Voce. After he recorded his first ever double-double to beat North Carolina, the fans stormed the court. Gary was engulfed by the mob because he had such a great game and he was one of the most popular players we ever had.

In the middle of the celebration, Gary felt someone tugging at his leg. He looked down and it was a student trying to take off one of his shoes. He laughed at the guy and said, "Go ahead, just loosen it up, but don't break my leg." So Gary spent the rest of the postgame in one shoe. He used to run into that student on campus and he told Gary he had the shoe prominently displayed in his dorm room. This was before ebay. Today it would have been up for auction an hour after the game.

Gary made a great improvement over his career. He was a native of Jamaica (the country, not New York), and didn't start playing basketball until he and his family moved to New York at age 12, the latest beginner to the game of all my players. When he moved to New York he was already 6-7, and everyone started telling him he should take up the game.

Pete Gillen recruited him, and when he came he was behind Barlow, Dolan and Kempton. After they graduated he had to step in and start. In the third game that year against BYU he played 35 minutes and didn't get a point or a rebound. But, thanks to John

Shumate, he made steady progress. The 1987 North Carolina game turned his career around, and his senior year he averaged 11.7 points a game, second to David Rivers. He scored 24 points against SMU in the NCAA Tournament in his last game at Notre Dame.

Gary Voce showed great improvement over his career, and it made me wonder after I left Notre Dame what Jon Ross, Joe Ross, Brooks Boyer and Carl Cozen might have done if I had had the opportunity to coach them longer than just one year.

But what struck me overall about Gary was his popularity with the students. His senior year, nearly every time he made a field goal or a free throw, the student body would extend their arms in the shape of a V. Sometimes, when he really got it going, they would chant, "Gary Voce" instead of the "Go Irish" cheer.

MONTY WILLIAMS, 1989-91

I still remember the first time I saw Monty Williams play. We were at an AAU tournament in Los Angeles during the summer and I was watching his D.C. All-Star team. Monty was a kid no one had heard much about, but he was dominating the game. I called over to Pete Gillen, who had been one of my assistants and was now the head coach at Xavier. I said, "Peter come watch this kid Williams. But don't get any ideas, he's mine."

When I got back to South Bend I checked his grades. He was near a 4.0 student, and in fact he made a 4.0 his senior year. At the time he was the all-time sleeper. We brought him out for a visit and he committed right away. Then his senior year he averaged 30 points a game and scored 56 against DeMatha. But he stayed true his commitment.

He had a terrific freshman year in 1989-90. He started 18 games and averaged almost eight points a game. He was second on the team in blocked shots, but he could play point guard. At 6-7 he could do just about everything. I could see that we were going to build our team around him down the road.

On September 4, 1990, just five weeks before practice, Monte had a routine physical with the rest of the team. During the physical our doctors discovered a problem with his heart. He was diagnosed with HCM (Hypertrophic Cardiomyopathy), a rare but potentially dangerous condition featuring a thickened muscle between chambers of the heart.

Hank Gathers of Loyola Marymount had just died of a heart problem the previous March. It was different from Williams's problem, but awareness was high. There was also a football player at Northeast Missouri State (Derringer Cade) who had dropped dead on the field that September as a result of this same condition. So, on September 28, 1990, after he had gone through many more tests, we announced Monty Williams was through with basketball. It was tough for Monty to accept because he didn't have any abnormal symptoms.

That year, I tried to involve Monty in the team as much as possible. At the beginning of the season I asked him to put his uniform on and to appear in the team photo. When all the players were dressed and ready to go, he was still back in the locker room. He couldn't bring himself to do it, so he put his jeans and shirt back on and left the building. He sat on the bench for most of the games and we took him on trips. But it was difficult.

After I left, he didn't want anything to do with the team. In fact, on nights Notre Dame played at home, he used to go to the Rockne Memorial and play pickup games. Sometimes he was all by himself just shooting jumpers pretending he was making moves against Grant Hill or Jalen Rose.

He sat out two years. Prior to the 1992-93 season, the Notre Dame physicians heard about the case of Steve Larkin, Barry's brother (and the brother of 1984 Notre Dame football captain Mike Larkin), who had the same problem as Monty. Steve had been cleared to play after having a test run at the National Institute of Health in Bethesda, Maryland, ironically just a few miles from Monty's hometown in Forest Heights, Maryland.

Monty had the test and the doctors determined he could play. It was quite a test. They basically shocked his heart, trying to give him a heart attack. There were 12 doctors in the room when they gave it to him. But he came through it just fine. He played the 1992-93 and 1993-94 seasons for John McLeod, averaging over 20 points a game for a 56-game period.

I always held my breath when I saw him play, but I was thrilled he was able to return to the court. He went on to play in the NBA through 2002-03, the last of my 22 guys to play in the NBA.

BROOKS BOYER, 1991-1994

I went to a White Sox vs. Mariners game on July 11, 2004, to see my son-in-law, Jamie Moyer, pitch for the Mariners. After the game I ran into Brooks Boyer, a guard on my last Notre Dame team. Soon after his graduation, Brooks got a job as an intern for the Chicago Bulls. He made some contacts, worked hard at each step, and is now vice president of marketing for the White Sox.

During our conversation before the game, I said, "You remembered. Don't assume, follow up, and always have a backup." He said, "Coach, follow me, I have to show you something in my office." Behind his desk on a cabinet was an old piece of paper from his first day as an intern. Written on it was: Don't assume, follow up, and always have a backup.

From my first day as head coach, we posted these "Keys to being Successful" above the blackboard in the Notre Dame locker room: 1) Listen, 2) Talk to each other, and 3) Concentrate on each situation. My last 10 years I taught my players that when dealing with any situation in life, don't assume, follow up, and always have a backup.

Seeing these keys to success in Brooks's office, 13 years after he played for me, certainly brought a smile to my face. He was one of my last players, in fact he scored the last basket in my last game.

There is more to life than just basketball. I sold that to parents and players for 20 years, and Brooks has used those keys every day since. On July 11, 2004, seeing Brooks made all those times I talked to the players about life seem worthwhile.

Chapter Seven

ODD BUT TRUE

I f you were a fan of the Dick Van Dyke show in the early 1960s, you might remember one of their most popular episodes, called "Odd But True."

It seemed like a fitting title to this chapter.

PAULEY PAVILION

One of the reasons I enjoyed playing at Pauley so much involved the UCLA students. They really got into the games, and I loved to play with them. Some of them would come by when we were practicing the day before and I would talk to them during breaks. I usually ended by saying, "See you tomorrow when we kick your..."

They had open seating in the student section at Pauley, so 90 minutes before the game UCLA would play the theme from the "Lone Ranger" over the PA as the students ran in to get the best seats. I used to go out on the court and watch this take place.

Whenever I went out to the court during pregame, they would boo me and hold up signs. I would hold my right hand up to my ear to signal to them that they weren't loud enough. If you could take the stress off the players and put it on yourself, I thought it would help. I learned that from Al McGuire.

One year they were booing me before a game and John Wooden was walking across the court and had to pass our bench. I knew they were going to cheer for him. So I made of point of going over to him and carried on a long conversion with him while they cheered.

Winning in Pauley Pavilion was like beating the Yankees in Yankee Stadium. It was always my goal to take the crowd out of the game, so players like Bill Hanzlik (42) didn't feel the pressure. Hanzlik and Rich Branning won four straight games at UCLA from 1976-80, and we won there six times overall in my Notre Dame career.

After he left, I nodded to the crowd as if I were acknowledging their cheers.

They had a lot of signs for our players and for me. In 1996, I went out to do a game for ESPN at Pauley and Jim Harrick, then the UCLA coach, took me to the cheerleading room just off the court. In the back of the room were a couple of signs that read, "Digger is a whimp."

Throughout the games at Pauley when I would complain to an official, they would yell, "Sit down, Digger!" They didn't pay attention to the game sometimes, so I would intentionally stand up and talk to an official while a UCLA player was shooting a free throw.

They wouldn't stop yelling at me when he was shooting and invariably the player would miss the free throw.

I saw former U.S. Open Champion Corey Pavin (a student at UCLA in the early 1980s) at the Los Angeles Open a few years back and he told me, "I can't believe I used to call you an A...hole."

Sam Gilbert

We won at Pauley Pavilion four years in a row from 1976-77 through 1979-80. UCLA was ranked in the top five in the country in each of the first three seasons, and the fourth year they went on to the national finals before losing to Louisville. I used to give Sam Gilbert, UCLA's No. 1 booster, a hard time whenever I saw him in Pauley. "Sam, when are they going to put a banner up in here for us? This is like our second home court. I think a banner shaped like a shamrock with our winning scores would be a nice addition."

I had secondary parties call me during my career at Notre Dame about coaching opportunities. I seriously looked at the New York Knicks job in 1980. Three times after Wooden left UCLA, Gilbert called me when they had a coaching opening. One of the conversations we had was during a women's U.S. Olympic basketball team game in Los Angeles in 1984. "How much money will it take?" he asked. But I was never interested in going to UCLA. I wanted to beat them.

EVEN BOOKER TURNER BELIEVED
WE COULD WIN

It seemed as if every year we went to play UCLA Booker Turner was the lead official. He was a very good official, but he worked a lot of UCLA games when John Wooden was "The Wizard of Westwood" and he had a mindset that UCLA was supposed to win.

I used to kid him before games. "Booker, have you finished your masters at UCLA yet? Booker, are you the commencement speaker this year?"

We were playing at UCLA in 1984-85, and David Rivers was a freshman. Late in the game there was a loose ball near our bench.

Rivers dove for the ball in an attempt to gain possession. Just as Booker was about to call traveling on Rivers, David had the presence of mind to call timeout. I looked at Booker and said, "He got you, you've got to give it to him." Booker started laughing and gave us the timeout. We won the game 53-52. We wouldn't have gotten that call when John Wooden was the coach.

WAKE-UP CALL

LaPhonso Ellis was ineligible for the fall semester of 1989-90. He was eligible going into summer school, taking classes so he could get ahead academically, but he did poorly, and the university placed him on academic probation. He was eligible by NCAA rules. That might be the only time someone became ineligible by going to summer school.

I went on a recruiting trip with Matt Kilcullen in September and while we were on the trip, Jeff Nix, another of my assistants, said we had some players cutting classes. I said, "Get the team together, we are going to straighten this out right now." I was really upset because we had just had a meeting on this subject in August when Ellis became ineligible.

I also told Matty to tell Nix to call Don Parcell at the Farmer's Market in South Bend and to get a rooster. We needed it for the meeting.

I told the team that I was disappointed they couldn't make their early morning classes. The rule was if you cut class, you missed two games. The second game that season was in the Hoosier Dome in Indianapolis on national TV, so I knew they didn't want to miss that. I told them they could see their professors and make up the work and I wanted a signed note from the professor, not something signed by their girlfriends.

I then told them I was going to give them some help as far as getting up in the morning. That is when I had Billy Parcells, Don's son, bring the rooster into the room in a cage.

"This rooster gets up every morning at 5 a.m., no matter what. Homes (Keith Robinson's nickname), you have it first. Everyone else sign up for it if you need it." With that I turned and walked out. At the end of the year, Scott Paddock told us the players all broke up when I left.

I didn't make the players take the rooster to the dorm. But I made my point to the team. They didn't miss any more 8 a.m. classes.

CARNATION TRADITION

I frequently went to lunch with Roger Valdiserri and Jim Gibbons, and most of the time we went to Bill Knapps, which was a family restaurant just up the road from campus on US 31. We went there a couple of days prior to Thanksgiving in 1975, and our waitress, Bonnie, was a big Notre Dame fan. Her husband was a big Irish fan as well and ran a flower shop in Roseland.

We were opening the 1975-76 season with Kent State at home the Saturday after Thanksgiving. Prior to the game someone brought in a box of green carnations to the locker room for the assistant coaches and me. They were from the Roseland Flower Shop. I looked at my assistants, Frank McLaughlin and Dick Kuchen, and said, "We have to wear them."

We won the game, so the next week I went back for lunch and thanked Bonnie and said that I was superstitious. "We have to keep this going." We kept winning and I kept wearing those carnations, home and away. The following year, I wore a green carnation for the NCAA Tournament game against North Carolina in College Park, a game that was played on St. Patrick's Day. We lost in the final seconds, so I retired the carnations from road competition. I wore them for most home games through my 18th year.

My last two years with the new administration, I decided not to wear the carnation until my last home game against Dayton in 1990-91. I brought one out for that game, and we won in overtime.

ADAM MILANI

John Milani was an accounting professor in the Notre Dame Business school. He had a son, Adam, who played hockey at South

Bend St. Joe High School, the high school that is just across the street from the old Notre Dame golf course.

One night Adam was playing a hockey game for St. Joe's. During one play he was body checked into the glass, hit his neck in the wrong place and was paralyzed. It was a shock to the entire community.

The next year, Adam enrolled at Notre Dame and came to most of our games. I saw him before the Indiana game in 1980-81 and I asked him if he wanted to sit behind our bench. Keith Penrod, the No. 1 Irish Fan, used to sit there, and I didn't see why we couldn't make room for Adam.

But Adam said he already had a ticket. I assumed it was in the lower arena. During the game I looked to the upper area in the handicapped section and there he was rooting as hard as he could for Notre Dame, especially when Orlando Woolridge made a good play. He didn't want to have a special seat, he wanted to sit upstairs with the other people in wheelchairs. After the game I got the game ball and went around the locker room and had all the players sign it. I didn't say what it was for.

I called Mrs. Milani and gave her the ball. Christmas was just a couple of weeks away, so I told her to wrap it up and put it under the tree.

Adam went on to graduate school at Duke, and he is now back in South Bend working at Notre Dame. He joins Mike Mitchell as the only people to get a game ball from my 20 years at Notre Dame.

CUTTING DOWN THE NETS
...AT MARQUETTE

We usually cut down the nets after we upset the No. 1 team. We did cut down the nets one other time in my career at Notre Dame, and it created some controversy. Looking back, I can see why. We did it at a rival's home arena.

We were ranked No. 2 in the nation in the January 8, 1979 poll behind Michigan State. Michigan State lost during the week, so we knew if we won at Marquette on Saturday, we would improve to No.

1 for the first time since we ended UCLA's streak in 1974, and just the second time in Notre Dame history.

We had been to the Final Four the year before and took pride in being No. 1. Marquette was ranked 11th in the nation, so this would not be easy. We trailed at the half, but Tracy Jackson came off the bench and made 9-10 from the field and scored 21 points to lead us to a 65-60 win.

After the game we met as a team, then the team showered and I did the postgame press conference. While I was doing the press conference, the players were plotting some mischief. On the way to the bus, they took a detour back to the court. The lights were dim and all the fans were gone, but there were some writers on press row working on their deadline stories.

One of the players, probably Tripucka, got a pair of scissors from our trainer and he convinced the others to go back and cut down the nets. They were stretching the tradition a bit. We hadn't beaten a No. 1 team, but we had won a game that was going to make us No. 1. And, the victory was against Marquette. Had we beaten Valpo they probably wouldn't have done it.

So, with the players lifting each other to the rim, they cut down the nets and walked out. Some of the writers noticed this and wrote about it the next day. The media gave me a hard time about it the next day. But even though it wasn't my idea, I approved.

EVEN PATTON COULDN'T GET US READY

I took pride in preparing my team for the opposition in all areas of the game. That means the Xs and Os aspect, but also from a motivational standpoint. The best known might be the 1974 UCLA game when we cut down the nets after practices leading up to that game, but there were other motivational speeches before games that had an impact. When they worked I told the media all about them in the postgame press conferences, and it made for great copy.

But, I'm not going to B.S. you. Not all the great ideas worked.

We were playing Fordham in South Bend my first year at Notre Dame. I had just left Fordham, so this game was huge, and I wasn't going to leave a stone unturned.

The movie *Patton* had just come out with George C. Scott, so I decided to play a tape of his speech in the locker room before the game. Tom O'Mara, who was from California, was an anti-war activist. I told him what I was going to do before the game because I didn't want to offend him. Plus, I didn't know if he would walk out or something. We needed his outside jumper.

He said he didn't care. So I played it. They were running onto the court with a purpose, nearly knocking me over. I could see the intensity in their eyes.

We were down by 18 at the half and lost by 20. It was obvious that anything I could have done as a pregame motivation for my team was woefully short of counteracting the motivation my former Fordham players had to beat me in my arena.

THE GREEN JERSEY GAME

Uniforms can be a motivational factor, and I was always looking for a way to get a motivational advantage. But, the most famous story involving uniforms during my Notre Dame career didn't have anything to do with my basketball team.

When Dan Devine came to Notre Dame to replace Ara Parseghian in 1975, I tried to help him any way I could. When I came to Notre Dame, Ara Parseghian took me under his wing and did anything he could to help our program. I wanted to do the same for Devine.

Before he ever coached a game at Notre Dame I went to see Devine and suggested that he should wear green jerseys for the biggest game of the year, Southern Cal at home. I thought it would be a way for him to establish his own identity. He declined.

The next year, 1976, Alabama and Bear Bryant were coming to Notre Dame Stadium for the first time ever, and I thought that would be the perfect game to break out the green jerseys. Again he said no. I decided, okay, I have said my piece.

In 1977, Notre Dame was meeting fifth-ranked Southern Cal in October at Notre Dame Stadium in Notre Dame's biggest game of the year. The week of the game, Devine came to me and asked if I would speak at the Pep Rally in Stepan Center. He wanted me to be the featured speaker and to tell the students to wear green the next day.

He then told me he had finally taken me up on my idea and that the team was going to wear green jerseys. I said, "Great, but do you know how to pull it off?

"First, have the team warm up in their normal blue jerseys," I told him. "Then have the managers put the green jerseys in their lockers while they are warming up. Second, don't tell the players what you are doing, just surprise them. You won't have to say a word. Don't even give a pregame talk, the jerseys will do all the motivating you will need. Finally, make sure Southern Cal is on the field first, even if you have to take a delay of game penalty."

The next day the student section was sea of green. Devine did just what I suggested. There was a Trojan horse leading the team out on the field. I have a framed two-foot picture in my basement (see color section of this book) of the reaction by Southern Cal coach John Robinson and the Trojan team. John had his hands on his hips and his mouth was wide open. It told the story of the game even before it started.

Final Score: Notre Dame 49, Southern Cal 19. Notre Dame went on to win the 1977 National Championship.

JOE MONTANA

Joe Montana was a terrific basketball player and he enjoyed the game. Dick DiBiaso saw him play a few times when he was scouting in Pennsylvania, but we knew his future was in football. We told Ara we would help if he wanted us to. His official visit as a high school senior was the weekend we ended UCLA's winning streak. Joe was at the game and the experience had to help in his decision to come to Notre Dame.

Joe loved to play hoops and played on three Bookstore championship teams before he graduated. He was competitive in everything he did in life, and it even carried over to pickup basketball.

He is certainly considered one of the greatest quarterbacks in the history of the sport. We can start with four Super Bowl Championships and work from there. He also led Notre Dame to a

National Championship in 1977. But his career at Notre Dame did not get off to a great start.

Ara saw Montana as the successor to Tom Clements, who was graduating after the 1974 season. Ara felt Joe could be Clements backup for a year, then take over. It was a great plan, but Ara decided to retire after the 1974 season and Dan Devine was hired.

Joe was not the greatest practice player and started the 1975 season far down the depth chart. By midseason, however, he came off the bench to lead Notre Dame to come-from-behind wins over Air Force and North Carolina on consecutive Saturdays.

He then suffered an injury and missed the last two games, Georgia Tech and Miami (FL). One of those games was the 1975 Georgia Tech game when Rudy Reuttiger sacked the Tech quarterback on the next-to-last play of the game. Joe was dropped from the roster that day and Rudy was added. They didn't mention that in the movie.

Despite the injuries, Joe had a strong finish and was expecting to be the starting quarterback in the fall of 1976. But after spring practice he was back at third string.

That summer, I saw Joe outside the sports information office. His wife at the time was one of the secretaries in the SID office, so he was there a lot. He even used to help stuff football and basketball guides and releases for mass mailing. Joe was wondering about his future and asked me about coming out for the basketball team. He just didn't see eye to eye with Devine on a number of fronts.

I told him to stick with football. He could have played for us, but he wouldn't have been a starter, not even in our top seven in 1976-77. Even though Adrian Dantley had just turned pro and I had a history of football players on the roster before (Mike and Willie Townsend my first two years were solid contributors), I told him to stay with with football.

Montana separated a shoulder during the preseason practice of 1976 and sat out the entire season. He was still third string at the beginning of the 1977 season. But in the third game, at Purdue, he finally got a chance when Rusty Lisch was ineffective and Gary Forystek was injured. He led the Irish to a 17-point fourth quarter and a come-from-behind 31-24 victory.

Notre Dame went on to beat South Cal in the Green Jersey game, then drubbed Texas, 38-10 in the Cotton Bowl to win the

National Championship. Notre Dame entered the bowl games that January 1 ranked fifth, then jumped all the way to No. 1 thanks to some upsets. They couldn't have done that in today's set up.

You know the rest of the Joe Montana story. But I do wonder how history would have changed had I encouraged him to join the basketball team in the summer of 1976.

•••

You could really stump some Indiana basketball fans if you asked the following question. What future Hall of Fame quarterbeck kept statistics for one of Indiana's games during the Hoosiers perfect 32-0 season of 1975-76? The answer is Joe Montana.

That year there were just 32 teams in the NCAA Tournament, so there were eight first-round sites that had two games apiece on a Saturday afternoon. Notre Dame was one of the host sites. There was a rule that you could not play a home game in one of those first rounds, so we went to Kansas to play Cincinnati.

The games happened to be played the first weekend of spring break at Notre Dame. So, combined with us playing on the road, Roger Valdiserri's staff was stretched pretty thin. Since Joe's wife had to work, Roger got Joe to work the tournament also.

After a quick tutorial from my co-author of this book, Joe kept assists, turnovers, blocks and steals for the first round games between Western Michigan and Virginia Tech, and St. John's vs. Indiana. Joe Montana had an effect on Quinn Buckner's assist total that year.

NOTRE DAME: THE RELIGIOUS ASPECT

When I was at Notre Dame we had a priest travel with us on the road, and we always had a pregame Mass just prior to the pregame meal. I had just one player who was an atheist in my 20 years at Notre Dame who refused to take part, so I told him to sit in the back of the room and meditate. Interestingly enough, he is not an atheist today.

I always had the players say the readings before the Gospel. We weren't trying to force Catholicism down anyone's throat, it was part of the educational process. Over the course of the year every player had to get up in front of the team at a Mass and give a reading. We started with the seniors and worked back to the freshmen. It was a great opportunity to learn public speaking, and I know it had a positive impact on a lot of my players.

The priests either lived in Corby Hall or in a dorm on campus where they served as Rector. Some of them used to keep track of how the team did when they traveled on the road. In 1976-77 Father Joe Carey made a road trip and we lost two games. When he got back to campus, the other priests said he had been fired. He never made another road trip.

I had some basic rules. I always wanted the priests to wear a Roman collar when they sat on our bench. That was a symbol of Notre Dame, and it was something Notre Dame people around the country wanted to see.

We gave the players and coaches medals during each pregame mass. That was also in the job description for the priests who came with us on the road. I always asked the priest if they remembered the medals. If they didn't they had until the pregame mass the next day to find some. It was easy on trips to New York, they just went to St. Patrick's Cathedral.

The players saved those medals. Bill Hanzlik's mother made a bracelet from the medals, one for each year Bill was on the team.

•••

I roomed with Jim Valvano's brother, Nick, when I was at Rider, and got to know the family because they used to come to campus. Bob Valvano works at ESPN now. I remember roughhousing with him in the Valvano car when he was a little kid. Jimmy was in high school at the time.

Mrs. Valvano would come to campus to see Nick and would bring us Italian food all the time, so I got on her good side. She was a great woman.

Whenever we played at NC State, Mrs. Valvano would come to the game. I would find her before the game and give her one of our game medals. Jim used to give her a hard time about that. "Did you root for Notre Dame tonight, Mom?" Jim would say. "You know why Digger is giving you those medals? He is trying to get you to pray for Notre Dame to beat us."

In 1983 we played in Raleigh, the year NC State won the NCAA Championship with that magic run that ended with the victory over Houston. We beat them in Raleigh that year 43-42 and I gave Mrs.

Valvano a medal before that game. We didn't even make the NCAA Tournament that year. Maybe Mrs. Valvano did pray for us that night!

•••

Father James Riehle is a Notre Dame institution. He was the head of the monogram association for many years. For much of my career he was the team chaplain and held that position for multiple Notre Dame teams, so he made a lot of road trips. A lot of the male students at Notre Dame used to say that if they could have Father Riehle's job, they would join the priesthood.

I only got mad at Father Riehle one time. We were playing Michigan State and Magic Johnson for the right to go to the Final Four in 1979. Somehow, the NCAA put us at a hotel that was flooded with Michigan State fans. Father Riehle was a friendly type and met some Michigan State fans in the lobby over the course of our stay.

The regional final was on a Sunday and we had Mass in one of the meeting rooms at the hotel. There were Michigan State fans everywhere. Some had brought pom-poms. I know a priest isn't supposed to keep people out of Mass, but it was not great mental preparation for our team. Playing Magic Johnson was going to be tough enough. I went up to Father and said, "Father, can't you say a second mass for these Michigan State sinners? Heck, have a collection and make some money."

Michigan State beat us 80-68 and went on to win the National Championship.

BUTCH WAXMAN

Stan Peziak was a friend who ran the Linebacker Bar in South Bend. In his spare time Stan used to volunteer at the Logan Center, a facility just south of campus for the mentally handicapped.

Just before Christmas my first year he asked me if I could get some coaches together from Notre Dame and play the Special Olympics Team from Logan Center in a basketball game.

One of the Special Olympians was Butch Waxman, a 24-year-old at the time who loved basketball, and we hit it off from the outset. The gym at Logan Center was packed with the disabled kids from the center. Before the game, I got our team together and told them how we were going to play this game.

"At the end, we will be up two points. Let Butch score, then I'll let him steal the ball from me and score again to put them up by two. Then I'll take a last shot and miss and they will win by two."

The plan went according to script and the place went crazy. After the game we had a Christmas party and dinner and Santa even showed up to give everyone gifts. I realized these people are God's little angels. I did some research and found that over six million people in this country are challenged in this way.

After the game I met Butch's parents, and they were terrific people. I asked them about Butch's life expectancy and they told me around 37 to 38 years old. I was very impressed with the people at Logan Center and the job they were doing, so I got more involved as the years went on. So did my team.

Butch Waxman (second from right) sat on the bench against Providence in 1985 and tried to call a timeout in the second half. He's hit the game-winner against me 33 straight years at the Logan Center Christmas game.

Butch came to a lot of the games, and sometimes he came in the locker room before the game. In January of 1984-85, we played a Saturday game at Maryland and we stunk. Rivers, Kempton and Royal shot 5-34 combined and Lefty Driesell's team beat us by 12 points. It was our second loss in three games and we were starting to feel sorry for ourselves.

We had a quick turnaround and were playing Providence at home on Monday night. It was a game we had to win. I was in the locker room with Eddie O'Rourke, an avid Notre Dame basketball fan who was a lawyer in Chicago. He came to all of our games home and away.

At about 7:30 p.m., Butch and his friend Tommy (who Gerry Faust always called Dome because he was bald), came in the locker room. "You got beat by Maryland," said Butch. I said, "We got killed by Maryland." He continued to give me a hard time about that game. I finally told him, "You want to talk to the team? They will be back in here in a couple of minutes."

When the team came back in, much to the shock of my assistant coaches, I let Butch and Tommy give the pregame talk. I thought Pete Gillen was going to pass out, because this was his game from a scouting and preparation standpoint.

Providence's game plan was on the board, so Tommy and Butch started reviewing it. They pointed to Kempton and called him Barlow, and pointed to Dolan and called him Royal. But the guys nodded their heads like they were following along. Finally I said, OK guys, let's go. If my team was feeling sorry for itself earlier in the day, they weren't now.

At halftime I was sitting on the bench looking at the stat sheet and Butch was sitting next to me. He always sat in the stands during the game with a social worker named Tim from Logan Center, but as time was winding down on the halftime clock, Tim was nowhere to be seen.

The horn sounded and still no Tim. I told Butch to take my seat on the bench. I didn't know what else to do. Butch was now sitting among my assistant coaches. They really thought I had lost it now.

The second half started and about three minutes in someone from our bench shouted, "Time out!" I looked at my assistants and they were all startled. It was Butch; he wanted a timeout. Fortunately, none of the officials heard it. "Butch, what are you doing?," I asked him.

"I want to talk to the team," was his reply. I told him he had to wait until the 16-minute mark on the clock for a TV timeout. I then went to the end of the bench and grabbed one of my managers. "Go find Tim. Now."

We went on to win the game 70-63. Tommy and Butch came into the locker room and high-fived all the players and coaches as if they had won the game.

After that first game against Butch in 1971, I told the people at Logan Center I would play in the Christmas game as long as Butch played. Every year it was played the Sunday before Christmas and I even worked our schedule around it. Two seasons I actually moved Notre Dame games to accommodate the Logan Center game, once for a road game at Valparaiso and once for a home game against UCLA.

In December of 2003, I played in my 33rd consecutive Christmas game against the Logan Center Olympic team. I am happy to report that Butch, now 57, was on the court also. For the 33rd straight year, he hit the game winner.

PISTACHIO UNIFORMS

Champion, the company that made our uniforms, called me before my last season and said they wanted to order us a special uniform for one big, national TV game during the 1990-91 season. They were planning to market some wacko uniforms for the NBA, and they wanted to try some out with us. They asked me what I thought about a pistachio green uniform.

I looked at the schedule and figured Syracuse would probably be our biggest game late in the season. Just like the Southern Cal football game of 1977, our players warmed up in their regular uniforms and came back into the locker room, where managers had placed these fluorescent green uniforms in their lockers. We kept everyone in suspense even longer by wearing our warmups over the uniforms the last time out. It wasn't until we went out for the introduction of the starting lineups that people saw the uniforms.

The ACC went crazy, but the TV people had some problems. Millions watching at home on CBS thought their sets had gone out. People were calling press row to find out what that color was.

Syracuse was ranked No. 7 in the nation entering that game and we had been struggling, but we hung with them. On the last play of the game Billy Owens, who scored 31 points, scored on an offensive rebound and we lost, 70-69. Had we won that game, people would have remembered that as a great game and those uniforms would have held legendary status. When we lost, those uniforms got uglier and uglier.

Monday, the athletic director sent me a memo. First, he asked if the equipment manager had received a bill for those uniforms. Champion had never planned to send us a bill, and with all the attention on them, they should have paid us to wear them. Later, I was told we couldn't wear green any more, just the traditional blue and gold.

IRISH VS. IRISH

When we played Houston at home in 1989, the game was one of the most unusual on record from a uniform standpoint. The game was scheduled for a 2 p.m. tipoff on a Sunday afternoon in February. Houston flew through Chicago on Saturday night. They got to South Bend just fine, but their luggage, including their game uniforms, didn't.

Houston's managers called the airline all Saturday night and Sunday morning, but by the time they left the hotel Sunday for the game, they still didn't have uniforms. They received word when they got to the ACC that the airline had found them, but there was no way they were going to get to South Bend by gametime.

The only solution was for Houston to wear our road uniforms. It was an odd sight, especially for the players, to see both teams on the floor wearing uniforms that said Irish. Some players were guarding players wearing their own road uniforms. It was a challenge for the announcers because the numbers didn't match their program rosters, which they had obviously memorized during their pregame preparation.

The uniforms arrived by halftime and Houston changed into their normal road uniforms. That changed all the numbers in the scorebooks, but the officials waived the rule. Otherwise we would have shot 10 technical fouls. We didn't need the technical fouls, and we won 89-80.

TRUCKER TRYOUT

Every year we had walk-on tryouts just before the annual October 15 beginning of practice. We would get about 100 candidates who would come to the ACC that day. We would run them through some drills, then take the top 15-20 guys and have them scrimmage. Before the scrimmage, we would get the names and addresses of each guy.

One year, we made the cut and as we were getting the names we came to one guy who had really impressed us in the early drills. We asked him his name and address, but the address he gave was not only off campus, it was from a city nowhere near South Bend. He finally said, "I got to tell you, I'm a trucker who heard about your tryouts on the radio. I just wanted to come by and see if I could make the team."

TERRY GANNON

Terry Gannon, now the preeminent voice of figure skating for ABC and a part-time college basketball play-by-play broadcaster for both ESPN and ABC, was a very good basketball player in his day. My problem was I didn't know how good.

Gannon grew up in Joliet, Illinois, in the late 1970s, the same hometown that sent Dan "Rudy" Ruettiger to Notre Dame. The movie about Rudy's life could easily have included Gannon, because he was close to the Ruettiger family, and Terry used to visit Rudy on campus when Rudy was a student in the mid-1970s.

When Terry was a youngster he came to campus for football weekends and stayed with Rudy. In the movie, Rudy lives in Notre Dame Stadium, but in reality he lived in the Joyce Center in an apartment. For insurance reasons, a student lived in every building on campus and Rudy was the student who lived in the Joyce Center. One Friday night he and Rudy turned on the lights of the main floor at the ACC at 2 a.m. and shot baskets, pretending they were taking Dwight Clay's shot from the corner to end UCLA's streak.

Terry continued to improve as a basketball player to the point where he was getting recruited heavily by some big-name schools on a national basis. I needed a replacement for John Paxson, but I looked at Terry as a shooting guard, not a point. So we signed Dan Duff, also from Illinois, instead.

Terry went to NC State where he played for Jim Valvano. He went on to play a big role for NC State's National Championship team in 1983. He was on the court when Lorenzo Charles made the game-winning dunk. Here was a kid who used to sleep in our own building who dreamed he was Dwight Clay, and I didn't even recruit him.

In March of 2004, Terry came back to Notre Dame to broadcast the Notre Dame vs. Purdue NIT game at the Joyce Center. The afternoon before the game he went to Notre Dame Stadium and sat in the same seat he used to have as kid. In fact, his parents still have season tickets.

Terry and I have worked some games together and as studio hosts at ABC. Every time I see him he reminds me that he would have crawled to Notre Dame.

Okay, Terry, I admit it. I should have given you a scholarship, but you did get a National Championship Ring with my good friend Jim Valvano.

YOU THINK WINNING IN CAMERON IS TOUGH?

We were playing in the championship game of the Zadir Cup in Yugoslavia in 1983, our third ever foreign trip. The score was tied, there were four seconds left on the clock, and it was our ball. We wanted to run a baseline screen where Tim Kempton would screen for Tom Sluby, and Sluby would come off the screen and take the jumper.

Jim Dolan was handed the ball by the official and looked to in-bound. A couple of seconds after he took the ball from the official, but before he in-bounded it, the horn sounded. Apparently the clock operator started the clock when the ball was handed to Dolan instead of waiting to start the clock after someone had touched it in-bounds.

About the time the horn sounded, Dolan in-bounded the ball. Sluby wasn't open, but Kempton was after he set the screen. Kempton swished the shot after the buzzer, but he had made it clear-ly within the four seconds because the operator had started the clock too soon.

I looked at everybody on the bench and I yelled, "Munich," just like I had when we beat Virginia in the Horizon in 1981. I had learned from Hank Iba's mistake.

We all ran downstairs to our locker room and locked the door, figuring that they would not make us come all the way back upstairs to replay the last four seconds or send the game into overtime. While the players knew what "Munich" meant, we left poor Father John Van Wolvear back on the bench with the valuables bag because he didn't know what we meant. I felt bad that he was left up there on the court with 4,000 angry fans. But he was a priest, who was going to bother him? And surely they weren't going to steal from a priest.

We could hear the crowd whistling, which is what they do in Europe instead of booing. I refused to come out, and we stayed in the locker room. Finally, after about 15 minutes, someone knocked on the door and simply said, "You won!" They knew we weren't going to leave the locker room in our uniforms because we felt we had made the shot within the four seconds.

When we finally came out of the locker room there were still angry fans on the court and we needed an armed police escort on our departure that night. We went on to win the tournament and the Zadir Cup is still on display in the Convocation Center at Notre Dame. You think it is tough to play at Duke? At least the Cameron Indoor Stadium ushers don't have guns!

OFFICIALS

Gary Muncy was calling our game with Lafayette at Notre Dame during the 1978-79 season. We had been to the Final Four the previous year and had just beaten Marquette in Milwaukee to get to No. 1, for the first time since we ended UCLA's 88-game winning streak in 1974.

This Lafayette game was our first since being ranked No. 1 so we had a high opinion of ourselves. In the first half, Lafayette was giving us a game. We were flat after an emotional win over Marquette.

The game was sold out, but the crowd was flat because we were supposed to blow out Lafayette. A couple of minutes into the second half, Orlando Woolridge inadvertently got hit in an area below the belt where men don't like to get hit. Play was stopped while he caught his breath and regained his deep voice.

I went to check on Orlando, but I also took the opportunity to do something to get the crowd into the game. We had to do something, this was embarrassing.

I went to Gary Muncy, a Big Ten referee who was the lead official on the game, and started acting like I was mad at him. I got right in his face and vehemently said with an fierce expression, "Gary, I am coming out to talk to you so the fans think I am on your case." I then pointed at him with my meanest face possible and said, "Gary, you guys are doing a terrific job tonight, just keep it up."

Our players didn't know what was going on because they were over at the bench and the crowd couldn't hear what I was saying, they just saw this demonstration of anger.

The crowd got into it and we went on a 20-point run and won 91-66. Ironically, Woolridge led us to the victory with eight-of-nine shooting and 16 points.

I did something similar with Steve Welmer, one of the top officials in the Big Ten, late in my career during a UCLA game. We knocked the ball out of bounds behind our bench, but the crowd thought a UCLA player knocked it out. I knew it was UCLA's ball. So did Steve. I went over to him at midcourt and in a fit of rage said, "Steve, did you see where that ball went out of bounds?" I pointed and said, "In the green section. Fourth row up, where the good-looking blonde is sitting." I was pointing and appeared to be all over him.

I then said, "OK, let's go." The students thought I was really on his case, and the crowd got back in the game.

We were playing Marquette in Milwaukee some time in the 1980s. David Hall, a rookie official from the Missouri Valley who was working his first national TV game, made what I thought was a bad call and I wanted to talk to him about it during a timeout. He was standing at the foul line across from our bench, but he would not pay any attention to me.

I said, "David, come here, I want to talk to you. Could you please explain that last call. David, don't you hear me?" Finally, after about 45 seconds of me barking at him, he came over, and we discussed the call. I ripped him because he was a rookie official, so I knew he wouldn't T me up.

In 1996, I was broadcasting a Marquette game for ESPN and David was the referee. We were talking before the game and he said, "I have a great Digger story. Do you remember that game here (Marquette) when I didn't pay any attention to you during a time-out? That game was on national TV. I didn't care about the 10,000 people in the arena seeing you chew me out, but I didn't want the millions of people watching at home on TV to see it, especially the people back home. So I waited until the commercial started to talk to you."

THE BEST OPPOSING CHEER

In 1973-74 we played Austin Peay (pronounced PEE) in the first round of the NCAA Tournament at Indiana State. The Governors were from Clarksville, Tennessee, and they had a good contingent of fans make the drive to Terre Haute.

Austin Peay had a player named Fly Williams, a free-wheeling wing player who could shoot the lights out from the outside. And, as was the case with a lot of players in that era, he liked to put up a lot of shots. He averaged 29 points a game that year, fifth in the country, but he also shot it about 25 times a game.

Fly was the star of the team and he had his own cheering section. They had the best cheer I ever heard for an opposing player. "Fly's open, let's go Peay."

Running Up the Score

I ran the score up on a team only one time. For our February 22, 1986 game at Miami (Florida), we were motivated and had a predetermined margin in mind.

The previous fall, Miami's football team, coached by future NFL Hall of Fame coach Jimmy Johnson, had beaten us 58-7. Gerry Faust had announced the previous Tuesday that he was stepping down as head coach. Miami was ranked fourth in the country heading into the game and would finish the season ranked ninth. Gerry's last team was 5-6, and the bubble burst that November afternoon in Miami.

Jimmy was in his second year at Miami and was trying to impress the voters as much as possible in hopes of getting to a national championship game. Vinnie Testeverde, who would win the Heisman the following year, was still throwing the ball with a 40-point lead. They scored their 51st point on a touchdown pass with 6:11 left and their 58th on a blocked punt with four minutes left.

They were out to embarrass our football team on national television, so it was payback time for the basketball team. This basketball game was broadcast on ESPN with Harry Kalas, now the Hall of Fame broadcaster from Philadelphia, doing the play by play.

A few days before the game, Tim Kempton came to me and said, "The football team really wants us to run it up on Miami." He didn't have to tell me that, I wanted to also. Gerry Faust was a good man. He didn't win at Notre Dame, but I don't know of a better person who served in that position.

When we got to Miami I called a team meeting. I did it while Father Riehle was off playing golf, because I didn't want him to hear what I had to say to the team. I told them that Miami had beaten our football team by 51 and we were going to beat them by at least that margin. I was not going to be satisfied until we had that margin. I was intense, and I could see our team had a collective smile. They shared my feeling.

This would not be easy because Miami was not an awful team. They were coached by Bill Foster, who finished his career with over 500 wins. His 1985-86 Miami team was 12-12 coming into the game and had just played at Duke the previous Wednesday, losing by only 22 to a Coach K-coached team that would lose in the national championship game. They were in the first year of the program after 15 years without a team, so they started five freshmen.

At our shootaround on Friday night, Jimmy Johnson came over to the gym to try to get into practice. But one of my managers, who had been at the meeting, wouldn't let him in. He said the practice was closed. I hadn't told him to keep Jimmy out, he just decided to do it on his own. I told him he had made the right decision. I certainly knew who Jimmy Johnson was, but we weren't friends by any means. Knowing how mad Notre Dame people were about the score of that football game, he must have been coming over to try to get me to hold the score down. I never saw him, and I'm glad I didn't. I would not have been very cordial.

The game was sold out, and when they announced our lineup, the crowd shouted the football score. Their Hurricane mascot held a football throughout the introductions and throughout the game. He even shot a football at the basket during timeouts. All that did was motivate our players.

Both teams got off to a hot start. It was 19-16 just five minutes in, but by halftime we had a 66-40 lead. As we walked off the court, Bill McMurtrie, a lawyer from Washington D.C. who traveled with us now and then, said to me within earshot of the Miami Athletic Director Sam Jankovich, "Well, you are halfway there." I said, "SHH-HHH, I don't want him to hear."

The team knew we could do this. The locker room was intense; starters were talking to the reserves, imploring them to be ready and play with intensity when they were in the game.

We continued to play lights out the second half. We went on a 30-8 run to start the second half. With 13 minutes left, we had scored 91 points and were 40-57 from the field. With 9:47 left we had already reached our goal, a 100-49 lead. Ken Barlow and David Rivers were on fire. Barlow had 28 points with 12 minutes left in the game, and Rivers had 19 points and nine assists at the same juncture.

I pulled Rivers and Barlow with 10 minutes left, and all the starters with eight minutes left, up by 50. If the score had gotten down to 40, I probably would have put the starters back in. Fortunately, I never had to make that decision. The subs, Sean Connor, Gary Voce, Jeff Peters, Michael Smith, and Matt Beeuwsaert kept up the intensity and played at the same level as the starters.

During the last TV timeout, we were up by 49. Kempton came over to Smith and grabbed him by the jersey and said intently, "Keep playing hard, you know what we want." With 15 seconds left we got the ball back, up 124-73. Most of my teams would have run the clock out, but not in this game. Smith drove the ball down the lane and threw a pass to Connor for a layup with eight seconds left, giving us a 53-point lead. Miami missed at the buzzer and we had beaten our predetermined spread.

I was very satisfied inside as I walked to the press conference, but never verified to the media that we had a specific goal in mind. We had beaten Manhattan 102-47 in the previous Wednesday in Madison Square Garden. When I was asked if we ran up the score to atone for the football game, I just said, "We are just playing very well right now. Hey, we beat Manhattan by a worse score than this."

Bill Foster was one of the nice guys in coaching, and it had nothing to do with him, his coaches or his players. This game was all about Jimmy Johnson.

Chapter Eight

HALL OF FAME OPPONENTS

I recommended that Notre Dame join the Big East in the mid-1980s. I thought it would be a natural marriage with the other Catholic schools already in the conference, plus I could see that it was becoming more and more difficult to recruit against those schools, because the conference was becoming a force nationally. I thought it would be a natural for DePaul to also join the league at that time as a travel partner and give us the Chicago market through WGN television. That would have been a strong combination with the East Coast. In 2005, it is finally taking place with DePaul joining the league.

That said, I did benefit from a coaching experience standpoint from being an independent. Father Ned Joyce allowed me flexibility in the schedule process, so we were able to go all over the country and take on the top teams nationally. I faced 20 coaches who are already in the Basketball Hall of Fame, and I am sure there will be more added over the shelf life of this book. I beat 17 of the 20 Hall of Fame coaches at least once. I'm not going to deceive to you, I didn't have a winning record against these coaches, but there were many memorable moments.

LARRY BROWN

I was riding in a cab in New York City in September of 1979 with Eddie Broderick, who was a lawyer in Chicago who used to work for Mike DeCicco in our academic tutoring department.

The topic of conversation in the cab was the UCLA game against then first-year Bruins coach Larry Brown. Eddie heard Brown was planning to outdress me for the game at Notre Dame on December 11. He had already bought an expensive suit just for that game. I decided that I wouldn't let that happen and I had just the outfit in mind.

At 5 p.m. the night of the game, I left the house wearing basic slacks, an open shirt and a winter jacket. I wasn't even taking a sports jacket, and my wife, Terry, asked me, "What are you doing?" I told her, "You will see at the game."

Before the game I was in the coaches locker room and Mike DeCicco gave me a curious look as I changed into a navy blue Notre Dame sweatshirt with bright yellow Notre Dame printed across the front, along with Navy blue slacks. It was the same coaching outfit Ara Parseghian wore when he was the Notre Dame football coach. He also wore this attire for the Ford commercials he did in the 1960s and 1970s. I had one subtle addition, however. My sweatshirt had a gold shovel (for Digger) on the upper half of the right sleeve.

Mike asked, "What in the world are you doing?" I said, "Larry Brown thinks he is going to outdress me tonight with some expensive suit, but I am going to wear something that is priceless to Notre Dame fans."

I had one other ploy for this game. The last time we went on the court, I usually went ahead of the team courtside by our bench and incited the crowd. I would give a gesture that I couldn't hear them, trying them to bring the noise to another level. This time there was quite a reaction to my attire, but there was also an element of surprise because the team was not in the tunnel behind me. None of the students knew where the team was.

I did my normal antics to get the crowd going, then pointed to the top of the student section. There, at the top of the concourse in two separate groups, was the Notre Dame team. Led by the two captains, Rich Branning and Bill Hanzlik, the team entered the arena through the student section from the top of the concourse. They shook hands with the students as they came down the steps. This was a first, and I hoped it would lead to a Notre Dame moment.

We were down by six points, 74-68 with just over two minutes left when we made a comeback behind Tripucka and Woolridge. With 15 seconds left we were trailing by one, but UCLA missed a free throw. John Paxson, then a freshman playing in just his fifth game, took an 18-footer that missed, but he was fouled on the play. Pax sank both free throws to put us up by a point, then stole the in-bounds pass and was intentionally fouled with two seconds left.

After he stole the in-bounds pass and was fouled, Tripucka ran over to congratulate him but inadvertently caught an elbow from one of the officials square in the mouth, dislodging two teeth. He went to the floor and was bleeding at an alarming rate. All hell broke loose because someone on our bench said a UCLA player had decked Kelly. I hadn't seen it, so I was going by that report and I was not a happy man. I got into a shouting contest with Brown.

Paxson made the free throws and we won, 77-74. Someone asked Larry in the press conference what happened at the end of the game when Tripucka got hit. He said, "I don't know, why don't you ask the cheerleader?" He was referring to my game attire.

Today, Larry Brown is one of the top coaches in basketball and is very deserving of his induction into the Hall of Fame. He is the only coach in history to win the NCAA Championship (at Kansas in 1988) and the NBA title (with the Pistons this past season). Memorial Day weekend 2004, Mark Shapiro and Bill Creasy of ESPN invited me to the Indy 500 and a Pacers vs. Pistons playoff game. Bill and I spent 45 minutes in the Pistons' locker room prior to the game. As I finish this book he is coaching our Olympic team. With all of these accolades, the one that gives testimony to his greatness came in Los Angeles early in his career. He took the Clippers to the playoffs, twice!

LOU CARNESECCA

Lou Carnesecca and I have something in common. We both lost exactly 200 games in our college careers as head coaches. We both handed each other one. I beat his St. John's team in 1975 by one point (68-67) and he beat my Notre Dame team by two points (57-55) in my last year. Both games were played in New York.

When Louie, who won 526 games over 24 years, was the head coach at St. John's—especially for games in the Garden—there were basketball rules and there were "Louie rules." He was famous for wandering during games. He was just oblivious to the coaching box.

Once in the early days of the Big East, Gary Williams brought his Boston College team to Madison Square Garden to face Louie and St. John's. Gary's star guard then was Michael Adams, a senior, who was aware of Louie's antics during games.

Late in this game on a key possession, Adams brought the ball up court near the St. John's bench. Louie was giving instructions to his team, but, as he often did, he had wandered a good seven feet out onto the court. Adams intentionally ran into Carnesecca, something Williams had told him to do if the opportunity arose. Gary thought he might get a technical foul out of it.

Adams saw the opportunity and ran into Louie. During the collision, Adams lost the ball out of bounds. The officials huddled, then gave the ball to St. John's. Gary of course went bananas. Gary then asked one of the officials, "How could you give them the ball?" The official responded, "That's just Louie."

CHUCK DALY

Chuck Daly coached the Gold Medal 1992 United States Olympic Dream Team, and won two NBA World Championships with the Detroit Pistons (with the help of Bill Laimbeer at center). He was Billy Cunningham's top assistant when the Philadelphia 76ers won the title in 1983, and as a college coach he won four Ivy League Championships in six years at Penn.

I have to rank as one of the few coaches who never lost to Chuck Daly. I was lucky, because I only had to coach against him one time.

When I was the head coach at Fordham in 1970-71 we played Daly's Boston College team at the Roberts Center in Boston. It was a midseason game and we were ranked 14th in the nation with a 15-1 record.

The Roberts Center seated about 4,000 and it had two tiers, a popular style for gyms built at that time. Jack Burik, a guard on our team from the Pittsburgh area, had a devout Catholic mother who came to most of our games.

Before the game I was on the bench giving the team its final instructions, when I felt drops of water hitting me in the top of the head. I looked up in the balcony and there was Mrs. Burik sprinkling the team with holy water. The players had their backs to her, so they didn't know where the water was coming from.

I brought them together and said, "Their fans hate you guys. They're spitting on you. Get out there and take it out on their team."

I don't know if it was that motivational ploy or Mrs. Burik's holy water, but we took Boston College out of their game early with our full-court press and jumped out to an 18-point halftime lead at 43-25. Burik had his best half of the year and had 17 points by intermission. But Jim O'Brien, who went on to become the head coach at Ohio State, led a second-half comeback, and Boston College tied it at the end of regulation on a late free throw.

Charlie Yelverton, only 6-2 but a great leaper, got the tip for us to start overtime and Bart Woytowicz scored. It was the first of a 10-0 run that put the game away, and we ended with an 84-80 victory.

MAGIC JOHNSON

Magic Johnson grew up about three hours from South Bend in Lansing, Michigan. He was a senior in high school in 1976-77 and we convinced him to come to Notre Dame for an official visit. Danny Nee drove to Michigan to pick him up and bring him back to campus. He was a very gregarious young man, just like he is today.

He stayed for a football weekend and seemed to fit in well with our players. Just before Danny was about to drive him back to Michigan, he called me. "Coach, we have a little problem with Magic," Danny said. "We went to check him out of the hotel and he had a $67 phone bill." Under NCAA rules I knew we could pay for two calls home, one to say the student-athlete had arrived and one to say he was headed back.

I met Magic at the Morris Inn and while driving him around campus I asked him how his weekend went. He replied with that big smile that he had a great time. "When did you have time to enjoy it because it looks to me like you spent the entire weekend in your hotel room talking on the phone?" I was upset and showed it, because he had to know the way we did things around here.

I told him he would have to pay the phone bill when he got back. Danny called me when he returned and said it was a quiet ride back. We called his high school coach the next day and told him what had happened and he said he would call Magic's father.

The next week, we got our money, but we didn't get Magic. He went to Michigan State and two years later eliminated us from the NCAA Tournament in the Regional Final. Notre Dame hasn't been to a regional final since.

BOB KNIGHT

I have known Bob Knight since we first met at Bill Foster's and Harry Litwack's basketball clinic in Valley Forge (near Philadelphia), Pennsylvania. Knight had just become one of Tates Locke's assistant coaches at Army and I was in graduate school at Rider College. Locke was friends with Tom Winterbottom, who got me interested in coaching the summer after I graduated from Rider.

We were both young, starving coaches in those days and I remember telling him if he wanted to make some extra money he could drive to Beacon and work a funeral for my dad. My dad paid $20 a funeral. That was good money in 1964!

We got together during the season when I would go to their practices, then in the offseason we would play golf together. One summer day we were playing the course at West Point. We were both taking our time on one of the holes loitering by a creek. Tates drove up and asked us what we were doing. He knew exactly what we were doing. We were both so poor we were looking for some free golf balls so we didn't have to buy any.

I coached against Bob Knight 18 times in my 20 years at Notre Dame. Two of the years (1978-79 and 1979-80) we couldn't agree on a date in the first semester so the games weren't played. I beat him five times and all the victories were memorable. We won only once in Bloomington, 73-67 in December of 1973. That was a special win because it was the first game we played at Indiana since we had lost by 65 points there two years previously.

I remember Father Jim Shilts had been our chaplain for that game in 1971 and he requested to be the chaplain for this game in 1973. He was just as excited as any of the players when we won that game. We won that game without Gary Brokaw, who was injured, and we started three freshmen, Dantley, Paterno and Ray Martin.

Bob Knight handed me my (and Notre Dame's) worst loss in history. But we have been friends since we first met at a basketball clinic in Valley Forge, Pennsylvania in 1964.

We also won in South Bend in December of 1976 when they were the defending national champions, then won four years later when they went on to win the national championship with Isiah Thomas.

For nearly 40 years Bob Knight and I have had tremendous respect for one another. We took the same approach to our profession from a priorities standpoint: don't cheat, work hard every day to the best of your abilities and graduate your players.

We both were big on remembering where we came from and who helped us along the way. Bob has been the best at taking care of the past coaches who helped him and the college game prosper. Whether it be Hank Iba or Pete Newell or Claire Bee, he treated them with respect and included those wise men in his important basketball decisions. This was especially true when he coached the 1984 Olympic team and made sure Coach Iba was involved. He felt Coach Iba was given unjustified criticism when the United States lost in the 1972 Olympics to the Russians in Munich.

If you are loyal and honest with Bob Knight, he will be your friend for life. There are many stories about his impact on his players. Landon Turner was a player who became paralyzed in an auto accident after his senior year. Prior to the NBA draft that summer (1982) Bob called Red Auerbach, the legend of the Boston Celtics, who had the last pick of the draft. He asked Red to draft Landon Turner. Sure enough, on draft day, Red took Landon Turner with the 225th selection.

Bob went out of his way to make sure Landon's insurance payments were provided in a timely manner. Landon, who will work from a wheelchair the rest of his life, has been helped professionally by Knight since the accident.

MIKE KRZYZEWSKI

The first time I saw Mike Krzyzewski was in the mid-1960s. He was playing in a scrimmage for Bob Knight's Army team against Pennsylvania. Penn scrimmaged against Army in basketball the morning of the Army-Navy football game whenever it was in Philadelphia.

We had a player named Pete Andrews, who drove in for a lay-up and was fouled by Krzyzewski. In true Bob Knight fashion, Mike was trying to draw a charge. But Mike got there a little late and Andrews took a hard fall and landed on his back. There was silence in the gym because we thought Pete was injured seriously. Mike and all the Army players were very concerned, but Pete was fine after he was helped off the floor.

The second time I saw Coach K was in the fall of 1974 when he was a graduate assistant under Coach Knight at Indiana. We were at a clinic in Valley Forge, Pennsylvania, where Knight was lecturing and I went to Bob's room. Mike was sitting on a bed counting money. Bob had a booklet on defensive strategies that he sold to the coaches and Mike was in charge of selling it. My, how far he has come in 30 years.

I coached against Coach K eight times when I was at Notre Dame and he was the head coach at Duke. We beat him just once, a 70-66 overtime win in 1986-87 in South Bend. It was just two weeks after we had beaten Dean Smith and North Carolina when they were number one. That was a pretty good fortnight of basketball for the Irish.

I never won in Cameron Indoor Stadium, but we came close in 1985-86. We had the ball down one for a final possession against a second-ranked Duke team. David Rivers took the final shot, but Billy King deflected his foul-line jumper.

No one has done what Mike Krzyzewski has accomplished in the last 20 years. It amazes me to watch Mike reload every year with the top talent in the country. It seems he has players turn pro early every year, but every year he is in the hunt for the national championship. What a perfect marriage this has been for Duke and Coach K for the last 20 years.

AL McGUIRE

If Bob Knight had the biggest impact on my coaching career from a strategy standpoint, Al McGuire had the biggest impact from a psychological perspective. He was the master at controlling the crowd, the students, the officials, the media, his players and your players.

He loved coming to Notre Dame because the students were into the game. Our students used to throw toilet paper on the court, and

Al would go on the court in front of his bench, pick up a roll and throw it back at them.

He had charisma, and he had magic. Many of my ideas from a motivational standpoint were ideas I got from Al or things I thought Al would do if he had the opportunity. Playing to the crowd before our team came on the court, giving the students specific chants ("29...and one") for a big game, or cutting down the nets before a UCLA game, these were all the result of the Al McGuire influence.

The Digger and Al show reached its high point during the 1973-74 season when Marquette came to South Bend. This game was played on a Tuesday night in South Bend, and it was just 10 days after we had ended UCLA's 88-game winning streak, and just three days after UCLA had defeated us in the return game in Los Angeles.

Marquette entered the game with a 16-1 record (only loss to Frank McGuire and South Carolina) and ranked fifth in the nation in both polls. We were ranked third, even after the loss at UCLA.

Before the game, Art White, the lead official and one of the best in the Big Ten during that time, called us together at midcourt while the teams were finishing their warmups. One of the Ali vs. Frazier fights had just taken place the night before, so Art said, "Gentlemen, the big fight was last night." Meanwhile, in the press room, the media conducted a pool as to who would get the first technical and how long it would take.

We had a circus atmosphere, and it didn't take Al long to move to the center of the ring. Just 60 seconds into the game, he got a technical foul after one of the officials called a foul on guard Marcus Washington. That had to be a record for the quickest technical he ever got, and that is saying something. I never heard who had Al and 60 seconds in the media pool.

In my first game against Al when I was at Fordham, he got a technical foul early and controlled the latter stages of the game while I sat on the bench and watched. Marquette beat us in overtime. I wasn't going to let that happen again, so I knew I had to counteract his technical with one of my own. I just had to find the right time to do it.

I actually got the upper hand twice in the second half. We had an eight-point lead at the half. But with 15:33 left in the game, Maurice Lucas hit a jumper and was fouled by Adrian Dantley, cutting the lead to two. I called for a timeout after the free throw, but Art White didn't see me call it.

The officials came to the scorer's table and asked, "Who called timeout?" I immediately yelled, "TV called timeout." Al had seen me signal for a timeout and wanted me charged with the timeout instead of TV. He was livid.

The game was not on national TV, as it was only televised back to Milwaukee. But White came to the scorer's table and extended both arms with his fists clenched, "TV Timeout." I looked at Al and said, "Gotcha." That evened the score for the 1971 Fordham-Marquette game in Madison Square Garden.

Ray Martin was fouled at the 10:19 mark and I started ranting and raving, earning the technical I wanted. After Bo Ellis made a free throw to make the margin three points in favor of Marquette, we went on an 9-0 run to take a 52-46 lead, culminated by a 20-foot jumper by Dwight Clay. Sound familiar?

We held a three- to seven-point margin the rest of the game and won, 69-63.

•••

My first year (1971-72) at Notre Dame I was looking for ways to create interest in the basketball program within the student body. I made it clear in a preseason article in *The Observer*, Notre Dame's student paper, that any student who wanted to come to a preseason practice was invited.

These were the days before Midnight Madness, but we had a thousand students show up for our first practice. Later in the semester on a good day we had 50 or so. It made the players excited that the students cared that much and it made them more intense during practice.

I kept the practices open for about three weeks until I received a package with a notebook full of pages and diagrams attached to a letter from Al McGuire, who we would be playing that season.

Dear Digger,

You need to be careful who you allow into your practices. There is a student on your campus from Milwaukee who has been a Marquette fan since he was in diapers. Guess he went to Notre Dame for its academic program.

Anyway, he has been coming to your practices everyday and diagramming your complete offense and defense for the 1971-72 season. He brought it to me last week when he was home, thinking it would help us in our preparation for this year's game at Notre Dame.

I am returning it to you because it is too complicated for me to figure out. But, someone smarter than me might use it against you.

Good luck this year,

Al McGuire

FRANK MCGUIRE

When I was a kid in Beacon, New York, I remember buying my first preseason college basketball magazine. In the mid-1950s, Tommy Kearns, a New York kid who was the star of Frank McGuire's North Carolina team, was on the cover. He had that crew cut and those high Tar Heel blue socks.

McGuire beat Wilt Chamberlain and Kansas in the NCAA Championship game in 1957 that put the ACC on the map. Say what you want about Everett Case of NC State and Vic Bubas at Duke, McGuire's national championship was the strongest building block of the ACC's now 51-year heritage. North Carolina was 32-0 that year, including two triple overtime wins in the Final Four (Michigan State and Kansas).

McGuire attended and coached at St. John's, where he coached the baseball team to the College World Series in 1949 and the basketball team to the Final Four in 1952. He coached St. John's before he went to North Carolina and established strong recruiting roots in the city. McGuire knew every Irish mother and cop in New York City, especially if they had a son who could play basketball. At both North Carolina and South Carolina (which played in the ACC during his first six years at the school) he had an "underground railroad in reverse" that brought him championships at both schools. He is still the only coach to win the ACC Championship at two different schools.

I coached against Frank McGuire nine times when I was at Notre Dame and we won seven of them. One of the losses was in 1977-78, the year we went to the Final Four. I benefited by facing him at the end of his career at South Carolina. Paul Dietzel had convinced the administration at South Carolina to leave the ACC and that eventually hurt their program.

In those days the NCAA only took one team from each conference, so it was easier to get in the NCAAs as an independent. South Carolina went to the NCAAs just one time as an ACC team, in 1971, their last year in the league. Their first three years as an independent (1972, 1973 and 1974) they went to the tournament, so it looked like a great move. But eventually they could not compete for recruits without the ACC tie-in.

Frank's final year, 1979-80, we beat them 90-66 in Columbia. We subbed a lot to keep the score that close. The decision to leave the ACC set South Carolina's program back and they didn't return to the NCAA Tournament until 1989. They finally figured it out and joined the SEC in 1992.

RAY MEYER

Ray Meyer and his wife, Marge, were like a second father and mother to me. As I said earlier, we wouldn't have gotten the San Francisco game on NBC in 1977 if Ray hadn't agreed to move our DePaul home game off a Saturday to a Monday night. And we made the move during the season.

What he accomplished over 42 years is amazing because he had great success in the 1940s through the 1980s. He went to the Final Four with George Mikan in 1945 and with Mark Aguirre in 1979. He had the ability to change with the game and relate to his players. He won all the way to his final year when he took DePaul to the Sweet Sixteen in 1984.

We had some great games against Ray Meyer, especially his last seven years as coach (1977-83), when the rivalry really got intense. One year we were playing in Alumni Hall in Chicago and a DePaul fan was sitting a few rows up behind our bench. He was probably in his late 50s and was calling me every name in the book. Alumni Hall was like a big high school gym, so a fan could stand out. Late in the game, I looked up in the stands during a timeout and there were medical personnel attending to this same guy who had been riding me. As it turned out he had suffered a heart attack and later died at the hospital.

In 1980 we beat DePaul in double overtime at the ACC when they were No. 1 and undefeated. After that game I met Ray at center court and hugged him. I told him that I was sorry and that I loved him. It's the only time I ever said that to an opposing coach.

Ray Meyer still comes back to Notre Dame for reunion weekend every year and he marches into the all-classes dinner carrying the flag for the class of 1938. Say what you want about Mike Ditka, Michael Jordan and Mayor Daley, Ray Meyer is Chicago.

He is near 90 now and John Wooden is 93. Every time I see Ray I tell him, "Ray, you have to keep going. You have to beat Wooden. You can't let him win the last one."

C.M. NEWTON

C.M. Newton is in the Basketball Hall of Fame as a contributor, and justifiably so. I can't think of a more deserving individual who made contributions in so many areas of the game. He was a head coach for 32 years at Transylvania, Alabama and Vanderbilt, worked as the manager of the 1984 Olympic team under Bob Knight, and later was the chairman of the Men's Basketball Committee when he was the Athletic Director at Kentucky.

He did so much for integration of college basketball in the South. He was the first coach to recruit African-American basketball players to Alabama. Bear Bryant wanted African Americans on his football teams, but convinced Newton to sign some first for the basketball program to start the process. Then, as athletic director at Kentucky, he brought in Tubby Smith as Kentucky's first African American basketball coach.

I first met C.M. when he was the head coach at Alabama in 1974 and we played at Alabama in the 1974 regional in Tuscaloosa. After our practice the day before the tournament, he gave me a tour of the athletic facilities and the campus. I wanted to meet Bear Bryant and see their athletic dorm, which was state of the art for the early 1970s. I didn't want one at Notre Dame, but I wanted to see what it looked like.

We went into that athletic dorm, and it was full of football players. We had just beaten Alabama 24–23 in the Sugar Bowl to win the national championship, so I decided I was going to have some fun with these guys. I walked right in the lobby and asked them if they would come out and root for Notre Dame in the NCAA tournament. I didn't expect a warm reception, and I didn't get one.

I finally got to meet the Bear. He was a legend with that deep voice. He had a big office and I told him it was twice as big as Ara's. I told him I was going to go back and tell Ara he needed to negotiate with Moose Krause and get better working conditions.

We lost the Sweet 16 game to Michigan in Tuscaloosa and played Vanderbilt in the regional third-place game. On the night in between games I went out to dinner with Newton and some other administrators. During the dinner, a woman professing to be a Vanderbilt fan came up to me and asked if I was Digger Phelps.

I replied affirmatively, and she proceeded to go on and on about how Vanderbilt was going to beat us the next day. She had had a few drinks and was pretty feisty about the matter. I finally told her to come to the game early because we were going to blow out Vanderbilt in the second half.

The next day we probably played our best game of the year. I wish we had used some of that offense against Michigan. Vanderbilt came into the tournament ranked sixth in the nation, but we beat them by 118-88. Shumate and Dantley took out their frustrations from 48 hours earlier and combined for 59 points.

After the game I thought about that woman in the restaurant. She was probably sitting in the stands thinking that she had made me mad the night before and this Vanderbilt drubbing was all her fault.

DRAZEN PETROVIC

In 1980, I did a clinic in Sibenek, Yugoslavia. During the clinic, I was mesmerized by a 16-year-old kid. He was just shooting and shooting, making everything so effortlessly. I asked our interpreter, Farak, about this kid and he replied, "Drazen Petrovic, the next great international player."

I knew from the first time I saw him shoot that I wanted him at Notre Dame. In 1982, I talked to him about coming to Notre Dame. His father was a retired Secret Police officer in Yugoslavia under President Tito. I developed a relationship with Drazen, and I convinced him when they came over to the United States with the national team that he should consider coming to Notre Dame.

We played the Yugoslavian national team at Notre Dame in the fall of 1982, and after the game the media was going crazy because Drazen indicated in the postgame interviews that he would be coming to Notre Dame the next year.

He didn't come that next year, because there was too much pressure to stay in Yugoslavia. I saw him at the 1984 Olympics. I told him about David Rivers, who was coming to Notre Dame as a freshman that fall. He could have played two years with Rivers and they would have been the best backcourt in the world, never mind the NCAA. "All I want you to do is shoot, David will handle the ball and all the passing."

But he signed with Real Madrid in Spain for $350,000 a year, which was $350,000 a year more than I could pay him. I was heartbroken that summer when he signed that pro contract. He was the missing piece in what could have been a Final Four season in either 1984-85 or 1985-86.

Of course, Drazen eventually came to the NBA and played with Portland and New Jersey. He was on his way to a great NBA career when he was tragically killed in an automobile accident in Germany after the European Championships of 1994.

It was a national tragedy in his country. There were 100,000 people in the square in Zagrad for his funeral. The war stopped the day of his funeral; it was a truce in his honor. I visited his grave in Szgreb in May of 1995 during the war. Yes, I had tears in my eyes.

ADOLPH RUPP

My first year at Notre Dame was Adolph Rupp's last year at Kentucky. We weren't a very good basketball team my first year. By the time we played Kentucky in Louisville on December 28 we were 2-5 and had lost to Indiana, 94-29 and to UCLA 114-56 the past two games.

Kentucky was ranked 12th in the country, and their fans, and probably their coaches, were expecting another 50-point blowout. But with Gary Novak and Tom O'Mara hitting some shots, along with some sound ballhandling by John Egart and Bob Valibus, we only lost by 16, 83-67.

When I got back to my hotel room after the game the phone rang. It was Adolph. When I first heard his voice I figured he was calling to congratulate me on playing his team tough and that he was going to encourage me to hang in there for the rest of the year.

"Digger, what is wrong with my team?" he said at the top of the conversation. Not knowing where he was going with this conversation, I answered, "What do you mean, Coach?" "Well, Indiana beat you by 65, UCLA by 58, we should have beaten you by 50. What is wrong with my team?" I was surprised by the phone call and basically told him I had enough problems of my own.

DEAN SMITH

Dean Smith is the NCAA record holder for coaching victories with 879, three more than Adolph Rupp. Dean beat me six times, and Adolph beat me once, so I contributed to Dean's margin of victory, or at least leadership until Bob Knight eclipses the record some day.

I beat Dean twice, in the 1973 NIT semifinals in New York and when North Carolina was No. 1 in 1987. We met twice in the NCAA Tournament in Sweet 16 games, and he won both games, in 1977 at College Park, MD, and 1987 at the Meadowlands.

When it came to innovation, Dean was the master. He was the first to use the Four Corners Offense, and he was the master of using his timeouts to milk the clock at the end of games. Defensively, his run-and-jump rotation defense forced many turnovers, especially late in games when he stole a lot of victories. He also was the master of substitutions, sometimes five at a time. His Tall Blue Team was the inspiration for our S.W.A.T team in 1976-77.

Dean adapted to changes in the game and the personalities of his players, who respected him in the 1990s just as they did in the 1960s. Not a bad career for someone who was hung in effigy by North Carolina students during his first season.

Dean Smith's most important contribution to college basketball might have been the recruiting of Charlie Scott in the 1960s. Thanks to Dean, who personally brought Scott to restaurants and to church,

Scott broke the barrier for African Americans at North Carolina, which led to more opportunities for African Americans at other schools in the South.

JOHN THOMPSON

We have reached the point in college basketball today that it is not big news when an African American gets a head coaching position. Whether it be in Mississippi, Alabama, South Carolina, it is not a big deal because African Americans have earned high-profile positions and they are excelling. When a coach is hired today, we don't think about him being black, white or whatever. He is the basketball coach.

Three coaches stand out in my mind when it comes to the development of the Black Coaches Association. George Raveling and Rudy Washington were early leaders of the movement, but John Thompson probably had the biggest impact because of what he had accomplished at Georgetown and the way he accomplished it. He gave the Black Coaches Association credibility.

He turned Georgetown into a national power, and he did it without cheating at a strong academic institution. I can attest to that improvement personally. In my third year we beat John's Georgetown team in South Bend 104-77, but in my 19th year he had Georgetown ranked No. 2 in the nation and they ended our 1988-89 season in the NCAA Tournament in Providence, 81-74.

Rudy Washington asked me to speak at one of the BCA conventions. Thompson and Raveling were pleased that I had given Gary Brokaw and John Shumate full-time assistant coaching positions. They would later become Division I head coaches.

During that talk at the BCA convention I told them how important it was to become involved in all aspects of coaching. "Don't let any coach label you as just a recruiter," I said. I went on to say how Gary Brokaw had scouted nine of our games every year.

I referred to five areas of emphasis to the group:

1. Put in the game plan from your scouting report.

2. Teach each phase of the game, as I did with Brokaw, who handled the guards.

3. Recruit.

4. Learn the administrative end of the game, including office management and developing a budget.

5. Deal with the media.

Thompson came to me after that presentation and said he had a lot of respect for me because I backed up what I believed in with action.

John Thompson won a national championship, coached first-round draft choices and put Georgetown basketball on the map. But, the most important thing he did for the game was wake up our sport to the excellent African American coaches in this country.

BILL WALTON

I coached against 77 players who eventually made first- or second-team consensus All-American during my Notre Dame coaching career and 10 players who were named National Player of the Year by at least one service.

One of the best players we faced was Bill Walton. He was the national player of the year all three years he played on the varsity and we faced him six times, winning once.

He was a dominant player with quick moves towards the basket, a great defender, possessed an unblockable shot, and one of the best passing centers I have ever seen. His abilities as a rebounder have been well documented, and he averaged 15.7 rebounds a game over his 90-game career at UCLA. Eighty-six of those games ended in UCLA victories. His outlet passes were among the best in basketball history, leading to UCLA's fast break.

We had a great rivalry with UCLA, and Bill had a lot to do with it. I get a kick out of his interviews concerning the 1974 game that ended the 88-game streak. In one of those *ESPN Sports Century* features he is quoted as saying, "Digger Phelps ruined my life on January 19, 1974."

In a feature in a Fort Wayne, Indiana, paper commemorating the 25-year anniversary of that 1974 game Walton said, "Every time I tried to discipline my kids when they were growing up, they would look back at me and say, 'Fine, I'm going to Notre Dame.'"

With all due respect to Bill Walton and the other nine National Players of the Year we faced in my Notre Dame career, Maryland's Len Bias (above, defended above by Tim Kempton) was the best opposing player we faced.

So you can see it is an easy choice for my selection as the best player we faced during my 20 years at Notre Dame. Wrong! When I am asked that question my answer is Len Bias of Maryland (1982–86), who is not one of the 10 National Players of the Year we faced.

I pick Bias because of his ability to score everywhere and create his own shot. Pound for pound, he had the most talent of any basketball player I coached against. He could score from anywhere on the court, defend, rebound, he could do it all.

We played Maryland all four years he was at Maryland and every time I watched the film when we were preparing to play them I was in awe at what he could do in so many facets of the game. We split the four games with Maryland during his career, but he was terrific. His senior year we won at South Bend, but he made 9–12 shots from the field and scored 25. He could score 25, and you would come away from the game feeling he was too unselfish.

If he had not died as the result of a cocaine problem, the course of professional basketball would have been drastically different. Larry Bird knew Bias was the link to keep the Celtics dynasty going. The Celtics haven't won a world championship since Bias's passing.

Sorry Bill, you were a great one, as were Scott May, Ralph Sampson, Mark Aguirre, and Butch Lee. But, my vote goes to Len Bias.

JOHN WOODEN

We defeated John Wooden each of his last two trips to South Bend, 1974 and 1975. The 1974 team was the better of the two with Walton and Keith Wilkes, but the 1975 team went on to win the National Championship.

Before we played UCLA in 1974, Wooden had a book published that was entitled, *They Call Me Coach*. There was another book about the UCLA program entitled, *The Real UCLA Story*. I read both books and they helped me during each victory. It was similar to the scene in the movie *Patton*, where Patton beats Rommel in World War II and yells to him, "I read your book, you dumb S.O.B."

In those books it was revealed that Wooden hated to call timeouts because it was a sign of weakness. He also didn't like to see his defense commit fouls. He thought putting a team in the bonus in the second half was giving away points.

In the 1974 game when we made that run in the last 3:22 of the game, he never called timeout until after Dwight Clay's jumper, so we just kept the pressure up and the momentum continued. You could see Walton look to the bench after we cut it to three, then motion to Wooden for a timeout after we cut it to one. Then, Walton just called one on his own (I think) after we took the lead on Dwight Clay's shot.

In the game at South Bend in 1975, which we won 84–78, we had the ball with four minutes left and were up by two points. I called for a four corners offense with Ray Martin doing the majority of the ballhandling. There was no shot clock then, so he just dribbled the time away out at halfcourt. They just weren't used to this situation.

The clock went under three minutes, then under two before Wooden saw what I was doing. With only two team fouls, they couldn't put us in the bonus. Finally, when it was too late, they started fouling in bunches because they could see we were just going to run out the clock. They kept fouling Billy Paterno, who was outstanding from the line. We won by six, 84–78, one of only three losses UCLA had that year.

DICK VITALE

My broadcasting colleague, Dick Vitale, was a finalist for the Basketball Hall of Fame in 2004. How he didn't get selected is beyond me. No one has done more for college basketball in the last 25 years than Dick Vitale. You can make the argument that he has had a positive impact and enhanced interest in the game at every university in this country. No one goes out of his way for the good of the game more than Dick. He made ESPN college basketball, and the sport as a whole, what it is today and continues to do so.

When you travel with Dick, it is like being around a rock star. He always takes the time to answer questions, sign autographs, anything he can do to help people. In December of 2003 my mother passed away. He must have called me four times that week to check on me, and then sent flowers and even made a donation to the Moyer Foundation in her honor.

He will be in the Hall of Fame, hopefully in 2005, and certainly within the shelf life of this book. So, even though I never coached against Dick, I am including him in this chapter. (Hey, it's my book, I can do whatever I want).

We were signing books at the Notre Dame Bookstore a few years back. I was signing the first edition of *Basketball for Dummies*, and Dick was signing whatever book he had written with Dick Weiss that year.

Dick is very popular at Notre Dame. His two daughters graduated from Notre Dame and they both married Notre Dame graduates. He gave a big contribution to the university one year and they made him an honorary alumnus. I told him if he gave $1 million they would let him give the commencement address.

This day at the bookstore, a gentleman came up to Vitale and said, "I will always cherish that game in 1974 when you upset UCLA. You did a magnificent job of coaching that day."

Dick decided to play along with the man and said, "You mean how I outcoached John Wooden, the Wizard of Westwood? I tell Dick Vitale that story all the time. I was phenomenal that day wasn't I?"

So the guy left for a couple of minutes to get his wife. He came back to Dick to pose for a picture and said, "Look honey, let's have our picture made with the coach who stopped UCLA's 88-game winning streak."

Dick was now in hysterics, but still carried on with this guy. He posed for the pictures, then grabbed the guy and said, "Sir, would you mind telling that story to this gentleman over there (me). So, not knowing who I was, he proceeded to relay the story of the game to me.

Finally we told him the truth. Vitale told him, "You had the wrong Dick."

Dick can get so wound up sometimes he doesn't even know what he is saying. This was the case during the 2004 NCAA Tournament. We had just finished our three-hour selection show on Sunday night and we were taping little segments for *SportsCenter* and ESPNEWS. Dick wanted to conclude the segment by talking about Pittsburgh, who was a physical, aggressive team.

Dick concluded his dissertation on the Panthers meaning to say, "When you play Pittsburgh you better come with your helmets and hard hats on." But, he transposed some important words and his eventual statement sent us into hysterics. (See photo in color insert.) We all lost it, even the camera guys, stage managers and the production people upstairs. It took 10 minutes before we could get our composure.

That tape never got any airtime, and it probably won't make a bloopers special either.

FUTURE HALL OF FAME COACHES

The following coaches have made their mark throughout many years in college basketball. These five, in my mind, deserve to be in the Basketball Hall of Fame.

• JIM CALHOUN, Connecticut: With the exception of Coach K at Duke, no college coach has had more success in the NCAA Tournament. He's won two national championships.

• JIM BOEHEIM, Syracuse: His record over two decades speaks for itself, including the 2003 national championship.

• TUBBY SMITH, Kentucky: History was made when an all-white Kentucky team lost to an all-black Texas Western team for the national championship in 1966. Today they've won a national championship with an African-American coach and players.

• GARY WILLIAMS, Maryland: To take a program on NCAA probation to a national championship, as well as his consistency each year in college basketball, he too belongs in the Hall of Fame.

• EDDIE SUTTON, Oklahoma State: Not just his record, but the way he has taught defense each year to new players and teams gives him instant credibility as a coach.

• ROY WILLIAMS, North Carolina: What he did at Kansas, and what he will do at North Carolina, will get him elected to the Hall of Fame.

Chapter Nine

ASSISTANT COACHES

JIM BARON, 1981-87

Jim Baron first caught my attention as a counselor at our summer camps at Notre Dame. He had been a very good player at St. Bonaventure. In fact, he won the NIT championship game against Houston in 1977 with two late free throws. He was a strong, hard-nosed guard who has been very successful as a head coach. He coaches the same way he played, and it has been a successful formula because he has taken St. Francis and St. Bonaventure to the NCAA Tournament, and I am sure he will do the same at Rhode Island very soon.

He became a member of my staff in 1980-81 as a part-time coach and stayed for six years overall. He was on the sidelines with me for 118 wins in six years (1981-87), more wins than any of my 13 assistant coaches at Notre Dame.

I was one of the first coaches to have meetings with my assistants away from the bench at the beginning of timeouts. I got the idea because we had so many games on television and those TV timeouts were sometimes over two minutes. It was a waste of time to talk with the players for two minutes, they just weren't going to retain more than a few seconds of strategy anyway. I used the first minute to talk strategy with my assistants. I then went to the team for the last 30 seconds and gave them our offense and defense, the timeout situation and other pertinent information just before they went back on the floor.

Ninety percent of the time these meetings were worthwhile. But in one game during the 1985-86 season, we had a huge lead late in

My 1981-82 staff included (from left) Pete Gillen, Gary Brokaw, John Shumate and Jim Baron. All four assistants later became Division I head coaches.

the second half of a game at Notre Dame, and there just wasn't that much to say.

Just after the game had started, a young lady in a black leather mini-skirt took her seat behind the press table opposite our bench. She was striking. It was one of those situations where you knew everyone on the staff noticed her, but you wanted to at least give the impression you were so into the game that you didn't say anything.

During this timeout late in the game, I took out my clipboard and pen and gave the impression, at least to the fans, I was going to diagram a play. While I was looking down at the clipboard, I said, "OK, where is she?" Immediately, Gary Brokaw said, "Section 10." Jim Baron added, "Row six." Matt Kilcullen said, "Seat 4." We all broke up.

GARY BROKAW
Player, 1972-74 • Coach, 1980-86

The 1973-74 team had 18 players on its roster including walk-ons and everyone had a nickname. There was John "The Big Shu" Shumate, Adrian "A.D." Dantley, Gary "Goose" Novak, and Billy "The Apple" Paterno. Even the walk-ons had nicknames: Ken "Geek" Wolbeck, Tom "TV" Varga and of course "Hawk" Stevens. Everyone called him "Hawk." I bet a lot of the ND grads from the 1970s don't remember his real first name (Chris).

But the most appropriate nickname in my book was Gary "Magic" Brokaw. He was Magic Johnson before Magic Johnson. He was 6-3, 180 pounds, could jump out of the gym, could go right or left, and could create his own shot anytime he wanted. He was unselfish, too. He could give us 25 points one night and seven assists the next. In our victory over UCLA in 1974, he scored 25 points in that head-to-head match-up with Keith Wilkes.

Gary had as much natural ability as any player I ever coached, and the pros agreed with me... unfortunately. Gary turned pro a year early and was the No. 14 pick of the entire NBA draft by the Milwaukee Bucks. He played that 1974-75 season with Kareem Abdul Jabbar. He thought he was going to get an NBA Championship ring in his rookie year, but they lost in the conference finals. Gary played four years in the NBA, averaging about eight points a game. When he retired in the late 1970s he came back to Notre Dame to finish his degree.

Coming back to finish his degree impressed me, and I thought he might make a good coach. What better example of a successful former Notre Dame student-athlete. Shortly after he earned his degree I hired him as an assistant coach. He worked for me for six years from 1980-86, and we won 117 games together, second among all my assistants in victories.

So, while Gary left me as a player a year early, he did return to coach by my side for six years, tied for the longest tenure of all my assistants.

After the 1985-86 season he became the head coach at Iona. He stayed there for five years, then returned to the NBA as a player personel director for the Orlando Magic. He is now an assistant coach with the Charlotte Bobcats, the expansion team that will begin play in 2004.

Dick DiBiaso, 1971-75

Dick DiBiaso was the JV coach at Beacon High School in Beacon, NY, my old high school. He worked under Tom Winterbottom, who had asked me to coach in the Beacon Summer League in 1963, my first job in coaching. We met through Tom and became good friends. When I was the head coach at St. Gabriel's in Pennsylvania, he was the head coach at Beacon. He and my dad drove to one of my state tournament games and that meant a lot to me.

During our friendship, we told each other that whoever got a college head-coaching job first would hire the other one as an assistant. When I got the job at Fordham, Dick was an assistant at Virginia under Bill Gibson, who coached Dick when he was a player at Mansfield State. He didn't want to leave Bill that soon, so he didn't come to Fordham when I got that job in 1970-71. But when I went to Notre Dame, he was hired the same day.

Dick was one of the most organized people I ever met, and I learned a lot from him about setting up an office. He taught my secretary, Dottie Van Paris, the system, and we used that system of office management for my 20 years at Notre Dame.

Dick was also the best coach I had when it came to teaching the fundamentals of the game to big men. He took films of Shumate and broke down his post moves into drills. He knew how to teach a big man to get open better than anyone.

Dick left Notre Dame in 1975 to become the head coach at Stanford. He worked in real estate in California for many years and is now retired. He came back for our 30-year reunion of the 1974 team. He has a little more gray hair today, but don't we all?

Pete Gillen, 1980-85

One of the top players on my 1970-71 Fordham team was Kenny Charles, a sophomore guard who averaged in double figures. Pete Gillen was the freshman coach at Brooklyn Prep when Kenny was a senior. Pete knew talent.

When I needed to hire an assistant in 1980-81, Pete was the guy. He was at Villanova prior to coming to Notre Dame, and had coached against us under Rollie Massimino. He was on the visiting bench the night Tracy Jackson hit a 30-foot shot at the buzzer that gave us a one-point win. Gillen recruited the best player I ever coached, David Rivers. Pete was a New York guy from Brooklyn and he had a strong relationship with Bob Hurley, David's coach.

Pete left Notre Dame in 1986-87 to become the head coach at Xavier, and he took that program to seven NCAA Tournaments in nine years. Then he took Providence to the Elite Eight in 1996-97. Now he is the head coach at Virginia where he has had five postseason tournament teams in six years.

Pete and I have a lot in common from a detail standpoint. He learned about the importance of paying attention to details after his first scouting trip for me in December of 1980. When he returned from his trip we had a staff meeting, and I asked him three simple questions.

"What brand of game ball did they use? Was it Wilson, McGregor or Spaulding?" He didn't have an answer. "Were the nets tight and how tight were the rims?" Again, he didn't have an answer. "Where did their band sit, behind our bench or opposite?" Now he started to turn white.

All those details were important to me. Different brands of balls had different seams, which made a difference when it came to ball handling and shooting. When we were going on the road we practiced with the ball we were going to use in their gym. Tight rims meant long rebounds and if the nets were tight that meant a home team could use that to their advantage if they liked to press. UCLA always had new tight nets in Pauley Pavilion so it would give them extra time to set up their press. The position of the band was also important for communication during a game.

Pete didn't have any of the answers that first trip, but he did the rest of his career and he still takes note of those details today.

Pete is a basketball guy through and through. He thinks hoops 24 hours a day. He met his wife, Ginnie, at the wedding of a former Fairfield teammate. When they met, he was at a table at the reception drawing basketball diagrams on a napkin.

DICK KUCHEN, 1975-78

Dick Kuchen was on the Rider team that ended NYU's 23-year home winning streak when I was a graduate assistant at Rider, so our relationship was long term even before I hired him in 1975. Dick was the best coach I had at teaching the motion offense. We had him put that offense in and it had a great deal to do with our run to the Final Four in 1978.

In the 1970s and early 1980s we had eight frontcourt players make it in the NBA. Our reputation with big men in the NBA was similar to Penn State's reputation with linebackers in the NFL. Dick Kuchen had a lot to do with that. He developed Dave Batton, Bruce Flowers, Bill Laimbeer, Orlando Woolridge, Kelly Tripucka... I could go on and on.

Our trip to the Final Four earned Dick a lot of notoriety. . .and he left after that season to become the head coach at California. He later coached at Yale and we faced each other late in my career. I had to coach against my former assistants twice (Shumate at SMU was the other). I won both games, but I hated the experience. You have feelings for those guys, because you had been in the war room with them. I never intentionally scheduled a game against a former assistant coach.

We had just lost at Washington in double overtime, 63-61, in January of 1984. I was talking to Dick Kuchen, who was by now the head coach at California and he warned me that the student section at Oregon, our next opponent, sat over the visiting locker room and they were there an hour before the game. They were relentless, stomping their feet, making noise, trying to psych out the opposing team. McCarthur Court is still considered one of the nation's toughest road venues.

He told me, "You can't even hear each other in the locker room. They can really get in your team's head if you aren't used to it." So I told Skip Meyer, our trainer my last 10 years and still Notre Dame's trainer today, that we would tape at the hotel and arrive at the gym at 7:30 p.m. for the 8:00 p.m. game. We walked into the gym, went straight to the bench and just put our warmups on the bench. We never went into our locker room.

The fans had been there screaming and yelling, thinking we were below them. Then we walked in wearing our warmups and holding our belongings in hand. They realized we hadn't been in the locker room...and we weren't going to the locker room. They calmed down because they knew we were way ahead of them in the head game. We got ahead of them early and won the game, 68-54.

MATT KILCULLEN, 1988-91

Matt Kilcullen was one of my assistants in the 1980s, and like me, he was born and raised in the New York area. Single most of his career as an assistant, he is now married with a family. He has gone on to be the head coach at Jacksonville, Western Kentucky and North Florida.

Matty was one of the best assistants I ever had when it came to scouting an opponent. We won twice at Syracuse in the 1980s over top-10 Jim Boeheim-coached teams, and he scouted both of those games.

In the 1980s, he lived the social life of an active bachelor. Whenever we played in Madison Square Garden, he had to get up to 40 tickets for his high school buddies. We were playing Manhattan in The Garden in 1986 and we were cheered on by countless Notre Dame Subway Alums and Matt's 40 high school friends, who were seated together in the upper deck.

We had a strong team that year with David Rivers and Ken Barlow leading the way. Manhattan was no match for us, and we had a 50-point lead with 10 minutes left, so many of the Garden fans left early. That gave the Kilcullen Clan time to move down from their perch to open seats behind our bench.

In the game's final minute, Matt's group started yelling for me to call a timeout. I thought they must be crazy. As it turned out, there was an injury that stopped the clock. As we met as a staff just off the team bench, Matt's group went into a prepared chorus to the tune of "Camptown Races":

"Matty should be head coach, do da, do da,
Matty should be head coach, all the do da day,
Even though he's gay, even though he's gay,

Matt should be head coach, all the do da day.

When someone asks Matty about his most embarrassing moment in sports, he can give a quick reply.

FRAN MCCAFFREY, 1988-91

Fran McCaffrey was on the staff of my last three teams at Notre Dame. He was also retained by John MacLeod so he coached at Notre Dame for 11 years, the longest tenure of any Notre Dame basketball assistant coach in history.

Fran was from Philly and he started his playing career at Wake Forest before transferring to Penn. Penn won two Ivy League championships during his playing career. He got his undergrad degree from Penn's Wharton School of business and later got a master's from Lehigh.

Fran was the only assistant coach I hired with previous head coaching experience. He became the head coach at Lehigh in 1985 at the age of 26. That year he was the youngest Division I head coach in the country. In his third year he led Lehigh to an NCAA Tournament berth and 21 wins. That certainly caught my eye.

In 1999 he left Notre Dame when Matt Doherty replaced John MacLeod. He is now the head coach at UNC Greensboro.

THE MCLAUGHLIN BROTHERS
Frank McLaughlin, 1971-77
Tom McLaughlin, 1978-81

The McLaughlin brothers both worked under me in the 1970s, but they never were on the same staff. Between 1971 and 81, I had a McLaughlin on my staff every year, and we won 183 games in those nine years, an average of over 20 per year, and went to seven NCAA Tournaments, including six trips to the Sweet 16.

Frank was an assistant at Holy Cross when I took the Fordham job in 1970. A 1969 Fordham grad, he grew up in New York. Frank's senior year there were two unanimous All-City players in New York,

Frank and Lew Alcindor. I thought he would be a perfect fit as an assistant at Fordham.

He was instrumental to my success at Fordham because he knew the school as well as anyone. Without him we never would have gone 26-3. It was Frank, my only assistant that year, who suggested that we go to a four-guard offense after the Holy Cross game. He was a big reason we beat Julius Erving and UMass that year. If we didn't have that level of success at Fordham, I wouldn't have gotten the Notre Dame job.

It took a little bit of convincing because I was asking him to leave his alma mater, but Frank joined me at Notre Dame. He became one of the best recruiters Notre Dame has ever had.

In 1977, he went back east and became the head coach at Harvard. We went to the Final Four the next year, and he came to the games, but he should have been on the bench with us. He had such a positive effect on that team.

One of the first persons he hired as an assistant coach at Harvard was Ray Martin, who he had recruited to Notre Dame. Frank is now the athletic director at Fordham.

I had known Tom McLaughlin through Frank, obviously. Tom had been a solid player at Tennessee. With three straight seasons of at least 22 wins during his time at Notre Dame, it didn't take him long to become a head coach. He became the head coach at UMass in 1981-82, so for two years Frank coached at Harvard, and Tom was at UMass.

DANNY NEE, 1976-80

Danny Nee was an assistant on my staffs between 1976-80. We won at least 22 games and reached at least the Sweet 16 all four years, including the 1978 Final Four season. He has been the head coach at Ohio University, Nebraska, and now Duquesne.

We played the Russian National team at Notre Dame in the 1970s, and it was Danny Nee's first game to scout. He worked as the part-time coach at the time, making the incredible sum of $3,000 a year.

Danny had scouted the Russians at Colorado, but his report had some gaps. He couldn't pronounce the names and didn't give us a very complete report.

The Russians scored the first eight points of the game, boom, boom, boom. They were quite a good team with Sergei Belov as the leader, and we didn't have a clue as to how to defend them. I was irate and got so mad. "You are bad luck, get off the bench," I said to Danny.

So Danny went to the end of the bench, like he was a kid sent to the corner of the room for detention. We called a timeout to stop the bleeding and Danny stayed out of the huddle at first. He must have been scared of me. But he was the only coach who knew anything about these guys, so I called him back to the huddle. We came back and won the game.

The next week, Nee was kidding with assistant football coach George Kelly about me banishing him from the bench. Kelly came up with the idea of using headsets. "Why not have a coach at the top of the Joyce Center watching the action, just like we do in football," said Kelly. So, the rest of the year for home games, Nee was in the old press box at the top of the ACC. He had a headset connected to a manager and when he saw some type of offense or defense he thought would work, he would make the call to the manager, who would then relay it to the staff.

We were the first team to have a coach at the top of the coliseum.

•••

Danny was a Brooklyn native who played at Power Memorial with Kareem Abdul Jabbar (then Lew Alcindor). He went to Marquette to play for Al McGuire in 1965, then joined the U.S. Marine Corps. His military career included a tour of Vietnam, where he won the Combat Air Crew Insignia and Air Medal. He returned to the United States and earned his degree from St. Mary of the Plains College in Dodge City, Kansas.

The effects of war on an individual's psyche are immense and Danny showed this to me when we played at West Virginia in 1979. The Mountaineers always got excited when they played Notre Dame, and our presence always meant they had a sellout. Before the game the Mountaineer mascot used to shoot off his rifle at a certain point during their pregame introductions.

I was used to it, but it can be shocking when you haven't seen it before. Right on cue the Mountaineer Mascot shot the rifle. I looked at our bench and Danny was under the chairs, face down. When the Mountaineer shot that gun, it was still a natural reaction from his Vietnam experience to take cover.

JEFF NIX, 1987-91

Jeff Nix, along with Dick Dibiaso, was one of the most organized coaches I had at Notre Dame. He was outstanding when it came to scouting, and he took that ability to the NBA with the New York Knicks for many years after he left Notre Dame.

Jeff was an assistant at Loyola of Maryland under Dave Magarity. We played Loyola one year and were lucky to beat them. Jeff had scouted the game and put a great effort into the preparation. After the game he was sitting there on the bench. I knew he was thinking about what else he could have done to win that game. That impressed me.

"Nixer" came to us in 1987 after two years at Xavier working for Pete Gillen on two NCAA Tournament staffs. Jeff also spent a lot of summers at our camps. The camps are the best recruiting grounds for future assistants, because you have time to spend with the young men and see what they are made of.

Jeff is now the assistant general manager of the New York Knicks. He deserves to be an NBA general manager someday.

JOHN SHUMATE
Player, 1972-74 • Coach, 1981-83, 1986-88

When I was in my last year as an assistant coach at Pennsylvania, one of the players I coveted was John Shumate. He was a strong, 6-8, 230-pound center from Elizabeth City, New Jersey and the son of a minister. Also recruiting him that year was Frank McLaughlin, then an assistant at Holy Cross, and Dick DiBiaso, then an assistant at Virginia. All three of us would coach Shumate at Notre Dame.

Shumate was going to be the star of my first Notre Dame team in 1971-72. He had averaged 22 points and 13 rebounds for the Notre Dame freshman team during my year at Fordham. But, in September of 1971, Shumate developed a blood clot in his left leg. He was hospitalized, and it became a life-threatening situation because he developed an infection around his heart. He was in the hospital for a long period of time and lost 45 pounds. "I was afraid to go to sleep some nights because I didn't know if I was going to wake up the next morning," he told me during that ordeal.

Shumate shared a room with a heart attack victim in the South Bend St. Joseph's Hospital, and the two of them used to encourage each other about surviving. When they both came out of it, Shumate discovered that his roommate was white. Shumate had grown up in the projects in New Jersey so it was a life-changing experience for more reasons than one.

"It had nothing to do with race, color or religion, but a will to live," Shu said. "We got each other through a life-and-death situation."

Shumate recovered from his ordeal, but it wasn't easy. John Markovich, the trainer my first two years, and Dr. Howard Engel did a grerat job in helping Shumate on a daily basis. For a long period of time he basically had to drag his left leg when he walked. He really had to learn how to walk again, then run, then learn to shoot and play defense. He played the 1972-73 and 1973-74 seasons for me at Notre Dame. He still had a year of eligibility remaining for 1974-75, but he had enough credits to graduate so he turned professional. Gary Brokaw also turned pro with a year remaining for the 1974-75 season. I often wonder if we could have won it all if those two players had returned for that season to join sophomore Adrian Dantley.

Shumate was my top center in 20 years at Notre Dame. He is still Notre Dame's leader in career field goal percentage. He was the MVP of the 1973 NIT, quite an accomplishment considering we didn't win the championship. He was 38-51 from the field in that tournament and scored 95 points. At one point he made 20 consecutive field goals in victories at Madison Square Garden against Louisville and North Carolina, still a Notre Dame record. His senior year he averaged 24 points, 11 rebounds and shot 63 percent from the field.

Shu was the No. 4 selection of the NBA draft by the Phoenix Suns. Shortly after Shumate began summer practice with the Suns, he developed chest pains. After playing two complete seasons at Notre Dame, the blood clots were back, this time in his left lung.

John missed the 1974-75 NBA season, what was supposed to be his rookie season in the NBA. But he returned for 1975-76 and made the All-Rookie team. The following year he was traded to the Buffalo Braves and averaged a career-best 15 points and 9.5 rebounds. He played seven years in the NBA, but missed two and a half due to the blood clot problems.

When John Shumate was a player for me from 1972-74, he always seemed to get hurt at the end of practice. He was like Redd Foxx on Sanford and Son. Remember when Redd would say, "Elizabeth, I think this is the big one"? That was Shumate near the end of practice. He would make a late dive into the fifth row for a loose ball, then lie in pain calling for our trainer, Arno Zoske.

One day when he was an assistant I decided to play a joke on him. During a break in practice I called over the players and told them I was going to have Shumate supervise sprints at the end of practice. I told them to goof off during the sprints, just jog, faint, pull up with a sprained ankle, anything to get out of doing sprints.

So practice ended, and I told Shu to run the players. I went up the tunnel out of sight. So the players did what I said, some of them even ran backwards. Shumate was furious and found me in the tunnel. Fearing a huge discipline problem and feeling a lack of respect, Shumate said, "Coach, they won't run the sprints." I said to him, "Well, they must have learned from the master."

Shumate was one of the best recruiters I ever had, even as a player. He recruited Adrian Dantley. Dantley was only going to stay for 24 hours on his official visit, but he had such a good time with Shumate that he stayed the extra day.

As an assistant, he recruited many of our top players, including LaPhonso Ellis. I was heartbroken when Shumate left to take the head coaching position at SMU in 1988-89. I understood it because it was the right professional move for Shumate, but Phonz could have benefited greatly from being coached by Shumate. Shumate won the Southwest Conference regular-season championship at SMU in 1993, and took the Mustangs to the NCAA Tournament.

John Shumate scored 24 points in the win over UCLA in my first win over a No. 1-ranked team, then served as an assistant coach when we beat North Carolina in 1987, the seventh and final win over No. 1.

When I left Notre Dame in 1991, I wanted John to succeed me. He was interviewed, but John and I both felt it was a token interview. John didn't return to campus again until our reunion in January, 2004. He was bitter over the interview process, but I convinced him that he needed to experience that UCLA game again. He received the loudest ovation of all of us. The crowd still called him, "Shu."

Of all my former players, I think Shumate was the one who appreciated the spirit and traditions of Notre Dame the most. You could see that during his speech at our luncheon last January. That's why it hurt him and me so much when he was not hired as my replacement.

SCOTT THOMPSON, 1977-80

Outside of Shumate and Brokaw, Scott Thompson was the best player that served as one of my assistant coaches. He played at Iowa from 1972-76 and was an All-Big Ten guard who averaged over 19 points per game. He was also Academic All-Big Ten, so he was a good role model for our players in the three years he coached at Notre Dame.

He was significantly involved in Fellowship of Christian Athletes and played for Athletes in Action his first year out of college. In 1976-77 when we beat San Francisco to end their 29-game winning streak, their only loss prior to that game was an exhibition game against Athletes in Action, a game Scott played in.

Scottie coached in 89 games with me, and we won 69. He took a job with Lute Olson at Iowa when he left Notre Dame, and later became the head coach at the Division I level at Rice, Wichita State and Cornell.

Scott developed colon cancer his last year at Cornell and he had to give up the profession because of the stress brought on by coaching and recruiting. He now works in athletic administration at Cornell.

Chapter Ten

DOMERS

MIKE DECICCO

Mike DeCicco was the "Godfather" of the Notre Dame Athletic Department, especially when it came to academics. He doubled as the fencing coach and the academic advisor for all athletes. He coached the fencing team to five national championships in his 34 years as head coach. It is amazing to see how the academic advising department has grown since the 1970s.

I am proud that all 56 of the basketball athletes who played four years for me at Notre Dame (I never took transfers) earned their degrees. Mike DeCicco had a lot to do with that because everyone respected him...or feared him. Whatever the reason, he was a tremendous asset to our program.

When I came in the locker room before practice and said, "DeCicco needs to see one of you," everyone stood still. I would pause for about a minute while the players squirmed, then I would call out the name or names. It didn't matter who it was, Kelly Tripucka—an Academic All-American as a sophomore—or LaPhonso Ellis—who was on probation twice, but got his degree in business on time with his class—the player went with Mike.

Sometimes he would show up on the court in the middle of practice and I would just say, "Mike, who do you need?" He would call out the player and he would be gone for the rest of practice. I was very serious about academics. If a player violated the cut policy of a class, he sat on the bench in street clothes.

December of his senior year Ken Barlow, my starting center from 1982-86, missed a class, so I suspended him the next game against Oregon. I never announced academic suspensions prior to a game. I had the player dress, but sit on the bench without entering the game. Of course, during the game the students started to yell for Barlow. Finally, in the second half, I called his name. He thought he was going into the game. I said, "Kenny, why don't you go up to the student section and find out what they want?" I didn't want players cutting class during the season.

After the game the media was dying to ask why Barlow didn't play. Joe Tybor of the *Chicago Tribune* finally asked the question and I simply said, "He cut a class last Thursday. Next question."

Today, coaches ask me how I graduated 100 percent of my players. The overall academic environment at Notre Dame was positive because the students were very goal oriented. But, we were also successful because I was serious about holding the line, even to the point of players missing games.

And I had a great academic advisor in Mike DeCicco.

JIM GIBBONS

No one wore more hats at Notre Dame during my tenure than Jim Gibbons. He played basketball and baseball at Notre Dame from 1950-53 and later served as an assistant coach in both sports from 1956-62. He recruited a lot of outstanding basketball players, but his most famous recruit was a baseball player named Carl Yastrzemski.

Gib recruited Yaz from Massachusetts in 1957 and he played on the Notre Dame freshman team in 1958. In those days there was no major league draft, so a baseball player could sign at any time, and Yaz did so after his freshman year. They kept in touch his entire career with the Red Sox, and when Yaz retired in 1983, Gib was at Fenway Park for the ceremony, and presented him a Notre Dame monogram blanket.

Gib and Roger Valdiserri were very close friends and when Notre Dame was looking for a replacement for Johnny Dee, Roger asked Gib to go to the Fordham-Marquette game in Madison Square Garden to see what he thought of me as a possible successor.

Gib was the Director of Special Projects at Notre Dame at the time he came to New York for that Marquette game, a position he held for nearly 30 years. He came back from that game and seconded Roger's nomination to Father Joyce.

Again, Gib wore many hats at Notre Dame. When President Gerald Ford spoke at the Joyce Center on St. Patrick's Day in 1976, he organized the entire event. He impressed the president's people so much that they offered him a job in the White House. He was the most congenial man I ever met. In the 1980s he worked on many of our games as a color analyst with Hall of Fame broadcaster Harry Kalas.

Roger, Gib and I had a lot of lunches together over my 20 years as Notre Dame's head coach. There were many decisions made that affected the course of Notre Dame athletic history made at Bill Knapp's Restaurant on US 31 in South Bend.

ANN HART

There is a tradition of outstanding student managers at Notre Dame. The system goes back to the Rockne era. Over 100 students would volunteer as freshmen to handle varied tasks, such as painting the gold helmets the Friday evening before a home game. Over the course of four years the number of managers is pared down, and about 15 seniors survived to run the varsity sports. Football got three head managers, and I got one, until the 1980s, when I got two.

Every Thanksgiving the outgoing senior managers would meet to rank the juniors to determine who would be head managers for the varsity sports the next year. Prior to that meeting before my final season (1990-91), I went to the seniors and told them I wanted a woman for my head manager for the next season. "This is too much of an old boys club," I told them. "We have been coed since 1972, and I have never had a female head manager. It's time that changed."

They listened to me and the following fall Ann Hart reported for duty. As head manager she was in charge of everything outside of Gate 6 at the ACC. Bob Schiewe, the other senior manager that year, was in charge of everything pertaining to practice. Ann's major task was to coordinate all the team travel, something assistant athletic directors do at most schools today.

Ann did an outstanding job in every task she faced. She was organized, efficient and knew the game. The transportation was always there, the hotel was set up and there were never any problems. Most of all, she had the respect of the coaches and the players.

We kept in touch after she graduated. One day she sent me a letter and told me she was having troubles with her knees. Tests revealed she had some form of cancer. But, after many treatments, it went into remission.

In the fall of 2003, I got a call through Notre Dame's sports information office that one of my former managers had passed away. I thought it was one of the men I had serve as head manager my first or second year. No one knew who had passed away, but they gave me a phone number to call. The man on the other end of the line was Ann Hart's husband.

On the one hand, I could believe it because I was aware of her earlier cancer problems. But, on the other hand, here was a beautiful woman of 34 years old, my last manager, almost 30 years younger than me, who was now gone.

I went to the wake in Chicago and met her husband, her parents and the rest of her family. Ann's brother, now a screenwriter in Hollywood, recalled a game at Syracuse in 1990, the game Elmer Bennett hit the game-winning shot. Her brother was a student at Syracuse, but Ann had gotten him a ticket behind our bench. He showed up in an orange Syracuse shirt and I gave him hell before the game. "Don't make me get security to throw you out of here," I said, kiddingly.

I had a lot of great managers during my 20 years at Notre Dame, Ann Hart stood out because she broke down a barrier and created an opportunity for future coeds. Mike Brey had a female manager in 2004. Ann made a significant contribution to Notre Dame.

I never had a player die during my career at Notre Dame, and all of my former players are still alive today. But my last manager, the first female head manager in the history of Notre Dame athletics, was the first to pass away.

Father Theodore Hesburgh is a living saint. As university president, he inspired me when I was the head coach and for many years beyond. He's still an inspiration today.

FATHER THEODORE HESBURGH

The mystique of Notre Dame was developed in three phases. It started with the University's founder, Father Edward Sorin, who arrived in South Bend in 1842 at age 28 with $310 and a short credit line. When he arrived on what is now the campus, he saw farmland that was blanketed in snow—so much so that he didn't even know St. Joseph's Lake was there. But, at age 34, his spirit and determination to establish a Catholic institution of higher learning set the foundation for what Notre Dame is today.

The second phase centered around Knute Rockne. He was far ahead of his time when it came to coaching innovation, but he was also at the cutting edge from a marketing standpoint. He made Notre Dame a national institution, promoting it across the country. He started the image of Notre Dame overcoming great odds as the underdog when he was a player. He and Gus Dorais engineered the upset of Army in 1913 and he continued that tradition as a coach from 1918-30.

Of course, he became the winningest coach in the history of college football and won four national championships. Then his tragic passing at age 42 enhanced his legend. I've seen footage of the funeral and the newspaper accounts; it was a national tragedy.

The third phase is the Father Hesburgh era. He studied Father Sorin and his basic values and teachings, then continued those teachings as a young priest when he became the president of Notre Dame in 1952. Father Hesburgh built respect for Notre Dame from inside and outside the Notre Dame community.

He traveled the world to bring the university's values and the teachings of the Catholic church to an international audience. He served on the United States Civil Rights Commission from 1957-72, including three years as chairman. He was given the nation's highest civilian honor, the Medal of Freedom, in 1964 by President Lyndon Johnson for his work on behalf of civil rights. He worked for six United States presidents in his career as a public servant and has the world record for honorary degrees with 150.

While Hesburgh was devoted to his mission in the national and international arenas from a civil rights and world hunger standpoint, he never lost sight of his chief role as president of the University of Notre Dame, and the chief mission of the university. He enhanced the university's standing from a research and development standpoint, but I always felt maintaining the quality of the undergraduate education was of utmost importance.

I was obviously close to the daily activities of many undergraduate students at Notre Dame, whether it be my student-athletes or my daughters Karen and Jennifer (My son Rick graduated from Toledo where he was a member of the football team).

I felt the quality of the undergraduate educational experience at Notre Dame was second to none, and I sold that when I went into homes to recruit. That came directly from Hesburgh.

•••

To me, Father Hesburgh is a living saint. What Mother Teresa was as a nun, Father Hesburgh is as a priest. There is something about him. He has a power of inspiration that he is able to convey to people. He can inspire people to dream and go beyond their own perceived limits.

In 1996, I saw Father Hesburgh at a function at Notre Dame. We had talked a few years earlier, just after I left the White House where I had worked for President George Bush (1992-93). During that two-hour visit, we spoke about subjects that ranged from world hunger to civil rights to the future of college athletics.

At this function in 1996, he asked me, "So, what have you been doing?" I told him I had been working for ESPN. He looked at me and said, "No, what have you *really* been doing?"

I had heard the story of Jose Duarte, a member of the Notre Dame Class of 1948 who had studied under Hesburgh when he was a student. Duarte returned to El Salvador, where he was employed as an engineer. But his homeland was in a chaotic state in terms of the political climate. Hesburgh and Duarte remained close friends, and it was Hesburgh who inspired him to become the country's president and bring democracy to El Salvador. He served his country with remarkable courage until his death due to cancer in 1990.

Hesburgh had inspired people to do great things over his lifetime. And now, on a smaller level, he was doing the same with me. I recalled that visit with him when I returned from the White House. We had discussed the educational crisis in this country and we talked about what it would take to improve the secondary school system. I told him how the schools not only needed better teachers, but the basic physical environment needed time, work and money. I could see that in the schools in South Bend.

Our discussion sparked an idea to improve the infrastructure of the schools in South Bend. I thought if I could establish a blueprint for success in South Bend, other cities across the country could adopt it, and we would have an impact nationally.

I took some ideas from Jimmy Carter's Habitat for Humanity, which builds homes for the poor, and the Christmas in April project, which involved hundreds of Notre Dame students who fixed up neighborhoods in South Bend during the spring.

I spoke to a Rotary Club luncheon in South Bend in early 1997 and challenged them to fix up the local schools and expand the after-school programs. The after-school programs were just as important because most of the juvenile crimes are committed between 3 p.m. and 5 p.m. during the week.

I convinced the corporate sector to become involved. I got Sherwin Williams of Ohio to donate $20,000 worth of paint and brushes. I told local corporations in South Bend I was putting down $5,000 of my own money and challenged them to match it. We had an initial goal of $175,000, but reached $200,000 by the end of the project.

I got the media involved—the news and the sports side. I had met Anne Thompson, a Notre Dame grad at NBC news and she contacted the *Today Show* about the program. Jack Ford interviewed me on the morning of June 20, 1998.

That was quite a day. Over 700 volunteers showed up to revitalize Lincoln Grammar School in South Bend. When I saw those busloads of volunteers pull in, it gave me a great feeling. We accomplished a lot that day, and worked through the summer on the project. We also established after-school programs, and today 70 percent of those kids are involved in some type of after-school program.

There were a couple of articles in the local papers about the project and I sent them to Father Hesburgh and former president George Bush, with whom I am still close friends from my days working for him at the White House. I still value their correspondence, which I have retained.

Dear Digger,

Thanks ever so much for sending me that interesting information about Lincoln School and all that you are doing as a true "Point of Light." I am so glad that you are still involved in helping students—but who's surprised?

Warmest regards, old friend. I miss our visits from the past.

Sincerely,

George

Dear Digger,

I finally had a few free moments tonight to read all those wonderful arti-
cles you sent to me. I am very proud of what you are doing. I wish you all
success in this endeavor, which could turn around the disastrous situation in
most of our schools, especially in poor neighborhoods.

I hope it is helpful to know that both Father Ned and I are very proud
of what you are doing and cheering loudly from the sidelines. The communi-
ty needs leadership like this and you are really giving it. I know the effect
will be outstanding.

Keep up the good work.
Ever devotedly in Notre Dame
Rev. Theodore M. Hesburgh, C.S.C.
President Emeritus, University of Notre Dame

It was one of the most rewarding projects of my career. And,
Father Ted Hesburgh had inspired it all.

FATHER EDMUND JOYCE

Father Joyce was the executive vice president in control of the fac-
ulty board of athletics. That was an impressive title, and he was an
impressive person. He was the first person from the state of South
Carolina to attend Notre Dame, and he graduated in 1938.

Father Joyce was Father Hesburgh's top assistant for 35 years. He
ran the University when Father Ted was away solving the problems
of the world. The students used to say jokingly that the only difference between God and Father Hesburgh was that God was everywhere and Father Hesburgh was everywhere but Notre Dame.

Father Ned trusted me with basketball and I trusted him. That
was the prime reason for our success. I had a great working relationship with both Hesburgh and Joyce because I never had to worry
about someone stabbing me in the back. In Chapter One I described
the first time I met Father Joyce. It was during my interview with
him at the Detroit Airport when he told me that he expected the
players to graduate, he expected me to play by the NCAA rules, and
to win about 18 games a year.

I earned respect with him, especially when it came to scheduling and balancing the budget. I used to give back about $100,000 to $200,000 a year to business managers Bob Cahill and Joe O'Brien. That earned credibility with Father Joyce.

We also helped the athletic department's budget by playing special games. In 1978 the Notre Dame and Michigan football series was resurrected, so I thought it might be a good idea to do the same thing in basketball. I was a good friend of Johnny Orr, the Michigan coach at the time. That might surprise some, because I never could beat him.

We played in a golf tournament together in the spring of 1978, and we talked about playing a basketball game in the Pontiac Silver Dome. We thought we might be able to break the all-time college basketball attendance record, which at the time was the 52,693 that attended the UCLA vs. Houston game in the Astrodome in 1968.

We scheduled the game for the season finale of the 1978-79 season. We didn't break the record, but we drew over 37,000 people, and each school took home $108,000. The four schools that went to the Final Four that year took home just $116,000. When Father Joyce got that check from Moose, he asked, "Where did this check come from, Moose?" Moose said, "It came from Digger and that Michigan game."

We did something similar when we played LSU in the Super Dome in 1990. We drew 68,112 for that game, the all-time regular season NCAA record. Bob Knight and I also put together some doubleheaders in the Hoosier Dome with Kentucky and Louisville and all four teams took home over $380,000 each year.

•••

Father Joyce passed away while I was working on this book, on May 2, 2004, just two days past the 33-year anniversary day of our first meeting in Detroit in 1971. I went to the wake and the funeral, and there were people from all over the country and all walks of life in attendance.

Father Hesburgh, who met Father Joyce one hour after Joyce was ordained at Sacred Heart Church in 1949, gave the eulogy. "I have never known anyone in my life who was as wonderful a human being as Ned Joyce," said Hesburgh. "He was always there when I was missing and managed to fill in the gap, and probably did a better job than I could have done."

MOOSE KRAUSE

Moose Krause was Notre Dame's greatest all-around athlete of the 20th century. How can I make that statement? He is still the only Notre Dame athlete to earn All-America honors in football and basketball. He was one of Rockne's last football recruits, as a center, and he also starred as the center on the Notre Dame basketball team.

Moose is in the Basketball Hall of Fame as a player and was a three-time consensus All-American, just the second in NCAA history after Purdue's John Wooden. Moose went on to coach Notre Dame for six years in the 1940s and he won 98 games, including four wins over Adolph Rupp when he was at Kentucky.

•••

My favorite story about Moose took place when he was a player. It was his junior year and Notre Dame was playing at Butler on March 1, 1933. Moose had a great game and scored the winning basket at the buzzer to give Notre Dame a 42-41 victory in overtime. The team spent the night at a hotel in Indianapolis, and the next morning, Moose walked through the lobby where he met a young man selling the *Indianapolis Morning Star*. The young man approached Moose, and, giving his best sales pitch said, "*Morning Star?*" With a high level of self-esteem in light of his game-winning shot the previous night, Moose replied, "Morning son."

•••

Moose was the athletic director at Notre Dame from 1948-80. While football and basketball paid all the bills, Moose was very supportive of the other sports. You would see him at track meets, baseball games, hockey games. After we beat Texas in the Cotton Bowl to win the 1977 National Championship in football, he would go to hockey games and sit in an area above the floor at the corner of the ACC wearing his 10-gallon cowboy hat that he had bought in Texas. He was omnipresent at sporting events while he was the athletic director and after he retired.

Moose was very supportive, but at the same time he let you do your job. He certainly didn't micro-manage. Moose had graduated from Notre Dame Cum Laude with a degree in journalism, so he knew the importance of public relations. He was the all-time AD when it came to public relations. He used to sit in the press box at football games home and away, because he knew how important it was to have a relationship with the press. That is something that has always been a key to Notre Dame's success. It went back to Rockne.

Perhaps Moose's management style wouldn't work today. He had one top assistant AD, Colonel John Stephens, who was a Colonel in World War II in India. I used to kid him about his height, "You were a colonel in *our* army?" He was about 5-6 and Moose, was about 6-5 so they were quite a Mutt-and-Jeff combination. There is a picture of the two of them sitting on a bench outside Notre Dame Stadium in the Book, *Notre Dame Football Today*. It is a classic.

By the end of my career and long after Moose had retired, it seemed you needed to go through five assistant athletic directors and three university vice presidents to schedule a game or make some personnel decision. With Moose you just went into his office and you made a decision in five minutes.

Those were the good old days!

Ara Parseghian

I've already mentioned the letter I wrote to Ara Parseghian in 1965. Shortly after I became the head coach at Notre Dame, Ara came to my office and said he would do anything he could to help our program. That meant a lot to me, and I told him I would do anything I could to help him and his football program. My first year he let me borrow the Townsend brothers, Willie and Mike, both outstanding players who later helped Notre Dame to the 1973 National Championship.

There are a lot of basketball coaches at schools with major football programs who think a good football program takes away from their basketball program. Rick Barnes at Texas is one of the few coaches at major football schools who has seen the light and views the school's football program as a recruiting advantage. When he was the coach at Clemson he used to ride a golf cart before football games and interview Tiger fans on the school's radio network. That promoted his program during the off season and endeared him and his team to Clemson fans.

That was my approach, because I thought Notre Dame football would help market Notre Dame basketball. I saw what television had done for Notre Dame football, so I worked with Roger Valdiserri to put together the No. 1 national college basketball TV package in the 1970s. We were tied to NBC long before the football team's contract began in 1991.

I brought kids in on recruiting visits on the biggest football weekend of the year. Ara was a legend, and I used to make sure the recruits met him during the visit. Before the football game I would bring recruits to the sideline and let them get the flavor of the game, and see some of what being a Notre Dame student was like.

When we started winning, it worked in reverse. When we played UCLA in 1974 and ended their streak, Joe Montana and Ken MacAfee were in the stands on their official visits. Ara was using our basketball games to help in his football recruiting.

From January 21-28, 1974 we were both ranked No. 1 in the nation. It is one of just two times in Division I history that the same school was ranked No. 1 in both major sports at the same time.

I was always proud of my office, which sparked an idea for a practical joke by Ara Parseghian in 1973.

•••

Notre Dame opened the 1974 football season in a nationally televised Monday night game at Georgia Tech. I took a recruiting trip
to the Atlanta area that weekend so I could go to the game. During
the course of the weekend, I saw Ara and asked him if there were any
extra rooms at the hotel because I had not made a reservation yet.
He said he had an extra bed in his room, so I stayed with him.

After the game, which Notre Dame won 31-7, we went back to
Ara's hotel room to unwind. I turned on the TV set and one of the
stations was playing the movie *Blazing Saddles*, which I had seen in a
theatre, but Ara had never seen it.

So there we were laying down in our respective twin beds watching the movie. At one point, I said to Ara, "Wait until you see this
next scene, you won't believe what Alex Karras does to the horse."
Of course that was the scene where the former Detroit Lion All-Pro
punches the horse and knocks him out.

I have never seen Ara laugh like that. He fell out of bed he was
laughing so hard. It is funny how you remember some things from
your younger days of coaching. Watching *Blazing Saddles* in an
Atlanta hotel room with Ara Parseghian is one of those memories.

•••

Ara had the image of the classic, no-nonsense coach when he was at
Notre Dame. He was one of the most organized men I have ever
met, but he was known to pull a few practical jokes now and then.

In the early 1970s I had a chance to visit the White House and
to see the Oval Office. When I returned, I contacted Dwayne Elliott
of a local furniture company and asked him to help redesign my
office. I wanted my own Oval Office with a Notre Dame motif that
started with a kelly green carpet. I was very proud of the finished
product and conveyed that to Ara and his staff.

The next day after I had it in perfect order, I came to work and
the office was a mess. I'm not talking about just rearranging the furniture that was already in the room. Someone had taken all of the
furniture and put a toilet bowl in the middle of the room, a broken
chair, and a damaged couch. There were papers everywhere and
some old pictures were hung upside down or sideways.

I went straight to the football office where Ara was having a staff
meeting. I walked in and said, "Where is my office?" Ara kept a
straight face, but the assistants started to snicker. He said he didn't

know what I was talking about. But I knew Ara. He and his assistants had come in at 6 a.m. and had taken my pictures and paintings, my desk, everything and put them in different rooms in the Joyce Center. I had to go on a two-hour scavenger hunt and it took me half a day to put my office back together.

KNUTE ROCKNE

Before I came to Notre Dame I had always lived back East and came to enjoy the Jersey Shore. When I worked at Penn I spent four summers working at the Brandt Yacht Club on Long Island. I loved being near the water, so we still went back for a couple of weeks during the summer when we lived in South Bend. But that was a long trip for a couple of weeks in the summer, so someone suggested that I look into getting a house on the lake in Michigan.

We called Rick Doolittle, a realtor who took us to Michigan to look at four houses. We started in New Buffalo, then he took us to a house in Stephensville. It was a very nice house that was right on the lake, owned by an executive at Whirlpool who was retiring and moving. The realtor gave us the square footage, etc., then said in passing that it had been built in 1929 by Knute Rockne. I said "What?" It was a little cabin that had been expanded over time, but it was Rockne's hideaway in the summers.

We did some further research, and Father Tom McNally, a CSE priest and a good friend of Father Bill Toohey's, said he remembered going up there when he was a kid. He confirmed it was Rockne's house. So, we bought it in 1979 and it was a perfect hideaway, a great place to unwind after a game or any time of the year. It was 37 miles from South Bend. It was not a bad drive for us, but I always wondered how long it took Knute to get there in his Studebaker back in the 1920s.

Sometimes I went up there during the season, especially after a loss. I'd sit on the back deck overlooking the lake, have a few cold ones and talk to Knute to see if he had something inspirational to say to me.

•••

I met with President Reagan and secret service director John Simpson at the White House in May of 1987, and personally invited the president to take part in the first day issue ceremony of the Knute Rockne Stamp in 1988.

Notre Dame has traditional ties between the football and basketball programs, and it dates to Rockne. Few realize he was an assistant basketball coach at Notre Dame in 1917-18, the academic year before he became the head football coach. He actually served as Jesse Harper's top assistant in both sports that year.

Of course Moose Krause was an All-American in both sports and three of the seven Notre Dame Heisman Trophy winners, Johnny Lattner, Paul Hornung and Johnny Lujack, also played basketball at Notre Dame. I had five basketball players who came to Notre Dame on football scholarships. That list included Willie and Mike Townsend, Frank Allocco, Oliver Gibson, and Joe Howard.

Conversely, one athlete who came to Notre Dame on a basketball scholarship, Sean Connor, left the basketball team and joined the football team. He was a reserve punter on the 1988 National Championship football team.

I felt the strong ties between Notre Dame football and basketball and had this unique tie to Rockne. I studied his career, and when it came time for the 100-year celebration of his birth, I took advantage of a unique opportunity.

I became a member of the Citizens Stamp Advisory Committee for the Postmaster General in 1983. Yes, I am one of the people who determine the topics and designs for stamps. You could stump a few people in a bar on that one, I know.

It takes almost two years to get something on a stamp, so in 1986 I started the process to honor Rockne with a commemorative stamp for his 100th birthday, which would be in 1988. It passed the committee easily.

During the 1986-87 season we played at Maryland and I arranged for the team to have a tour of the White House. During the tour, I spoke with John Simpson, then director of the Secret Service. I told him about the Rockne stamp and thought it would add a great deal to the first day of issue celebration at Notre Dame if Ronald Reagan could attend.

John agreed, but said to get it on the president's schedule I needed to contact him six months in advance in writing. In May of 1987 I went the extra mile. I personally went to the White House and gave President Reagan the letter. In the letter I asked him to attend, not as the president of the United States, but as George Gipp. He couldn't turn that down. He accepted, and on March 9, 1988, we had over 11,000 people in the Joyce Center for the first day of issue ceremony.

They drove the president to the back of the ACC and I had the team there to greet him. Reagan made a great speech and told some stories about the making of *Knute Rockne: All-American*. At his conclusion he said, "Where is Tim Brown?" Brown had won the Heisman Trophy the previous fall. President Reagan then took a football from under the podium and threw a perfect spiral to Brown.

FATHER BILL TOOHEY

When Father Bill Toohey was in charge of campus ministry from 1971-80 you couldn't get into the 12:15 p.m. Mass at Sacred Heart. He had this long, silver hair and had a certain presence about him where you hung on every word he said during his homilies. You could hear a pin drop when he gave his sermons each Sunday. He was very outspoken, and I am not sure Father Hesburgh agreed with everything he said in the pulpit because he had some views that were on the edge.

Father Toohey was the perfect game priest, because he was an ex-Marine who knew sports. He knew what to say to the players from a motivational standpoint, whether it was during the trip on the plane, or in his pregame Mass. When we won at Maryland and at UCLA in 1976-77, he was our priest. I really thought he had a positive impact on our team.

•••

While Father Toohey was one of my closest friends, I was not immune to some of his good-natured ribbing, even in front of the team. We were coming back from a game at NC State one year and I said to him during the plane trip, "Hey Father, heck of a sermon tonight. I liked that stuff about building inner strength. Where'd you steal that from, the Pope?"

Without skipping a beat, he deadpanned, "No, Digger, I stole it from Al McGuire, the same guy you steal your best lines from." The entire plane broke into laughter.

•••

When Father Toohey died in 1980, it was the biggest funeral at Sacred Heart since Rockne's in 1931. I was honored to be chosen as one of the pall bearers. Everyone marched from Sacred Heart to the north side of campus where all the Notre Dame priests are buried. I vividly remember that walk because it was an emotional time. He died in the prime of his life so it was sad, but at the same time we all celebrated such a vibrant life. That was the only Father Toohey any of us had ever known.

ROGER VALDISERRI

Roger Valdiserri is a legend among sports information directors in this country. He is the reason I got the job at Notre Dame. We have been close friends since the day I sat next to him at that Notre Dame vs. Marquette game in Milwaukee in 1971. He is retired and recently built a new home in South Bend. We kid each other about growing old and senile. One day I called him recently and he answered the phone and I said, "Rog," He said, "Hold on, I'll go get him."

My second game at Notre Dame we were playing Valparaiso. We all knew we were going to struggle that year and we were losing to Valpo, a game we later won, 81-71. During the middle of the game when I must have looked a bit frustrated, he passed a note from press row. "We are lucky to have you." That was all it said, but it meant so much. I will never forget that.

Roger was my confidant and my advisor. He had been at Notre Dame dating to the 1950s when he was an administrator under Terry Brennan. He knew what Notre Dame was all about and knew what it took to be successful.

•••

When Roger Valdiserri retired from Notre Dame in 1996, the university arranged a dinner for him in the area between the two domes of the Joyce Center. It was quite an affair, a meaningful one for me because everyone who had meant so much to me during my career at Notre Dame was present. Father Joyce, Father Hesburgh and I were among the speakers. Joe Montana and Joe Theismann sent video messages and Regis Philbin, a good friend of Roger's during his undergrad days, was the Master of Ceremonies. You know you are big when Regis is the emcee of your retirement dinner.

Of all the testimonials, the one that must have meant the most to Roger was given by Chris Zorich, then a starting defensive lineman with the Chicago Bears. Chris had grown up in Chicago in a poor neighborhood. He was an only child and was raised by his mother Zora, who was the light of his life.

An undersized middle guard, Chris had an All-America career (1988-90) at Notre Dame because of his incredible intensity and will to succeed. He did not come to Notre Dame with a strong academic background, but his will to succeed carried over to the classroom and he graduated in four years. In fact, since his playing days ended, he returned to Notre Dame and earned his law degree.

When Chris returned home to Chicago after his final Notre Dame game, a heartbreaking 10-9 loss to Colorado in the 1991 Orange Bowl, he found his mother lying on the floor of their house. She had died while he was playing his final game.

When Roger learned of Zora's death, he got in his car and drove to Zorich's home outside Chicago. Roger spent considerable time with Chris as he grieved and helped him organize his mother's funeral arrangements. He basically watched over Chris like a father for the rest of his time at Notre Dame and beyond.

When Chris Zorich spoke at Roger's retirement dinner, you could hear a pin drop. He spoke of Roger's help during his mother's sudden death and the many other areas of his life where he had made a difference. He concluded by saying, "Roger, you made me a man." Then the 5-8 Valdiserri and the 6-4 Zorich hugged. Chris Zorich spoke for countless student-athletes whom Roger had helped during his 30 years supervising the Notre Dame sports information office.

DOTTIE VAN PARIS

I had the same secretary my entire 20 years at Notre Dame. That alone should qualify her for sainthood. Dottie Van Paris had been the basketball secretary under Johnny Dee, so she made our transition an efficient process from an administrative standpoint. We did things differently from our predecessors, especially from a correspondence standpoint, so the transition was probably harder on her than it was on us.

Dick DiBiaso was a master at setting up an office, and he worked with Dottie in the early stages, but it didn't take her long. I prided myself on returning phone calls and letters promptly. She was the best at running the office, because she could deal with all kinds of people. Over her career she took calls from the White House and from the Pancake House, and she had the same demeanor regardless of the situation.

When we made it to the Final Four in 1978 we had a tremendous amount of correspondence. One day she brought in a letter from a fan who said he was naming his dog after me. She got a kick out of that, "Digger the Dog." Dottie supervised the activities of many other secretaries in our office, and they all contributed to our success. The list includes Marilyn Bumbaca, Patricia Ham, Teresa Haus, Cathy Fairchild, Sharon Nyberg, Janis Vergon, Carolyn Maglioa, and Karen (Chavis) Wesolek.

When we had our 30-year reunion for the 1974 team in January of 2004, she was the first person I introduced at the luncheon. Out of all the players, coaches and administrators who attended that luncheon, she probably received the loudest applause.

EPILOGUE

WHY I LIVE IN SOUTH BEND

During the course of the basketball season, I travel every week, mostly to ESPN in Bristol, Connecticut. I often get the question, "Why do you still live in South Bend?" My tongue-in-cheek answer is always, "The weather, of course."

I could live in Florida, Palm Springs, the Napa Valley… anywhere I want. But I love this community. I am a person who enjoys the changing seasons, I love going to the farmer's market, and I love the people in this town because they are good, hard-working, honest people.

But, most of all, I love living just two blocks from the University of Notre Dame. I have the best piece of real estate in the world in my own backyard. When I come home from a road trip I can't wait to walk on that campus because it recharges my battery. There are two lakes in the middle of campus and I walk the lake path to check out the swans. Sacred Heart Church, The Grotto and the Golden Dome are in the same area. Those places and all they represent give me inner peace and fulfillment.

Being around this campus keeps me young because I interact with young people all the time. Every day I am in South Bend I work out at the Joyce Center. Invariably I run into athletes, usually members of the basketball team. Mike Brey has done an outstanding job in bringing in good kids to that program. I remember the first time I went to one of his practices. I marched on the court and said, "Where's the varsity?"

I have a great relationship with Mike Brey, but I don't go to games. Al McGuire told me he didn't go to games after he retired out of fairness to the new coach. This particularly hit me in 1998 when we had a 20-year reunion for the Final Four team. I got a great ovation during that game, and I just felt bad for John McLeod, who was going through a tough season. The only other game I have been to was the Kentucky game in 2004 when we had the 30-year reunion of the team that ended UCLA's streak.

In early fall and late spring, I receive invitations to speak on campus in front of various student groups, usually dormitories, invitations I gladly accept. In late April of 2004 I spoke to the Notre Dame band at their year-end banquet. I discussed the spirit of Notre Dame, its heritage and its positive effect on the lives of so many people over the years. The Notre Dame band is one of the most tangible examples of that spirit. I talked informally for about an hour, then remained for another hour to talk with the students about a variety of subjects.

The next day I got a letter from two of the band members, Sarah Colson and Elizabeth Lefleur, who said the band director told them I was the most dynamic speaker they have ever had.

That note made me feel good, but it was nothing compared to what happened the following Monday night.

Each year the Notre Dame concert band has a season finale program at Washington Hall, and it is one of the major events of the year on campus. It is always sold out and the band members and some of the patrons wear formal attire. This particular night, I sat in the balcony wearing a leather Planet Hollywood jacket and blue jeans.

Near the end of the concert, Dr. Ken Dye, director of Notre Dame's symphonic bands, made an announcement that a special guest would later lead the band in the finale of the evening, the Notre Dame Victory March. Soon a student came to me and asked that I follow her. We walked downstairs to the backstage area. This was a complete surprise to me.

On the stage, Dr. Dye introduced me and I walked out on stage and was handed a baton.

With the crowd standing and joining in the song, I led the band in the "Notre Dame Victory March." I hope they really weren't following my lead because I didn't have a clue what I was doing. But, when it was over, I had to fight back some tears.

If you were in Washington Hall that night, you would have seen why I live in South Bend. I came to Notre Dame in 1971 and I will die here.

DIGGER'S ALL-TIME NOTRE DAME TEAMS

Here it is—my all-time teams for my 20 years at Notre Dame. Let me say from the outset that this was difficult to do, and I bet the fifth team could beat the first team. I picked the teams by position.

Three of the players on the first team played in 1973-74, one of the reasons I said earlier in this book that it was my most talented team. The five players on the first team went on to play 40 years in the NBA, but the second team has John Paxson and Bill Laimbeer, who combined to win five NBA Championship Rings.

Hanzlik played 10 years in the league and along with Laimbeer and Jim Dolan would be considered the smartest players I ever had in terms of basketball acumen. The only reason the first team might beat the second team in a fictitious game is because Hanzlik couldn't guard all five guys at the same time. Everyone on the first three teams went on to play in the NBA with the exception of Rich Branning, who was a great college point guard.

I hope some computer geek puts together a program that would match these teams up. I would like to see how it would come out.

First Team

Pos.	Name	Ht.	Years	PPG	RPG	FG%	FT%
PG	David Rivers	6-0	1984-88	17.4	#5.0	.442	.813
SG	Gary Brokaw	6-3	1972-74	17.3	4.6	.487	.713
C	John Shumate	6-9	1972-74	22.6	11.6	.610	.688
SF	Adrian Dantley	6-5	1973-76	25.8	9.8	.562	.800
PF	Kelly Tripucka	6-7	1977-81	15.3	5.4	.548	.798

Second Team

Pos.	Name	Ht.	Years	PPG	RPG	FG%	FT%
PG	John Paxson	6-2	1979-83	12.2	#3.7	.526	.736
SG	Bill Hanzlik	6-7	1976-80	5.9	2.4	.500	.765
C	Bill Laimbeer	6-11	1975-79	7.4	6.3	.538	.704
SF	Orlando Woolridge	6-9	1977-81	10.6	5.0	.595	.669
PF	Dave Batton	6-9	1974-78	10.6	5.8	.533	.700

Third Team

Pos.	Name	Ht.	Years	PPG	RPG	FG%	FT%
PG	Rich Branning	6-3	1976-80	10.8	#4.1	.483	.715
SG	Tracy Jackson	6-5	1977-81	11.3	5.0	.531	.705
C	Bruce Flowers	6-8	1975-79	8.8	5.7	.574	.692
SF	Donald Royal	6-8	1983-87	9.5	4.9	.559	.780
PF	Laphonso Ellis	6-8	1988-92	15.5	11.1	.577	.675

Fourth Team

Pos.	Name	Ht.	Years	PPG	RPG	FG%	FT%
PG	Dwight Clay	6-0	1972-75	9.2	#2.6	.401	.737
SG	Duck Williams	6-3	1974-78	12.5	1.9	.483	.749
C	Toby Knight	6-9	1973-77	9.4	7.3	.511	.692
SF	Monty Williams	6-8	1989-93	16.1	6.8	.487	.738
PF	Ken Barlow	6-10	1982-86	11.2	5.4	.527	.786

Fifth Team

Pos.	Name	Ht.	Years	PPG	RPG	FG%	FT%
PG	Elmer Bennett	6-0	1988-92	12.0	#4.2	.442	.717
SG	Billy Paterno	6-6	1973-77	9.8	4.7	.467	.707
C	Tim Kempton	6-9	1982-86	8.6	5.5	.516	.756
SF	Tom Sluby	6-4	1980-84	9.4	2.0	.495	.650
PF	Keith Robinson	6-9	1987-90	12.2	8.1	.582	.741

Notes: Heights are from final year at Notre Dame. All statistics are for entire Notre Dame career. # denotes career assist average

Celebrate the Heroes of Notre Dame
and Indiana Sports in These Other Releases from Sports Publishing!